3B

Grammar in Context

4TH EDITION

SANDRA N. ELBAUM

THOMSON

HEINLE

Australia • Canada • Mexico • Singapore • Spain • United Kingdom • United States

THOMSON
HEINLE

Grammar in Context 3B, Fourth Edition
ELBAUM

Publisher, Adult & Academic, ESL: *James W. Brown*
Senior Acquisitions Editor, Adult & Academic, ESL: *Sherrise Roehr*
Director of Product Development: *Anita Raducanu*
Associate Development Editor: *Yeny Kim*
Production Manager: *Sally Giangrande*
Director of Marketing: *Amy Mabley*
Marketing Manager: *Laura Needham*
Senior Print Buyer: *Mary Beth Hennebury*

Development Editor: *Charlotte Sturdy*
Compositor: *Nesbitt Graphics, Inc.*
Project Manager: *Julie DeSilva*
Photo Researcher: *Connie Gardner*
Illustrators: *Ralph Canaday, James Edwards, Larry Frederick, and Brock Nichol*
Interior Designer: *Jerilyn Bockorick*
Cover Designer: *Joseph Sherman*
Printer: *Edwards Brothers*

Cover Image: Edward Hopper: Lighthouse and Buildings, Portland Head. Museum of Fine Arts, Boston, Massachusetts, USA/Bequest of John T. Spaulding/Bridgeman Art Library.

Printed in the United States of America.
1 2 3 4 5 6 7 8 9 10   09 08 07 06 05

For more information contact Thomson Heinle, 25 Thomson Place, Boston, Massachusetts 02210 USA, or you can visit our Internet site at elt.thomson.com

Photo credits appear at the end of the book, which constitutes an extension of this copyright page.

For permission to use material from this text or product, submit a request online at http://www.thomsonrights.com

Any additional questions about permissions can be submitted by email to thomsonrights@thomson.com

ISBN: 1-4130-0823-2

Contents

Lesson 2   57

Lesson 3   97

Lesson 4   137

Lesson 5   183

Lesson 6   223

Lesson 7   273

Lesson 8   327

Lesson 9   371

Lesson 10   423

Appendices

In memory of
Meyer Shisler—teacher, scholar, inspiration

Acknowledgements

Many thanks to Dennis Hogan, Jim Brown, Sherrise Roehr, Yeny Kim, and Sally Giangrande from Thomson Heinle for their ongoing support of the *Grammar in Context* series. I would especially like to thank my editor, Charlotte Sturdy, for her keen eye to detail and invaluable suggestions.

And many thanks to my students at Truman College, who have increased my understanding of my own language and taught me to see life from another point of view. By sharing their observations, questions, and life stories, they have enriched my life enormously—*Sandra N. Elbaum*

Thomson Heinle would like to thank the following people for their contributions:

Marki Alexander
Oklahoma State
   University
Stillwater, OK

Joan M. Amore
Triton College
River Grove, IL

**Edina Pingleton
Bagley**
Nassau Community
   College
Garden City, NY

Judith A. G. Benka
Normandale Community
   College
Bloomington, MN

**Judith Book-
Ehrlichman**
Bergen Community
   College
Paramus, NJ

Lyn Buchheit
Community College of
   Philadelphia
Philadelphia, PA

Charlotte M. Calobrisi
Northern Virginia
   Community College
Annandale, VA

Sarah A. Carpenter
Normandale Community
   College
Bloomington, MN

Jeanette Clement
Duquesne University
Pittsburgh, PA

Allis Cole
Shoreline Community
   College
Shoreline, WA

**Jacqueline M.
Cunningham**
Triton College
River Grove, IL

Lisa DePaoli
Sierra College
Rocklin, CA

Maha Edlbi
Sierra College
Rocklin, CA

Rhonda J. Farley
Cosumnes River College
Sacramento, CA

Jennifer Farnell
University of Connecticut
American Language
   Program
Stamford, CT

**Abigail-Marie
Fiattarone**
Mesa Community College
Mesa, AZ

Marcia Gethin-Jones
University of Connecticut
American Language
   Program
Storrs, CT

Linda Harlow
Santa Rosa Junior
   College
Santa Rosa, CA

Suha R. Hattab
Triton College
River Grove, IL

Bill Keniston
Normandale Community
   College
Bloomington, MN

Walton King
Arkansas State
   University
Jonesboro, AR

Kathleen Krokar
Truman College
Chicago, IL

John Larkin
NVCC-Community and
   Workforce
   Development
Annandale, VA

Michael Larsen
American River College
Sacramento, CA

Bea C. Lawn
Gavilan College
Gilroy, CA

Rob Lee
Pasadena City College
Pasadena, CA

**Oranit
Limmaneeprasert**
American River College
Sacramento, CA

Gennell Lockwood
Shoreline Community
   College
Shoreline, WA

Linda Louie
Highline Community
   College
Des Moines, WA

Melanie A. Majeski
Naugatuck Valley
   Community College
Waterbury, CT

Maria Marin
De Anza College
Cupertino, CA

Karen Miceli
Cosumnes River College
Sacramento, CA

Jeanie Pavichevich
Triton College
River Grove, IL

Herbert Pierson
St. John's University
New York City, NY

Dina Poggi
De Anza College
Cupertino, CA

Mark Rau
American River College
Sacramento, CA

John W. Roberts
Shoreline Community
   College
Shoreline, WA

Azize R. Ruttler
Bergen Community
   College
Paramus, NJ

Ann Salzmann
University of Illinois,
Urbana, IL

Eva Teagarden
Yuba College
Marysville, CA

Susan Wilson
San Jose City College
San Jose, CA

Martha Yeager-Tobar
Cerritos College
Norwalk, CA

A word from the author

It seems that I was born to be an ESL teacher. My parents immigrated to the U.S. from Poland as adults and were confused not only by the English language but by American culture as well. Born in the U.S., I often had the task as a child to explain the intricacies of the language and allay my parents' fears about the culture. It is no wonder to me that I became an ESL teacher, and later, an ESL writer who focuses on explanations of American culture in order to illustrate grammar. My life growing up in an immigrant neighborhood was very similar to the lives of my students, so I have a feel for what confuses them and what they need to know about American life.

ESL teachers often find themselves explaining confusing customs and providing practical information about life in the U.S. Often, teachers are a student's only source of information about American life. With **Grammar in Context, Fourth Edition,** I enjoy sharing my experiences with you.

Grammar in Context, Fourth Edition connects grammar with American cultural context, providing learners of English with a useful and meaningful skill and knowledge base. Students learn the grammar necessary to communicate verbally and in writing, and learn how American culture plays a role in language, beliefs, and everyday situations.

Enjoy the new edition of **Grammar in Context!**

Sandra N. Elbaum

Grammar in Context

Students learn more, remember more, and use language more effectively when they learn grammar in context.

Learning a language through meaningful themes and practicing it in a contextualized setting promote both linguistic and cognitive development. In **Grammar in Context**, grammar is presented in interesting and culturally informative readings, and the language and context are subsequently practiced throughout the chapter.

New to this edition:

- **New and updated readings** on current American topics such as Instant Messaging and eBay.
- **Updated grammar charts** that now include essential language notes.
- **Updated exercises and activities** that provide contextualized practice using a variety of exercise types, as well as additional practice for more difficult structures.
- **New lower-level** *Grammar in Context Basic* for beginning level students.
- **New wrap-around Teacher's Annotated Edition** with page-by-page, point-of-use teaching suggestions.
- **Expanded Assessment CD-ROM** with ExamView® Pro Test Generator now contains more questions types and assessment options to easily allow teachers to create tests and quizzes.

Distinctive Features of *Grammar in Context*:

Students prepare for academic assignments and everyday language tasks.

Discussions, readings, compositions, and exercises involving higher-level critical thinking skills develop overall language and communication skills.

Students expand their knowledge of American topics and culture.

The readings in **Grammar in Context** help students gain insight into and enrich their knowledge of American culture and history. Students gain ample exposure to the practicalities of American life, such as writing a résumé, dealing with telemarketers and junk mail, and getting student internships. Their new knowledge helps them adapt to everyday life in the U.S.

Students learn to use their new skills to communicate.

The exercises and Expansion Activities in **Grammar in Context** help students learn English while practicing their writing and speaking skills. Students work together in pairs and groups to find more information about topics, to make presentations, to play games, and to role-play. Their confidence in using English increases, as does their ability to communicate effectively.

Welcome to **Grammar in Context, Fourth Edition**

Students learn more, remember more, and use language more effectively when they learn grammar in context.

Grammar in Context, Fourth Edition connects grammar with rich, American cultural context, providing learners of English with a useful and meaningful skill and knowledge base.

An **Audio Program** allows students to hear the readings and dialogs, and provides an opportunity to practice their listening skills.

Readings on American topics such as Instant Messaging, eBay, and The AIDS Ride present and illustrate the grammatical structure in an informative and meaningful context.

Grammar charts offer clear explanations and provide contextualized examples of the structure.

Language Notes refine students' understanding of the target structure.

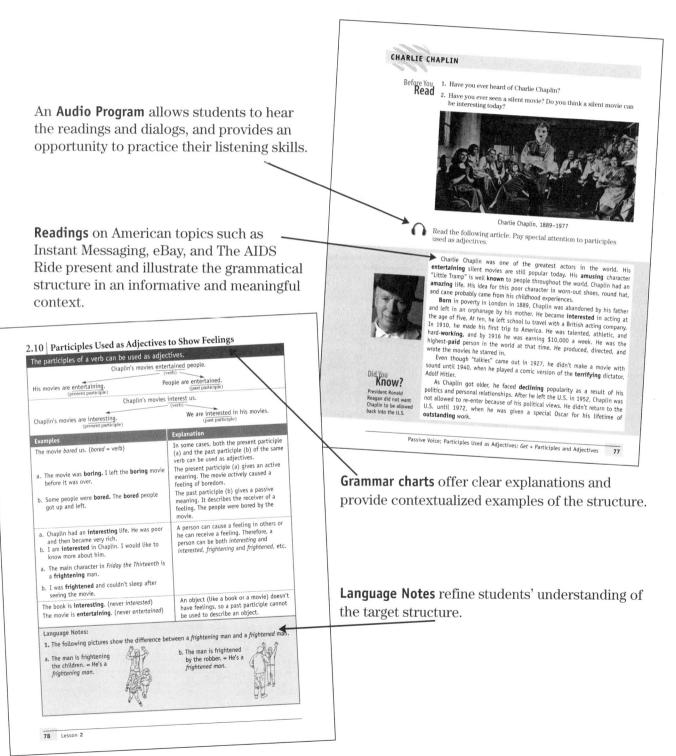

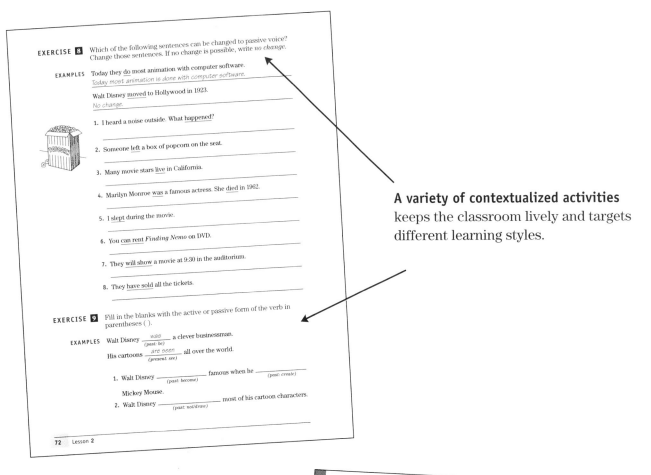

EXERCISE 8 Which of the following sentences can be changed to passive voice? Change those sentences. If no change is possible, write *no change*.

EXAMPLES Today they <u>do</u> most animation with computer software.
Today most animation is done with computer software.

Walt Disney <u>moved</u> to Hollywood in 1923.
No change.

1. I heard a noise outside. What <u>happened</u>?

2. Someone <u>left</u> a box of popcorn on the seat.

3. Many movie stars <u>live</u> in California.

4. Marilyn Monroe <u>was</u> a famous actress. She <u>died</u> in 1962.

5. I <u>slept</u> during the movie.

6. You <u>can rent</u> *Finding Nemo* on DVD.

7. They <u>will show</u> a movie at 9:30 in the auditorium.

8. They <u>have sold</u> all the tickets.

EXERCISE 9 Fill in the blanks with the active or passive form of the verb in parentheses ( ).

EXAMPLES Walt Disney ___*was*___ a clever businessman.
        (past: be)
His cartoons ___*are seen*___ all over the world.
              (present: see)

1. Walt Disney _____ famous when he _____
             (past: become)   (past: create)
   Mickey Mouse.

2. Walt Disney _____ most of his cartoon characters.
             (past: not/draw)

72   Lesson 2

A variety of contextualized activities keeps the classroom lively and targets different learning styles.

A **Summary** provides the lesson's essential grammar in an easy-to-reference format.

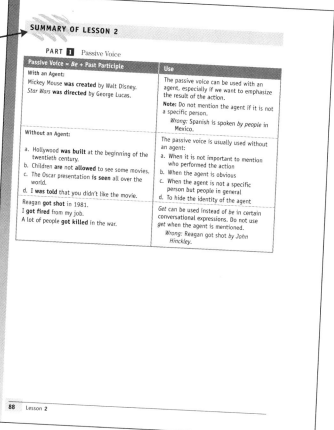

SUMMARY OF LESSON 2

PART 1 Passive Voice

Passive Voice = *Be* + Past Participle	Use
With an Agent: Mickey Mouse **was created** by Walt Disney. *Star Wars* **was directed** by George Lucas.	The passive voice can be used with an agent, especially if we want to emphasize the result of the action. **Note:** Do not mention the agent if it is not a specific person. 　*Wrong:* Spanish is spoken *by people* in Mexico.
Without an Agent: a. Hollywood **was built** at the beginning of the twentieth century. b. Children **are** not **allowed** to see some movies. c. The Oscar presentation **is seen** all over the world. d. I **was told** that you didn't like the movie.	The passive voice is usually used without an agent: a. When it is not important to mention who performed the action b. When the agent is obvious c. When the agent is not a specific person but people in general d. To hide the identity of the agent
Reagan **got shot** in 1981. I **got fired** from my job. A lot of people **got killed** in the war.	*Get* can be used instead of *be* in certain conversational expressions. Do not use *get* when the agent is mentioned. 　*Wrong:* Reagan got shot *by John Hinckley.*

88   Lesson 2

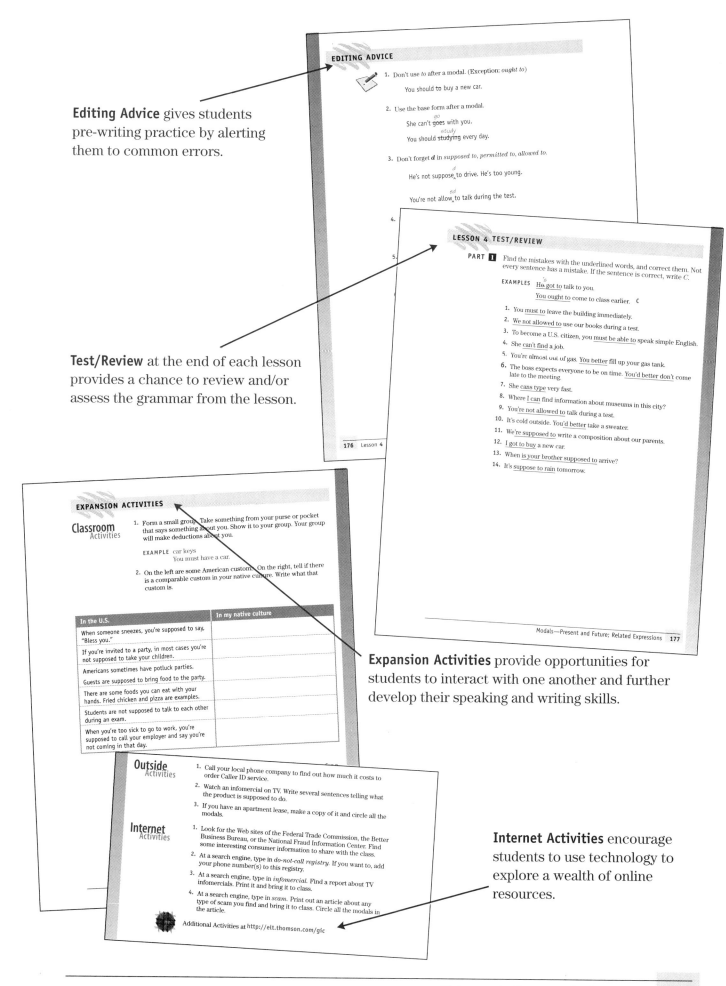

Editing Advice gives students pre-writing practice by alerting them to common errors.

EDITING ADVICE

1. Don't use *to* after a modal. (Exception: *ought to*)

   You should ~~to~~ buy a new car.

2. Use the base form after a modal.

   She can't ~~goes~~ *go* with you.

   You should ~~studying~~ *study* every day.

3. Don't forget *d* in *supposed to, permitted to, allowed to*.

   He's not suppose*d* to drive. He's too young.

   You're not allow*ed* to talk during the test.

176 Lesson 4

LESSON 4 TEST/REVIEW

PART 1 Find the mistakes with the underlined words, and correct them. Not every sentence has a mistake. If the sentence is correct, write *C*.

EXAMPLES   ~~He~~ *s* got to talk to you.

You ought to come to class earlier.   *C*

1. You <u>must to</u> leave the building immediately.
2. <u>We not allowed to</u> use our books during a test.
3. To become a U.S. citizen, you <u>must be able to</u> speak simple English.
4. She <u>can't</u> find a job.
5. You're almost out of gas. <u>You better</u> fill up your gas tank.
6. The boss expects everyone to be on time. <u>You'd better don't</u> come late to the meeting.
7. She <u>cans type</u> very fast.
8. Where <u>I can find</u> information about museums in this city?
9. <u>You're not allowed to</u> talk during a test.
10. It's cold outside. <u>You'd better</u> take a sweater.
11. <u>We're supposed to</u> write a composition about our parents.
12. <u>I got to buy</u> a new car.
13. When <u>is your brother supposed to</u> arrive?
14. It's <u>suppose to rain</u> tomorrow.

Modals—Present and Future; Related Expressions   **177**

Test/Review at the end of each lesson provides a chance to review and/or assess the grammar from the lesson.

EXPANSION ACTIVITIES

Classroom Activities

1. Form a small group. Take something from your purse or pocket that says something about you. Show it to your group. Your group will make deductions about you.

   EXAMPLE   car keys
   You must have a car.

2. On the left are some American customs. On the right, tell if there is a comparable custom in your native culture. Write what that custom is.

In the U.S.	In my native culture
When someone sneezes, you're supposed to say, "Bless you."	
If you're invited to a party, in most cases you're not supposed to take your children.	
Americans sometimes have potluck parties. Guests are supposed to bring food to the party.	
There are some foods you can eat with your hands. Fried chicken and pizza are examples.	
Students are not supposed to talk to each other during an exam.	
When you're too sick to go to work, you're supposed to call your employer and say you're not coming in that day.	

Expansion Activities provide opportunities for students to interact with one another and further develop their speaking and writing skills.

Outside Activities

1. Call your local phone company to find out how much it costs to order Caller ID service.
2. Watch an infomercial on TV. Write several sentences telling what the product is supposed to do.
3. If you have an apartment lease, make a copy of it and circle all the modals.

Internet Activities

1. Look for the Web sites of the Federal Trade Commission, the Better Business Bureau, or the National Fraud Information Center. Find some interesting consumer information to share with the class.
2. At a search engine, type in *do-not-call registry*. If you want to, add your phone number(s) to this registry.
3. At a search engine, type in *infomercial*. Find a report about TV infomercials. Print it and bring it to class.
4. At a search engine, type in *scam*. Print out an article about any type of scam you find and bring it to class. Circle all the modals in the article.

Additional Activities at http://elt.thomson.com/gic

Internet Activities encourage students to use technology to explore a wealth of online resources.

Grammar in Context Student Book Supplements

Audio Program
- Audio CDs and Audio Tapes allow students to listen to every reading in the book as well as selected dialogs.

More Grammar Practice Workbooks
- Workbooks can be used with *Grammar in Context* or any skills text to learn and review the essential grammar.
- Great for in-class practice or homework.
- Includes practice on all grammar points in *Grammar in Context*.

Teacher's Annotated Edition
- New component offers page-by-page answers and teaching suggestions.

Assessment CD-ROM with ExamView® Pro Test Generator
- Test Generator allows teachers to create tests and quizzes quickly and easily.

Interactive CD-ROM
- CD-ROM allows for supplemental interactive practice on grammar points from *Grammar in Context*.

Split Editions
- Split editions provide options for short courses.

Instructional Video
- Video offers teaching suggestions and advice on how to use *Grammar in Context*.

Web Site
- Web site gives access to additional activities and promotes the use of the Internet.

Toolbox
- A WebTutor™ Toolbox available on WebCT™ or Blackboard® provides chapter-by-chapter quizzes and support.

LESSON

6

GRAMMAR

Adjective Clauses
Descriptive Phrases

CONTEXT: Computers and the Internet

Spam
eBay
Handwritten Letters or E-mail?
Creating the World Wide Web

6.1 | Adjective Clauses—An Overview

An adjective clause is a group of words that describes or identifies the noun before it.

Examples	Explanation
I have a friend **who is a computer programmer.**	Here the adjective clause tells you about the friend.
You should buy a computer **that has a big memory.**	Here the adjective clause tells you about the computer.
People **who send e-mail** usually write letters **that are short.**	The adjective clause can describe any noun in the sentence. In the sentence to the left, an adjective clause describes both the subject (*people*) and the object (*letters*).

SPAM

Before You Read

1. Do you get unwanted e-mail asking you to buy products or order services?

2. What do you do with this e-mail?

Read the following article. Pay special attention to adjective clauses.

Do you ever get e-mail **that promises to make you rich or thin?** Do you get e-mail **that tries to sell you a mortgage or a vacation package?** Do you ever receive an offer **that will give you a college diploma in a year?** This kind of advertising through e-mail is called "spam." Spam is e-mail **that you haven't asked for.** It is the electronic equivalent of junk mail or telemarketing calls. About half of the e-mail sent today is spam. In 2002, 260 billion spam e-mails were sent. A year later, in 2003, this number rose to 4.9 trillion. Bill Gates, the founder of Microsoft, calls spam "pollution of the e-mail ecosystem."

How do spammers get your e-mail address? They use several methods. When you buy something online, you are often asked for an e-mail address when you place an order. Spammers buy addresses from online companies. In addition, spammers search chat rooms, bulletin boards, and newsgroups for e-mail addresses. Spammers regularly sell lists of e-mail addresses to other spammers.

Where does spam come from? It comes from companies **that want your money.** Many of these companies try to take your money by making false claims ("Lose 50 pounds in 10 days!"). But most people delete this kind of e-mail without even reading it. So why do spammers send e-mail **that nobody wants to read?** The answer is simple: Some people *do* read this mail and a very small percentage even buy the product or order the service **that is offered.** And a small percentage of trillions of e-mails means money. One spammer **who lives in Florida** made so much money that he sold his business for $135 million dollars and retired at the age of 37.

What can you do to eliminate spam?

- You could simply delete it.
- You could get anti-spam software. (Some software is free, offered by the Internet service provider **you use.**)
- You can get a separate e-mail address to give to retailers **who require an e-mail address,** and use your primary e-mail address just for people **you know.**
- On a Web site, when you see a box **that asks you if you want more information,** make sure to uncheck the box.

Many people **who are unhappy with the amount of spam they receive** are asking their lawmakers to enact laws **that would stop spam.**

6.2 | Relative Pronoun as Subject

The relative pronouns *who*, *that*, and *which* can be the subject of an adjective clause.

I received an e-mail. *The e-mail* promises to make me rich.

I received an e-mail | **that** **which** | promises to make me rich.

People ....often give out their e-mail addresses.

┌─*People* buy things online.

People →| **who** **that** | buy things online often give out their e-mail addresses.

Language Notes:
1. Use the relative pronouns *who* and *that* for people. Use the relative pronouns *that* and *which* for things. (*Which* is less common than *that*.)
2. A present tense verb in the adjective clause must agree in number with its subject.
   People who **buy** things online should have a separate e-mail address.
   A person who **buys** things online should have a separate e-mail address.

EXERCISE **1**   Fill in the blanks with *who*, *that*, or *which* + the correct form of the verb in parentheses ( ) to complete the adjective clause.

EXAMPLE   Spam comes from companies ___*that want*___ to sell you something.
(*want*)

1. Companies _____ you spam want your money.
(*send*)

2. People _____ spam are often annoyed.
(*receive*)

3. People _____ products and services online give
(*buy*)

   out their e-mail addresses.

✔ 4. Sometimes you see a box _____ a check in it already.
(*have*)

   Don't forget to uncheck the box if you don't want more information.

5. I know a student _____ all her textbooks online.
(*buy*)

   She never goes to the bookstore anymore.

6. A spammer _____ in Florida became very rich
(*live*)

   and retired young.

7. You shouldn't believe an offer _____ you that
(promise)

you will lose 50 pounds in a week.

EXERCISE 2 Use the phrase below to write a complete sentence.

EXAMPLES a computer that has a small memory

A computer that has a small memory is not very useful today.

a company that promises to make me rich in three weeks

I wouldn't want to do business with a company that promises

to make me rich in three weeks.

1. e-mail that comes from friends and relatives

_____

2. companies that send spam

_____

3. students who don't have a computer

_____

4. children who spend all their time on the computer

_____

5. people who have a high-speed Internet connection

_____

6. Web sites that offer free music downloads

_____

7. "colleges" that offer a four-year diploma in six months

_____

8. people who don't know anything about computers

_____

EXERCISE 3 ABOUT YOU Fill in the blanks with an adjective clause.
Discuss your answers.

EXAMPLE I don't like people *who say one thing but do something else.*

1. I don't like people _____

2. I don't like apartments _____

3. I don't like movies _____

4. I like movies _____

5. I don't like teachers _____

6. I like teachers _____

7. I don't like teenagers _____

8. I like to have neighbors _____

9. I don't like to have neighbors _____

10. I like to receive mail _____

11. I have never met a person _____

12. I can't understand people _____

13. I like classes _____

14. I like to be around people _____

15. I don't like to be around people _____

16. A good friend is a person _____

17. I have a good friend _____

18. I once had a car _____

EXERCISE **4** Work with a partner. Write a sentence with each of the words given to describe the ideal situation for learning English. You may use singular or plural.

EXAMPLES class *Classes that have fewer than 20 students are better than large classes.*

teacher *I prefer to have a teacher who doesn't explain things in my language.*

1. teacher _____

2. college / school _____

3. textbook _____

4. class _____

5. classroom _____

6. computer lab _____

7. school library _____

8. classmate _____

9. dictionary _____

10. study group _____

6.3 | Relative Pronoun as Object

The relative pronouns *who(m)*, *that*, and *which* can be the object of an adjective clause.

Object

I don't read all the e-mail.   I receive *e-mail*.

I don't read all the e-mail | **which** **that** Ø | I receive.

Object

I don't know *a person*.

A person...sent me an e-mail with her picture.

A person | **who(m)** **that** Ø | I don't know   sent me an e-mail with her picture.

Language Notes:

1. While all ways shown above are grammatically correct, the relative pronoun is usually omitted in conversation when it is the object of the adjective clause.

    I don't read all the e-mail ~~that~~ I receive.

    A person ~~whom~~ I don't know sent me an e-mail with her picture.

2. *Whom* is considered more correct than *who* when used as the object of the adjective clause. However, as seen in the above note, the relative pronoun is usually omitted altogether in conversation.

    A person *whom* I don't know sent me an e-mail. (Formal)

    A person *who* I don't know sent me an e-mail. (Less Formal)

    A person I don't know sent me an e-mail. (Informal)

3. In an adjective clause, omit the object pronoun.

    The computer that I bought ~~it~~ has a large memory.

EXERCISE 5   Fill in the blanks to make an appropriate adjective clause.

EXAMPLE   My friend just bought a new dog. The last dog _____*he had*_____ died a few weeks ago.

1. I have a hard teacher this semester. The teacher _____ last semester was much easier.

2. I studied British English in my native country. The English _____ now is American English.

3. The teacher gave a test last week. Almost everyone failed the test _____ .

4. When I read English, there are many new words for me. I use my dictionary to look up the words I _____ .

5. I had a big apartment last year. The apartment _____ _____ now is very small.

6. Did you contact the owner of the wallet _____ on the street?

7. I write poetry. One of the poems _____ won a prize.

8. The last book _____ was very sad. It made me cry.

9. She has met a lot of people at school, but she hasn't made any friends. The people _____ are all too busy to spend time with her.

6.4 | Comparing Pronoun as Subject and Object

Examples	Explanation
Compare: a. I receive a lot of e-mail **(that)** I delete without reading. b. I receive a lot of e-mail **that** promises to make me rich.	In sentences (a), the relative pronoun is the object of the adjective clause. It is often omitted, especially in conversation. The new subject introduced (*I*) indicates that the relative pronoun is an object and can be omitted.
a. A student **(whom)** I met in my math class doesn't want to own a computer. b. A student **who** has good grades can get a scholarship.	In sentences (b), the relative pronoun is the subject of the adjective clause. It cannot be omitted. The fact that there is no new subject after *that* or *who* indicates that the relative pronoun is the subject. *Wrong:* A student has good grades can get a scholarship.

EXERCISE **6** Fill in the blanks with an adjective clause.

A: I'm so tired of all the spam _____*I get*_____.
(example)

B: Do you get a lot?

A: Of course, I do. Doesn't everyone?

B: I don't.

A: How is that possible?

B: I have an e-mail address _____ just
(1)
for shopping online. I don't use it for anything else. The e-mail

address _____ to my friends is private.
(2)
I don't give it to anyone else.

A: I never thought about having different e-mail addresses for different things. Don't you have to pay for each e-mail account?

B: There are a lot of e-mail providers _____
(3)
_____ for free.

For example, you can use Hotmail™ or Yahoo™ for free. But they have limited space and aren't good for everything. I like to send a lot of

photos. The photos _____ are often
(4)
too big for my free Hotmail account, but it's perfect for the shopping

_____ online.
(5)

A: Do you do a lot of shopping online?

B: Yes. For example, I buy a lot of textbooks online. The textbooks

_____ online are often cheaper than
(6)
the ones in the bookstore.

A: How can I get one of these free accounts?

B: You just go to their Web site and sign up. Choose a username and password. If the username ———————————————(7)——— has already been chosen by someone else, you can choose another one or simply add some numbers to it. For example, I chose SlyFox, but it was already taken, so I added the year of my birth, 1986. So I'm SlyFox1986.

B: Why did you choose that name?

A: That's the name ———————————(8)———————— when I was a child. My older brother was always giving people nicknames. After you choose a username, choose a password. Make sure it's a number or word ———————————(9)———— easily. If you forget your password, you won't be able to use your account. The password ———————————(10)———— should never be obvious. Never, for example, use your birth date, address, phone number, or Social Security number.

B: What password did you choose?

A: The password ———————————(11)———— is a secret. I will never tell it to anyone.

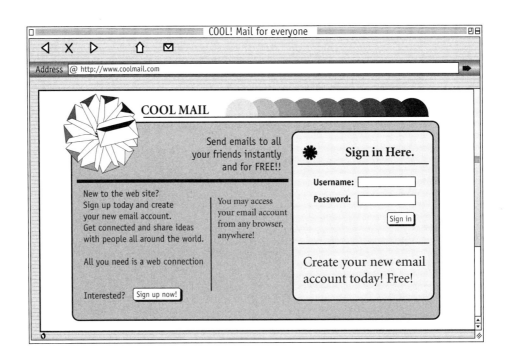

6.5 | Relative Pronoun as Object of Preposition

The relative pronouns can be the object of a preposition (*to, about, with, of, for*, etc.).

Prep. Object

Spam is commercial e-mail.   You don't ask **for** spam.

Spam is commercial e-mail | that / ∅ / which | ← you don't ask **for.**

Spam is commercial e-mail **for which** you don't ask. (*Very formal*)

Prep. Object

I wrote **to** a friend.

The friend..sent me a quick reply.

The friend | that / ∅ / who(m) | ← I wrote to   sent me a quick reply. (*Informal*)

The friend **to whom** I wrote sent me a quick reply. (*Very formal*)

Language Notes:

1. Informally, most native speakers put the preposition at the end of the adjective clause. The relative pronoun is usually omitted. The most common way to say the sentences in the above chart is:

   Spam is commercial e-mail you don't ask **for.**

   The friend I wrote **to** sent me a quick reply.

2. In very formal English, the preposition comes before the relative pronoun, and only *whom* and *which* may be used. *That* is not used directly after a preposition.

   The person **to whom** I spoke was very helpful.

   The college **to which** I applied is in California.

   Wrong: The college to *that* I applied is in California.

EXERCISE 7   ABOUT YOU   Complete each statement.

EXAMPLE   The class I was in last semester _____ *was very crowded.* _____

1. The city I come from _____

2. The school I graduated from _____

3. The house / apartment I used to live in _____

4. The elementary school I went to _____

5. The teacher I studied beginning grammar with _____

_____

6. Most of the people I went to elementary school with _____

_____

7. _____ is a subject I'm very interested in.

8. _____ is a topic I don't like to talk about.

EXERCISE 8 Make these sentences more informal by taking out the relative pronoun and putting the preposition at the end of the adjective clause.

EXAMPLE He applied to several colleges in which he was interested.
He applied to several colleges he was interested in.

1. I don't understand a word about which you are talking.

_____

2. The gym to which I used to go raised its fee.

_____

3. The pen for which you are looking is in your pocket.

_____

4. Those are the children for whom the babysitter is responsible.

_____

5. There is very little of which I'm sure.

_____

6. That is the counselor with whom you need to speak.

_____

EXERCISE 9 This is a conversation between two friends. One just came back from an island vacation where he had a terrible time. Fill in each blank with an adjective clause. Answers may vary.

A: How was your trip?

B: Terrible.

A: What happened? Didn't your travel agent give you good advice?

B: I didn't use a travel agent. I asked some friends for cheap ways to take a vacation. One friend I ___*talked to*___ told me to look for
(example)

vacations online. So I did. There was a choice of hotels. The name of

the hotel _____ was "Ocean View," so I thought I would
        (1)

see the ocean from my window. The view _____ from my
                                                (2)

window was of a brick wall. I didn't see any water at all. The only

water _____ was in the bathroom sink.
        (3)

A: What kind of food did they serve?

B: The food _____ made me sick.
                    (4)

A: Did you meet any interesting travelers?

B: I didn't like the other travelers _____. They were
                                            (5)
unfriendly.

A: Did you travel with an interesting companion?

B: The person _____ was boring. We weren't
                    (6)
interested in the same things. The things _____
                                            (7)
were different from the things _____.
                                    (8)

A: Did you take pictures?

B: The pictures _____ didn't come out.
                        (9)

A: Did you find any interesting souvenirs?

B: The souvenirs _____ were cheaply made.
                        (10)
I didn't buy any.

A: Could you communicate with the people on the island? Do they
speak English?

B: No. I don't understand the language _____.
                                              (11)

A: Did you spend a lot of money?

B: Yes, but the money _____was wasted.
                            (12)

A: Why didn't you change your ticket and come home early?

B: The ticket _____couldn't be changed.
                    (13)

A: Are you going to have another vacation soon?

B: The next vacation _____will be in
                            (14)
December. I think I'll just stay home.

Before You Read

1. What do you do with old things of yours that you no longer want? Do you sell them or throw them away?

2. Do you collect anything (coins, stamps, dolls, etc.)? Where can you buy your collectibles?

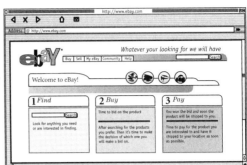

 Read the following article. Pay special attention to *when* and *where*.

Did You Know?

Pierre Omidyar was ranked the second richest man under 40 years old in 2002. His wealth was estimated to be $3.82 billion dollars. (The richest man under 40 in the same year was Michael Dell, the founder of Dell Computer.)

Did you ever want to sell an ugly lamp that your aunt gave you for your birthday? Or an old toy that is taking up space in your closet? Or are you trying to buy another train for your toy train collection? In the old days, buyers and sellers were limited to newspapers, garage sales, and flea markets[1] in their area to buy and sell unusual things. But since 1995, eBay has provided an online global community **where** people buy and sell almost anything. People are no longer limited to finding buyers and sellers in the local area **where** they live.

The creator of eBay, Pierre Omidyar, graduated from Tufts University in 1988 with a degree in computer science. He got his idea of an online trading community in 1995, **when** his wife, a collector of plastic candy dispensers, was trying to buy a piece for her unusual collection. From his California home, Omidyar developed an online trading site, and, within a short period of time, his wife was able to find what she was looking for, and Omidyar made a little money on the trade.

Using this idea, Omidyar created eBay, a Web site **where** people can put a photo of the object they want to sell, and give a starting price for an auction. In an auction, the person who makes the highest offer within a

Pierre Omidyar

[1] A *flea market* is a large area where individuals rent a space to sell used goods. It is usually outdoors.

certain period of time gets to buy the item. Not everything on eBay is sold by auction. Some items have fixed prices too. eBay makes its money by charging the seller a small percentage of the final price.

Meg Whitman

By 1998, eBay had become so big that Omidyar and his partner could no longer handle it without expert help. They brought in Meg Whitman, whose knowledge of business helped make eBay the success it is today. She changed eBay from a company that sold several categories of used things to a large marketplace of 11 million items in 18,000 categories of both new and used merchandise. Every day more than half a million items are sold. In the year 2001 alone, over $9 billion worth of merchandise changed hands on eBay, including cars, jewelry, toys, computers—and anything else you can imagine.

Not only can you buy and sell on eBay, you can also meet people whose interests you share. Whitman is proud of the online communities she has created. For example, doll collectors all over the world can "meet" each other and exchange information on bulletin boards and in chat rooms. Friendships are formed on eBay among people who share an interest in the same collectibles.

eBay is now among the top 10 Web sites visited.

6.6 | *Where* and *When* in Adjective Clauses

Examples	Explanation
eBay is a Web site **where people can buy and sell things.** eBay is a community **where you can meet people who share your hobby.**	*Where* means "in that place." *Where* cannot be omitted.
There was a time **(when) collectors were limited to their local areas.** Do you remember the day **(when) you saw a computer for the first time?**	*When* means "at that time." *When* can be omitted.

EXERCISE 10 Tell what information you can find on certain Web sites. If you're not sure, go to the Web site. Or you can take a guess and check it out later.

EXAMPLE WhiteHouse.gov is a Web site _____*where you can read about*_____ *the White House and the president.*

1. Weather.com is a Web site _____
2. Mapquest.com is a Web site _____
3. CNN.com is a Web site _____
4. USPS.gov is a Web site _____
5. Hotmail.com is a Web site _____
6. Travelocity.com is a Web site _____
7. Newsweek.com is a Web site _____
8. IRS.gov is a Web site _____
9. Redcross.org is a Web site _____
10. Harvard.edu is a Web site _____

EXERCISE 11 Fill in the blanks.

EXAMPLE I like to use the computer lab at a time ____*when it isn't crowded.*____

1. The teacher shouldn't give a test on a day when _____
2. I like to study at a time when _____
3. Saturday is the day when _____
4. _____ is the season when _____
5. Between 7 and 9 a.m. is the time when _____
6. _____ was the year when _____

EXERCISE 12 ABOUT YOU Fill in the blanks to tell about yourself.

EXAMPLE ____*June*____ is the month when I was born.

1. _____ is a place where I can relax.
2. _____ is a place where I can have fun.
3. _____ is a place where I can be alone and think.
4. _____ is a place where I can meet my friends.

5. _____ is a place where I can study undisturbed.

6. _____ is a time when I can relax.

7. _____ is a time when I like to watch TV.

8. _____ is a day when I have almost no free time.

9. _____ is a time when I like to use the Internet.

6.7 | *Where, When, That,* or *Which* in Adjective Clauses

Examples	Explanation
a. In 2002, Pierre gave the graduation speech at the college **where he had gotten his degree.** b. In 2002, Pierre gave the graduation speech at the college *from* **which he had gotten his degree.** c. In 2002, Pierre gave the graduation speech at the college **(that) he had gotten his degree** *from*.	Instead of *where* (a), the adjective clause can have preposition + *which* (b) or *that* + preposition (c). If you use *where*, don't use a preposition (in this case, *from*). The meaning of (a), (b), and (c) is essentially the same.
a. 1995 is the year **when eBay got its start.** b. 1995 is the year *in* **which eBay got its start.** c. 1995 is the year **(that) eBay got started** *in*.	Instead of *when* (a), the adjective clause can have preposition + *which* (b) or *that* + preposition (c). If you use *when*, don't use a preposition. The meaning of (a), (b), and (c) is essentially the same.

Compare:
a. She lives in a home **where** people use the computer a lot.
b. She lives in a home **that** has three computers.
	In sentence (a), *where* means *there* or *in that place.*
	     People use the computer a lot *there.*
	In sentence (b), *that* means *home.*
	     The *home* has three computers.

a. February is the month **when** I was born.
b. February is the month **that** has only 28 days.
	In sentence (a), *when* means *then* or *in that month.*
	     I was born *then.*
	In sentence (b), *that* means *the month.*
	     The month has only 28 days.

EXERCISE 13 Fill in the blanks with *where*, *that*, or *which*.

EXAMPLE The home _____*where*_____ I grew up had a beautiful fireplace.

1. The store _____ I bought my computer is having a sale now.

2. Do you bookmark the Web sites _____ you visit often?

3. The box at the top of your browser is the place in _____ you write the Web address.

4. There are Web sites _____ you can compare prices of electronics.

5. The city _____ I was born has a lot of parks.

6. I don't like cities _____ have a lot of factories.

7. I like to shop at stores _____ have products from different countries.

8. I like to shop at stores _____ I can find products from different countries.

9. A department store is a store in _____ you can find all kinds of goods—clothing, furniture, toys, etc.

10. I have a photograph of the home _____ I grew up.

11. The office _____ you can get your transcripts is closed now.

12. She wants to rent the apartment _____ she saw last Sunday.

13. I would like to visit the city _____ I grew up.

14. The town in _____ she grew up was destroyed by the war.

EXERCISE 14 Fill in the blanks with *when* or *that* or nothing.

EXAMPLE December 31, 1999 was a time _____*when*_____ people celebrated the beginning of the new century.

1. Six o'clock is the time at _____ the auction stops.

2. Do you remember the year _____ Meg Whitman started to work for eBay?

3. 2004 was a year _____ had 366 days.

4. New Year's Eve is a time _____ I love.

5. February is the only month _____ has fewer than 30 days.

6. My birthday is a day —————— I think about my past.

7. December is a time —————— a lot of Americans buy gifts.

8. My parents' anniversary is a date —————— has a lot of meaning for them.

9. Do you give yourself the time —————— you need to write a good composition?

10. She wrote about a time —————— she couldn't speak English well.

11. Our vacation to Paris was the best time —————— we had ever had.

HANDWRITTEN LETTERS OR E-MAIL?

Before You Read

1. What are some differences between a handwritten letter and an e-mail?

2. Do you ever use instant messages?

Part 1: Read the following handwritten letter, instant message, and e-mail.

May 14, 2005

Dear Fran,

I was so happy to receive the letter you sent me with the photos of your adorable children. They've grown so big since the last time I saw them. How do they like their new school?

As you know, our wedding is planned for September 12. We hope you'll be able to come. I've been so busy planning for the wedding, working, and studying that I haven't had much time to write lately. I hope you can understand.

I'm enclosing a picture of my fiancé. He has a sister **whose daughter goes to the same school as your son in Oakland.** I wonder if they know each other. Her name is Wanda Chen. Ask your son if he knows her.

I'm working now as a babysitter. The family **whose daughter I take care of** is from Japan. I'm even learning a few words in Japanese.

I'm also taking math classes at City College. The teacher **whose class I'm taking this semester** is very young. She just graduated from college, but she teaches very well.

(continued)

Adjective Clauses; Descriptive Phrases **241**

```
JoeP: how r u
NetSan: fine. i have a joke 4 u
JoeP: dont have time now. brb
JoeP: back
NetSan: wanna hear the joke now?
JoeP: e-mail it 2 me. dont 4-get gotta go now
NetSan: y?
JoeP: gotta talk 2 a co-worker whose laptop I fixed
NetSan: k. i'll send my joke 2 u later 2-day. g'bye 4 now
```

```
From:    jill
Subject: attachment

    fran,
    attached <attachment> r the pics i promised u. wanna
    see more? i'll call u tomorrow nite will u b home?
    jill
```

 Part 2: Read the following article. Pay special attention to adjective clauses beginning with *whose*.

When was the last time you received a handwritten letter in your mailbox? Are there people **whose letters you've saved for years?** The art of letter writing seems to be dying for many people as more and more of us are using e-mail, instant messages, and text messages for fast, easy communication.

You might think the United States is a country of serious Internet users. But there are many people **whose only online activity** is sending and receiving e-mail and chatting. When people send e-mail and instant messages, they often don't give much thought to how they write; many people use abbreviations and omit punctuation and capital letters. They  simply write the first thing that comes into their head, click, and send it. There are people **whose only experience with writing letters** is by e-mail.

Letter writing usually takes longer, but people love to receive handwritten letters that are long and full of news. The paper is often attractive, the handwriting is personal, and the contents are interesting and detailed.

On the other hand, writing quick, short e-mail notes is a great way to keep in touch with distant friends and relatives. But e-mail exposes us to the danger of viruses. There are people **whose enjoyment seems to come from creating viruses that cause problems for the rest of us.** Some viruses have shut down hundreds of thousands of computers in one day. You should never

open an attachment from a sender **whose name you don't recognize.** Postal letters never contain viruses. And they provide a personal, intimate connection with a friend or relative.

Regardless of whether you prefer to send and receive handwritten letters or e-mails, it is important and fun to stay connected with friends and family.

6.8 | *Whose* + Noun in an Adjective Clause

Whose is the possessive form of *who*. It stands for *his, her, its, their,* or the possessive form of the noun.

Whose + noun can be the subject of the adjective clause

Subject

There are people. *Their enjoyment* comes from creating viruses.

↓

There are people **whose enjoyment comes from creating viruses.**

Subject

Companies can lose a lot of money. *Their computers* are infected with a virus.

Companies **whose computers are infected with a virus** can lose a lot of money.

Whose + noun can be the object of the adjective clause

Object

Don't open an attachment from a sender. You don't recognize *the sender's name.*

Don't open an attachment from a sender **whose name you don't recognize.**

Object

I've saved *my friends' letters* for years. They are amazed that I still have their mail.

Friends **whose** letters I've saved for years are amazed that I still have their mail.

EXERCISE 15 Underline the adjective clause in each sentence.

EXAMPLE Companies <u>whose sites you visit</u> may sell your e-mail address to spammers.

1. Spammers send e-mail to all the people whose names are on their lists.

2. On eBay you can meet people whose interests you share.

3. I sent an e-mail to all the people whose e-mail addresses are in my address book.

4. I only open attachments of senders whose names I recognize.

5. The person whose e-mail I forwarded to you got angry at me for not asking her permission first.

6. A company whose Web site I visit often sends me coupons by e-mail.

7. Companies whose computers are affected with a virus can lose all their data.

8. I have to talk to a co-worker whose laptop I borrowed.

EXERCISE 16 Use the sentence in parentheses to form an adjective clause.

EXAMPLE eBay is a company ___*whose customers buy and sell thousands*___ ___*of items a day*___. (Its customers buy and sell thousands of items a day.)

1. Pierre Omidyar is a creative person _____. (His idea for eBay made him a very wealthy man.)

2. My friend has a sister _____. (Her daughter is studying to be a computer programmer.)

3. The teacher _____ uses a computer in the classroom. (I'm taking his class.)

4. There are some people _____. (Their idea of fun is to infect other people's computers with a virus.)

5. The police have arrested people _____. (Their viruses have infected thousands of computers.)

6. The person _____ got angry with me. (I forwarded her letter to everyone in my address book.)

7. I received a letter with an attachment from a sender _____

_____. (I don't recognize his or her name.)

8. The family _____ has three computers in their house. (I babysit for their daughter).

6.9 | Adjective Clauses After Indefinite Pronouns

An adjective clause can follow an indefinite pronoun: *someone, something, everyone, everything, no one, nothing, anything.*

Examples	Explanation
IP RP Everyone **who received my e-mail** knows about the party. IP RP I don't know anyone **who has never used e-mail.**	The relative pronoun (RP) after an indefinite pronoun (IP) can be the subject of the adjective clause. The relative pronoun cannot be omitted.
IP RP Something **(that) he wrote** made me angry. IP RP I didn't read anything **(that) I received** today.	The relative pronoun (RP) after an indefinite pronoun (IP) can be the object of the adjective clause. In this case, it is usually omitted.

Language Notes:

1. An indefinite pronoun takes a singular verb (the –s form).

   Everyone who **uses** e-mail has an e-mail address.

   I don't know anyone who **doesn't** have a computer.

2. An adjective clause does not usually follow a personal pronoun, except in very formal language and in some proverbs.

   He who laughs last laughs best.

   He who hesitates is lost.

EXERCISE 17   Fill in the blanks with an adjective clause. Use information from nearby sentences to help you. Answers may vary.

A woman (W) is trying to break up with a man (M).

M: I heard you want to talk to me.

W: Yes. There's something _____*I want to tell you*_____
(example)

M: What do you want to tell me?

W: I want to break up.

M: Are you angry at me? What did I say?

W: Nothing _____ made me angry.
(1)

M: Did I do something wrong?

W: Nothing _____ made me mad.
(2)

M: Then what's the problem?

W: I just don't love you anymore.

M: But I can buy you anything _____.
                                                    (3)

W: I don't want anything from you. In fact, I'm going to return

everything _____.
                                 (4)

M: But I can take you anywhere _____.
                                                    (5)

W: I don't want to go anywhere with you.

M: What about all the love letters I sent you by e-mail?

W: I deleted everything _____.
                                              (6)

M: Didn't you believe anything _____?
                                                    (7)

W: I found out that you said the same thing to three other women.

M: That's not true. Everything _____ was sincere.
                                              (8)

W: How can it be sincere? You wrote the same thing to my cousin's best
friend, my neighbor, and my classmate. The only thing you changed

was the name after "Dear." Everything else _____
                                                                    (9)

was the same. So goodbye!

EXERCISE 18 Fill in the blanks with an adjective clause. Answers may vary.

EXAMPLE I don't send e-mail to everyone ____*I know*____.

1. You should read everything _____ in an e-mail before
   sending it.

2. When sending an e-mail, you shouldn't write anything

   _____.

3. I received 20 e-mails today. Nothing _____ was
   important. It was all spam.

4. Some people delete everything _____ after they read it.

5. If you have a buddy list, you can send an instant message to

   someone _____.

6. People you don't know may send you attachments. You shouldn't

   open an attachment from anyone _____.
   It may contain a virus.

EXERCISE 19   Fill in the blanks with an adjective clause.

EXAMPLE   I know someone ____*who can help you with your car problem*____.

1. I don't know anyone _____.

2. I know someone _____.

3. Everyone _____ can go to the next level.

4. Anyone _____ should ask the teacher.

5. Everything _____ is useful.

EXERCISE 20   *Combination Exercise.* Circle the correct word in parentheses ( ) to complete the sentences. Ø means no word is necessary.

EXAMPLE   What is a computer virus? A virus is a computer code (what, (that,) who, whose) attaches itself to other programs and causes harm to programs, data, or hardware.

1. Viruses are written by people (they, who, whom, whose) enjoy causing problems for the rest of us.

2. What is spam? Spam is commercial e-mail (who, where, what, Ø) you haven't asked for.

3. Who is Bill Gates? Bill Gates is the man (who, whom, which, what) created Microsoft.

4. Bill Gates was born at a time (when, that, which, then) personal computers were not even in people's imaginations.

5. Who is Meg Whitman? She is the woman (to who, whom, to whom, to which) Pierre Omidyar turned over the operation of eBay in 1998.

6. Omidyar needed to bring in someone (who, whose, who's, who his) knowledge of business was greater than his own.

7. A computer is a tool (Ø, whom, about which, whose) most of us use today for fast access to information.

8. The Internet is a tool (that, what, when, Ø) has been around since the 1970s.

9. What is eBay? eBay is a Web site (that, where, there, which) you can buy and sell items.

10. The Internet can be slow at times (where, when, that, which) there is a lot of traffic.

11. The people (Ø, which, whose, where) you meet in chat rooms are sometimes very rude.

12. I have all the letters (that, what, where, whose) my parents have sent to me.

13. The computer lab is never open at a time (which, then, where, when) I need it.

14. I always delete the spam (who, that, when, whose) I receive.

15. On eBay, you can meet people (who, whom, who they, they) have the same interests as you do.

16. You can create an address book (when, that, where, whose) you can keep the e-mail addresses of all your friends.

17. You can create an address book (which, in which, there, in that) you can keep the e-mail addresses of all your friends.

18. There are chat rooms (there, where, which, that) people with the same interests can meet each other.

19. A virus writer is a person (his, whose, who, whom) enjoyment comes from creating problems for computer users.

20. Do you know anyone (Ø, who, whom, which) doesn't own a computer?

21. A man (who, whom, whose, who's) in my math class doesn't own a computer.

22. Don't believe everything (what, who, whom, Ø) you read on the Internet.

EXERCISE 21 *Combination Exercise.* Fill in the blanks with an adjective clause by using the sentences in parentheses or the context to give you clues.

A: How was your move last month?

B: It was terrible.

A: Didn't you use the moving company ___*I recommended*___?
   (example)

   (I recommended a company.)

B: The company _____ (1) _____ was not available on

   the day _____ (2) _____. *(I had to move on*

   this day.) I used a company _____ (3) _____.

   (I found the name on the Internet.)

A: What happened?

B: First of all, it was raining on the day —————————————.

                                                      (4)

That made the move take longer, so it was more expensive than I thought it would be.

A: It's not the company's fault that it rained.

B: I know. But there are many other things —————————————.

                                                           (5)

(Things were their fault.) The movers broke the mirror

————————————————. *(I had just bought the mirror.)* And

                        (6)

they left muddy footprints on the carpet —————————————.

                                                            (7)

(I had just cleaned the carpet.) I thought I was getting professional

movers. But the men *(They sent these men to my home.)* ————————

——————————————— ———— were college students. They

                                 (8)

didn't have much experience moving. Because the move took them so long, they charged me much more than I expected to pay. The

information *(They have information.)* —————————————

                                                            (9)

on their Web site says $100 an hour. But they charged me $800 for six hours of work.

A: You should talk to the owner of the company.

B: I called the company several times. The woman *(I talked to a*

woman.) ————————————— said that the owner would

                                    (10)

call me back, but he never has.

A: You should keep trying. Make a list of everything —————————

———————————————. *(They broke or ruined things.)*

                                    (11)

Their insurance will probably pay for these things.

B: I don't know if they have insurance.

A: You should never use a company —————————————.

                                                         (12)

B: Everyone ————————————— *(I've talked to people.)*

                                    (13)

tells me the same thing.

A: Don't feel so bad. Everyone makes mistakes. We learn from the

mistakes —————————————. Why didn't you ask

                                    (14)

your friends to help you move?

B: Everyone —————————— (15) ———————————— *(I know people.)* is so

busy. I didn't want to bother anyone.

A: By the way, why did you move? You had a lovely apartment.

B: It wasn't mine. The person *(I was renting her apartment.)*

—————————————————————— spent a year in China,
(16)

but when she came back last month, I had to leave.

A: How do you like your new place?

B: It's fine. It's across the street from the building

——————————————————. *(My sister lives in that*
(17)

building.) So now we get to see each other more often. Why don't
you come over sometime and see my new place?

A: I'd love to. How about Saturday after 4 p.m.? That's the only time

——————————. *(I don't have too much to do at that time.)*
(18)

B: Saturday would be great.

CREATING THE WORLD WIDE WEB

Before You
Read

1. Besides computers, what other inventions have changed the way people communicate with each other?

2. When you think about computers and the Internet, what famous names come to mind?

Tim Berners-Lee

Read the following article. Notice that some adjective clauses are separated from the main clause with a comma.

Most people have never heard of Tim Berners-Lee. He is not rich or famous like Bill Gates.

Berners-Lee, who works in a small office at the Massachusetts Institute of Technology, is the creator of the World Wide Web. The creation of the Web is so important that some people compare Berners-Lee to Johann Gutenberg, who invented printing by moveable type in the fifteenth century.

Berners-Lee was born in England in 1955. His parents, who helped design the world's first commercially available computer, gave him a great love of mathematics and learning.

In 1980, Berners-Lee went to work at CERN, a physics laboratory in Geneva, Switzerland, where he had a lot of material to learn quickly. He had a poor memory for facts and wanted to find a way to keep track of things he couldn't remember. He devised a software program that allowed him to create a document that had links to other documents. He continued to develop his idea through the 1980s. He wanted to find a way to connect the knowledge and creativity of people all over the world.

In 1991, his project became known as the World Wide Web. The number of Internet users started to grow quickly. However, Berners-Lee is not completely happy with the way the Web has developed. He thinks it has become a passive tool for so many people, not the tool for creativity that he had imagined.

In 1999, Berners-Lee published a book called *Weaving the Web,* in which he answers questions he is often asked: "What were you thinking when you invented the Web?" "What do you think of it now?" "Where is the Web going to take us in the future?"

6.10 | Nonessential Adjective Clauses

Examples	Explanation
Berners-Lee, **who was born in England**, now lives in the U.S.	Some adjective clauses are not essential to the meaning of the sentence. A nonessential adjective clause adds extra information. The sentence is complete without it.
Berners-Lee's parents, **who helped design the first computer**, gave their son a love of learning.	
Berners-Lee went to work at CERN, **which is a physics laboratory in Geneva.**	A nonessential adjective clause is separated by commas from the main part of the sentence.
Berners-Lee was born in 1955, **when personal computers were beyond people's imagination.**	
Pierre Omidyar, **who created eBay**, was born in France.	A nonessential adjective clause begins with *who, whom, which, where, when,* or *whose. That* is not used in a nonessential adjective clause.
Pierre Omidyar, **whose wife is a collector**, got his idea for eBay in 1995.	
Pierre brought in Meg Whitman, **whose knowledge of business helped make eBay the success it is today.**	

EXERCISE 22 Put commas in the following sentences to separate the adjective clause from the main part of the sentence.

EXAMPLE The abacus, which is a wooden rack with beads, was probably the first computer.

1. The abacus which was created about 2,000 years ago helped people solve arithmetic problems.

2. The first modern computer which was called ENIAC took up a lot of space (1,800 square feet).

3. ENIAC was created in 1942 when the U.S. was involved in World War II.

4. ENIAC which helped the government store important data was built at the University of Pennsylvania.

5. Personal computers which were introduced in the 1970s are much smaller and faster than previous computers.

6. Bill Gates went to Harvard University where he developed the programming language BASIC.

7. Bill Gates dropped out of Harvard to work with Paul Allen who was his old high school friend.

8. Together Gates and Allen founded Microsoft which has made both of them very rich.

9. In 1984, Apple produced the first Macintosh computer which was easier to use than earlier computers.

10. In 1990, Bill Gates introduced Windows which was Microsoft's version of the popular Macintosh operating system.

11. Berners-Lee whose name is not widely recognized made a great contribution to the world.

12. The Internet which has been around since the 1970s was not available to most people until the Web was created.

Bill Gates

6.11 | Essential vs. Nonessential Adjective Clauses[2]

Examples	Explanation
Bill Gates, **who created Microsoft,** never finished college. Berners-Lee, **whose parents helped design the first computer,** loved mathematics. Berners-Lee works at MIT, **where he has a small office.** eBay was in Omidyar's hands until 1998, **when he turned over the operation of the company to Meg Whitman.**	In the examples to the left, the adjective clause is **nonessential** because, without it, we can still identify the noun in the main clause. Try reading the sentences without the adjective clause. The sentences are complete. The adjective clause adds extra information to the sentence. A nonessential adjective clause is set off from the rest of the sentence by commas.
The people **who built the first computers** worked at the engineering department of the University of Pennsylvania. There are many people **whose only online activity is sending and receiving e-mail.**	In the examples to the left, the adjective clause is **essential** because, without it, we can't identify the noun. Try reading the sentences without the adjective clause. If we take it out, the noun isn't properly identified and the idea isn't complete.
Compare: a. The computer, **which was invented in the 1940s,** has become part of our everyday lives. (Nonessential)	Example (a) refers to the whole class of computers as an invention.
b. The computer **(that, which) I bought two years ago** is slow compared to today's computers. (Essential)	Example (b) refers to only one computer, which is identified by the adjective clause.
Compare: a. A person who invents something is very creative and intelligent. (Essential)	In sentence (a), the adjective clause is essential in order to explain which person is creative and intelligent.
b. Berners-Lee, who invented the Web, is not rich. (Nonessential)	In sentence (b), the adjective clause is nonessential because it provides extra information. Berners-Lee is unique and does not need to be identified. The adjective clause is nonessential.
Compare: a. The computer **(which or that)** she just bought has a big memory. (Essential)	In an essential adjective clause (a), the relative pronouns *which* or *that* can be used or omitted.
b. Microsoft, **which** Bill Gates helped create, is a billion-dollar company. (Nonessential)	In a nonessential adjective clause (b), only the relative pronoun *which* can be used. It cannot be omitted.

[2] Nonessential adjective clauses are often called nonrestrictive adjective clauses.

Language Note: Here are some questions to help you decide if the adjective clause needs commas or not. If the answer to any of these questions is *yes*, then the adjective clause is set off by commas.

- Can I put the adjective clause in parentheses?

  Bill Gates **(who created Microsoft)** never finished college.
- Can I write the adjective clause as a separate sentence?

  Bill Gates created Microsoft. **He never finished college.**
- If the adjective clause is deleted, does the sentence still make sense?

  Bill Gates never finished college.
- Is the noun a unique person or place?

  Berners-Lee, who works at MIT, invented the Web.
- If the noun is plural, am I including all members of a group (all my cousins, all my friends, all Americans, all computers)?

  My friends, who are wonderful people, always help me. (All of my friends are wonderful people.)

  Compare:

  I send e-mail to my friends **who have home computers and Internet service.**
  (Not all of my friends have home computers and Internet service.)

EXERCISE 23 Decide which of the following sentences contains a nonessential adjective clause. Put commas in those sentences. If the sentence doesn't need commas, write *NC*.

EXAMPLES   People who send e-mail often use abbreviations.   **NC**

         My father, who sent me an e-mail yesterday, is sick.

1. Kids who spend a lot of time on the computer don't get much exercise.

2. My grammar teacher who has been teaching here for 20 years knows a lot about computers.

3. Viruses which can be sent in attachments can destroy your hard drive.

4. People who get spam every day can get very annoyed.

5. My best friend who gets at least 30 pieces of spam a day wrote a letter to his senator to complain.

6. Berners-Lee whose parents were very educated loves learning new things.

7. Marc Andreesseon created Netscape which is a popular Web browser.

8. Berners-Lee worked in Switzerland where the CERN physics laboratory is located.

9. The Instant Message which was a creation of America Online is available to many e-mail users.

10. Did you like the story that we read about Berners-Lee?

11. The computer you bought three years ago doesn't have enough memory.

12. The computer which is one of the most important inventions of the twentieth century has changed the way people process information.

13. Bill Gates who created Microsoft with his friend became a billionaire.

14. My best friend whose name is on my buddy list contacts me every day through an instant message.

EXERCISE 24 Combine the two sentences into one. The sentence in parentheses ( ) is not essential to the main idea of the sentence. It is extra information.

EXAMPLE eBay is now a large corporation. (It was started in Pierre Omidyar's house.)

eBay, which was started in Pierre Omidyar's house, is now

a large corporation.

1. Marc Andreessen was only 24 when he became rich. (He founded Netscape.)

   _____

   _____

2. The World Wide Web is used by millions of people around the world. (It was created by Tim Berners-Lee.)

   _____

   _____

3. Tim Berners-Lee was born in England. (We saw his picture on page 250 and 251.)

   _____

   _____

4. The book *Weaving the Web* answers a lot of questions about the creation of the Web. (It was written by Berners-Lee in 1999.)

   _____

   _____

5. Berners-Lee knew about computers from an early age. (His parents helped design one of the first computers.)

_____

_____

6. Tim Berners-Lee works at MIT. (He has a small office there.)

_____

_____

7. Pierre Omidyar got his idea for eBay in 1995. (His wife couldn't find one of her favorite collectibles at that time.)

_____

_____

8. eBay hired Meg Whitman in 1998. (More expert business knowledge was needed at that time to run the company.)

_____

_____

9. E-mail did not become popular until the 1990s. (It was first created in 1972.)

_____

_____

10. Bill Gates often gets spam asking him if he wants to become rich. (He's the richest man in the U.S.)

_____

_____

11. Pierre Omidyar came to the U.S. when he was a child. (His father was a professor of medicine.)

_____

_____

6.12 | Descriptive Phrases

Some adjective clauses can be shortened to descriptive phrases. We can shorten an adjective clause in which the relative pronoun is followed by the verb *be*.

Examples	Explanation
Compare: a. People **who are unhappy with the amount of spam they receive** should write to their lawmakers. b. People **unhappy with the amount of spam they receive** should write to their lawmakers. a. Pierre Omidyar, **who is the founder of eBay,** is one of the richest men in the world. b. Pierre Omidyar, **the founder of eBay,** is one of the richest men in the world.	Sentences (a) have an adjective clause. Sentences (b) have a descriptive phrase.
a. One-half of all of the e-mail **that is sent today** is spam. b. One-half of all the e-mail *sent* **today** is spam. a. There are about 11 million items **that are listed on eBay.** b. There are about 11 million items *listed* **on eBay.**	A descriptive phrase can begin with a **past participle.** Compare sentences (a) with an adjective clause to sentences (b) with a descriptive phrase.
a. A man **who is living in Florida** retired at the age of 37 after making millions in the spam business. b. A man *living* **in Florida** retired at the age of 37 after making millions in the spam business. a. Shoppers **who are using eBay** can locate a hard-to-find item. b. Shoppers *using* **eBay** can locate a hard-to-find item.	A descriptive phrase can begin with a **present participle** (verb *-ing*). Compare sentences (a) with an adjective clause to sentences (b) with a descriptive phrase.
a. Spam, **which is unwanted commercial e-mail,** is an annoying problem. b. Spam, **unwanted commercial e-mail,** is an annoying problem. a. eBay, **which is an auction Web site,** is very popular. b. eBay, **an auction Web site,** is very popular.	A descriptive phrase can give a definition or more information about the noun it follows. This kind of descriptive phrase is called an **appositive.** Compare sentences (a) with an adjective clause to sentences (b) with an appositive.
a. A man **who is in Florida** retired at the age of 37. b. A man *in* **Florida** retired at the age of 37. a. Pierre, **who is from France,** created eBay. b. Pierre, *from* **France,** created eBay.	A descriptive phrase can begin with a preposition (*with, in, from, of,* etc.) Compare sentences (a) with an adjective clause to sentences (b) with a prepositional phrase.

Language Notes:

1. A descriptive phrase can be essential or nonessential. A nonessential phrase is set off by commas.

   People **unhappy** with the amount of spam they receive should write to their lawmakers. (*Essential*)

   Pierre Omidyar, **the founder of eBay,** is one of the richest men in the world. (*Nonessential*)

2. An appositive is always nonessential.

   Amazon.com, **an online store,** is a very popular Web site.

EXERCISE 25 Shorten the adjective clauses by crossing out the unnecessary words.

EXAMPLE On eBay, people ~~who are~~ living in California can sell to people ~~who are~~ living in New York.

1. Netscape is a popular Web browser which is used by millions.

2. Bill Gates, who is one of the richest people in the world, gets spam asking him if he wants to become rich.

3. There are a lot of dishonest companies which are trying to take your money.

4. eBay takes a percentage of each sale that is made on its Web site.

5. A virus is a harmful program which is passed from computer to computer.

6. Tim Berners-Lee, who was born in England, now works at M.I.T.

7. M.I.T., which is located in Cambridge, Massachusetts, is an excellent university.

8. Berners-Lee developed the idea for the Web when he was working at CERN, which is a physics lab in Switzerland.

9. Berners-Lee's parents worked on the first computer that was sold commercially.

10. People who are using the Web can shop from their homes.

11. People who are interested in reading newspapers from other cities can find them on the Web.

12. The World Wide Web, which is abbreviated WWW, was first introduced on the Internet in 1991.

13. Computers which are sold today have much more memory and speed than computers which were sold 10 years ago.

14. Marc Andreessen, who was the creator of Netscape, quickly became a billionaire.

15. You can download Netscape, which is a popular Internet browser.

EXERCISE 26 Combine the two sentences. Use a phrase for the sentence in parentheses ( ).

EXAMPLE Microsoft Windows made personal computers easy to use. (Windows was created by Bill Gates.)

Microsoft Windows, created by Bill Gates, made personal computers

easy to use.

1. Google is very easy to use. (It is a popular search engine.)

   _____

   _____

2. Have you ever used Mapquest? (It is a Web site that gives maps and driving directions.)

   _____

   _____

3. "Melissa" infected a lot of computers in 1999. (It is a virus.)

   _____

   _____

4. Tim Berners-Lee was born in 1955. (This is the same year Bill Gates was born.)

   _____

   _____

5. Marc Andreessen quickly became a billionaire. (He is the creator of Netscape.)

   _____

   _____

Marc Andreessen

EXERCISE 27 *Combination Exercise.* Combine these short sentences into longer sentences using adjective clauses or descriptive phrases.

EXAMPLE Pierre Omidyar came to the U.S. when he was a child. His father was a professor of medicine.

Pierre Omidyar, whose father was a professor of medicine, came to the U.S. when he was a child.

1. Pierre Omidyar was born in France. He wrote his first computer program at age 14.

2. *Business Week* named Meg Whitman among the 25 most powerful business managers. *Business Week* is a popular business magazine.

3. Bill Gates was born in 1955. His father was a lawyer.

4. Bill Gates wrote his first computer program in 1967. He was only 12 years old at that time.

5. Bill Gates has three children. His wife was a marketing executive at Microsoft.

6. Marc Andreessen is the co-founder of Netscape. He taught himself BASIC programming at the age of nine.

7. Andreessen and James Clark created Netscape. It was originally called "Mosaic."

_____

_____

8. Netscape went public in 1995. Andreessen was only 24 years old.

_____

_____

9. Michael Dell created Dell computers. He dropped out of college after his first year.

_____

_____

10. Dell's parents were worried about Michael. His grades were dropping.

_____

_____

11. Dell's business started to perform well at the end of his first year of college. At that time, his business was making over $50,000 a month.

_____

_____

12. Dell Computers was one of the first companies to sell computers online. It was selling about $18 million of computers a day by the late 1990s.

_____

_____

13. In 2000, _Forbes_ named Dell Computers the third most admired company in the U.S. (_Forbes_ is a business magazine.)

_____

_____

	Essential	Nonessential
Pronoun as subject	People (**who** or **that**) **write e-mail** aren't careful about spelling. I just bought a computer **that (**or **which) has a very big memory.**	Bill Gates, **who created Microsoft,** is one of the richest people in the world. eBay was created in San Jose, **which is a city near San Francisco.**
Pronoun as object	The first computer **(that** or **which) I bought** didn't have a mouse. The people **(who, whom, that) you meet in chat rooms** are sometimes very silly.	My first computer, **which I bought in 1996,** is much slower than my new computer. My father, **whom you met at the party,** is a programmer.
Pronoun as object of preposition	The person **to whom I sent an e-mail** never answered me. (Formal) The person **(whom, who, that) I sent an e-mail to** didn't answer me. (Informal)	Berners-Lee, **about whom we read,** is an interesting person. (Formal) Berners-Lee, **whom we read about,** is an interesting person. (Informal)
Where	The store **where I bought my computer** has good prices.	Berners-Lee works at the Massachusetts Institute of Technology, **where he has a small office.**
When	I'll never forget the day **(when) I saw a personal computer for the first time.**	The Web was created in 1991, **when most people did not have home computers.**
Whose + noun as subject	Children **whose parents are poor** often don't have a home computer.	Berners-Lee, **whose parents worked on computers,** learned a lot in his home.
Whose + noun as object	There are friends **whose letters I've saved for years.**	My mother, **whose letters I've saved,** died two years ago.
Adjective clause after indefinite compound	I don't know anyone **who has a Macintosh computer.** Everything **I learned about computers** is useful.	———————
Descriptive phrase	Home computers **made 20 years ago** didn't have a big memory.	Bill Gates, **the founder of Microsoft,** became a billionaire.

1. Never use *what* as a relative pronoun.

   who
   She married a man ~~what~~ has a lot of money.

   that
   Everything ~~what~~ you did was unnecessary.

2. You can't omit a relative pronoun that is the subject of the adjective clause.

   who
   I know a man ˄speaks five languages.

3. If the relative pronoun is the object of the adjective clause, don't put an object after the verb.

   The car that I bought ~~it~~ has a stick shift.

4. Make sure you use subject-verb agreement.

   I know several English teachers who speak~~s~~ Spanish.

   has
   A car that ~~have~~ a big engine is not economical.

5. Put a noun before an adjective clause.

   The student w
   ~~W~~ho wants to leave early should sit in the back.

6. Put the adjective clause near the noun it describes.

   The teacher ˄speaks Spanish (whose class I am taking).

7. Don't confuse *whose* with *who's*.

   whose
   A student ~~who's~~ grades are good may get a scholarship.

8. Put the subject before the verb in an adjective clause.

   my cousin bought
   The house that ~~bought my cousin~~ is very beautiful.

9. Use *whose*, not *his*, *her*, or *their*, to show possession in an adjective clause.

   whose
   I have a friend ~~who his~~ knowledge of computers is very great.

PART 1 Find the mistakes with the underlined words, and correct them. Not every sentence has a mistake. If the sentence is correct, write *C*.

EXAMPLES   The students should correct the mistakes <u>that they make them</u>.

The students <u>about whom we were speaking</u> entered the room.   **C**

1. The teacher <u>what we have</u> is from Canada.

2. Five students were absent on the day when <u>was given the final test</u>.

3. The room <u>where we took</u> the test was not air-conditioned.

4. <u>Who</u> missed the test can take it next Friday.

5. Students <u>who knows</u> a lot of English grammar can take a composition course.

6. The teacher <u>whose class I'm taking</u> speaks English clearly.

7. A tutor is a person <u>whom helps students</u> individually.

8. Everyone wants to have a teacher <u>whose pronunciation is clear</u>.

9. The student <u>whose sitting</u> next to me is trying to copy my answers.

10. A teacher helped me at registration <u>who speaks my native language</u>.

11. The teacher gave a test <u>had 25 questions</u>.

12. The student <u>which</u> sits near the door always leaves early.

13. I have a neighbor <u>who his</u> son plays with my son.

14. Do you know <u>anyone who has</u> a German car?

15. The textbook <u>we are using</u> has a lot of exercises.

16. The people <u>who lives</u> upstairs make a lot of noise in the morning.

PART 2 Fill in the blanks to complete the adjective clause. Answers may vary.

EXAMPLES   A: Do you like your new roommate?

B: Not really. The roommate _I had last year_ was much nicer.

A: Are there any teachers at this school _who speak Spanish_?

B: Yes. Ms. Lopez speaks Spanish.

1. **A:** I heard you had a car accident. You hit another car.

   B: Yes. The woman whose _____ wants me to pay her $700.

2. **A:** I bought a laptop for $1,500.

   B: That's a lot of money. The laptop _____ only cost $1,000.

3. **A:** Did you buy your textbooks at Berk's Bookstore?

   B: No. The store _____ is about ten blocks from school. Books are cheaper there.

4. **A:** My husband's mother always interferes in our married life.

   B: That's terrible. I wouldn't want to be married to a man whose _____.

5. **A:** What did the teacher say about registration?

   B: I don't know. She spoke very fast. I didn't understand everything _____.

6. **A:** Do you remember your first day in the U.S.?

   B: Of course. I'll always remember the day _____ in my new country.

7. **A:** The teacher is talking about a very famous American, but I didn't hear his name.

   B: The man _____ is John Kennedy.

8. **A:** Did you buy the dictionary I recommended to you?

   B: No. The dictionary _____ is just as good as the one you recommended.

9. **A:** Do you remember the names of all the students?

   B: No. There are some students _____.

PART 3 Complete each statement. Every sentence should have an adjective clause.

EXAMPLE The library is a place ———— *where you can read* ————.

1. The teacher _____ doesn't teach here anymore.

2. Everything _____ is important to me.

3. Teachers _____ aren't good for foreign students.

4. The teacher will not pass a student whose _____.

5. I would like to live in a house _____.

6. The classroom _____ is clean and pleasant.

7. I will never forget the day _____.

8. I never got an answer to the question _____ about the test.

9. Everyone _____ had a great time.

10. I don't like the dictionary _____, so I'm going to buy a better one.

11. Computers _____ ten years ago are slow compared to today's computers.

12. A laboratory is a place where _____.

13. There's so much noise in my house. I need to find a place

_____.

14. Small children whose _____ learn to read faster than children who sit in front of the TV all day.

PART 4 Combine each pair of sentences into one sentence. Use the words in parentheses ( ) to add a nonessential adjective clause to the first sentence.

EXAMPLE   Pierre Omidyar got the idea for eBay in 1995. (His wife is a collector.)

Pierre Omidyar, whose wife is a collector, got the idea

for eBay in 1995.

1. Berners-Lee was born in 1955. (Most people knew nothing about computers in 1955.)

_____

2. The Internet changed the way people get their information. (It became popular in the 1990s.)

_____

3. Berners-Lee studied physics in college. (His parents were programmers.)

_____

4. Berners-Lee is not a well-known person. (We read about him in this lesson.)

_____

5. Berners-Lee works at MIT. (He has a small office there.)

_____

PART 5 Some of these adjective clauses can be shortened. Shorten them by crossing out unnecessary words. Some of the adjective clauses cannot be shortened. Do not change them. Write "no change" (*NC*).

EXAMPLES Thanksgiving, ~~which is~~ an American holiday, is in November.

Everyone who came to dinner enjoyed the food. **NC**

1. The English that is spoken in the U.S. is different from British English.

2. A lot of people like to shop on eBay, which is an auction Web site.

3. Do not disturb the students who are studying in the library.

4. In the U.S. there are many immigrants who are from Mexico.

5. The computer that you bought has a very big memory.

6. She doesn't like the music that her daughter listens to.

7. Everyone who saw the movie liked it a lot.

8. Everyone whom I met at the party was very interesting.

9. Children who watch TV all day don't get enough exercise.

10. Parents whose children are small should control the TV programs that their kids watch.

11. The teacher with whom I studied beginning grammar comes from Canada.

12. The Web, which was introduced in 1991, has changed the way many companies do business.

PART 6 Some of the following sentences need commas. Put them in. If the sentence doesn't need commas, write "no commas."

EXAMPLES The last article we read was about the Internet.

no commas

Alaska, which is the largest state, has a very small population.

1. Ms. Thomson who was my English teacher last semester will retire next year.

2. I don't like teachers who give a lot of homework.

3. I studied engineering at the University of Michigan which is located in Ann Arbor, Michigan.

4. The computer I bought last month has a very big memory.

5. The computer which is one of the most important inventions of the twentieth century can be found in many American homes.

6. eBay is a Web site where people can buy and sell items.

7. My mother who lives in Miami has a degree in engineering.

8. I have two sisters. My sister who lives in New Jersey has three children.

9. Our parents who live with us now are beginning to study English.

10. The American flag which has 13 stripes and 50 stars is red, white, and blue.

11. The city where I was born has beautiful museums.

12. St. Petersburg where I was born has beautiful museums.

EXPANSION ACTIVITIES

Classroom Activities

1. **Game. Yes, but . . .** Work with a partner. One person will finish the sentence giving a point of view. The other person will contradict the first person by saying, "Yes, but . . ." and giving a different point of view.

   EXAMPLE   People who get married when they are young . . .
   A: People who get married when they are young have a lot of energy to raise their children.
   B: Yes, but people who get married when they are young are not very responsible.

   a. Couples who have a lot of children . . .

   b. People who immigrate to the U.S. . . .

   c. English books that have the answers in the back . . .

   d. People who have a lot of money . . .

   e. People who have a car . . .

   f. People who live in the same place all their lives . . .

   g. Teachers who speak fast . . .

   h. People who use credit cards . . .

   i. Cities that have a lot of factories . . .

   j. Movies that have a lot of violence . . .

   k. Parents who do everything for their children . . .

   l. Couples who have children when they're in their 40s . . .

   m. People who use the Internet a lot . . .

2. Fill in the blanks and discuss your answers in a small group.

a. People ———————————————————— have an easy life.

b. No one likes or respects people ————————————————

c. People who ———————————————— want to come to the U.S.

d. There are a lot of people who ——————————————————

3. **Dictionary Game.** Form a small group. One student in the group will look for a hard word in the dictionary. (Choose a noun. Find a word that you think no one will know.) Other students will write definitions of the word. Students can think of funny definitions or serious ones. The student with the dictionary will write the real definition. Students put all the definitions in a box. The student with the dictionary will read the definitions. The others have to guess which is the real definition.

EXAMPLE   nonagenarian
            Sample definition: A nonagenarian is a person who has none of the characteristics of his generation.
            Real definition: A nonagenarian is a person who is between 90 and 99 years old.

(**Alternate:** The teacher can provide a list of words and definitions beforehand, writing them on small pieces of paper. A student can choose one of the papers that the teacher has prepared.)

Talk About it

1. In what ways does the computer make life better? In what ways does it make life worse?

2. Discuss the differences between using e-mail and postal mail. In what cases is it better to use e-mail? In what cases is it better to write a letter, put it in an envelope, and mail it?

Write About it

1. Write a paragraph telling the different ways you use your computer (or the computers at this school).

2. Write about an important person you know about who didn't receive much attention or money for his or her work.

3. Write about an important invention. How did this invention change society?

Internet Activities

1. Find Tim Berners-Lee's Web site. What kind of information can you get from his Web site?

2. Go to a Web site that sells books. Find Berners-Lee's book, *Weaving the Web*. How much is it? Find a review of his book and print it out.

3. If you don't use AOL, type in *AOL Instant Messenger* at a search engine. Find out how to use this service.

4. Bring in a copy of a spam e-mail you received. Talk about the offers. Are they believable?

5. Go to eBay and find an item you might be interested in buying. Find the starting price.

6. At a search engine, type in *How Stuff Works*. Look up an article about spam. Circle all the adjective clauses in the article.

Additional Activities at **http://elt.thomson.com/gic**

LESSON

7

7.1 | Infinitives—An Overview

An infinitive is *to* + base form: *to go, to be, to see.*

Examples	Explanation
I want **to help.**	An infinitive is used after certain verbs.
I want him **to help.**	An object can be added before an infinitive.
I'm happy **to help.**	An infinitive can follow certain adjectives.
It's important **to help** others.	An infinitive follows certain expressions with *it.*
Do you volunteer your time in order **to help** others?	An infinitive is used to show purpose.
He's old enough **to help.** She's too young **to help.**	An infinitive is used after expressions with *too* and *enough.*

ANDREW CARNEGIE, PHILANTHROPIST[1]

Before You Read

1. Who are some of the richest people today?
2. Should rich people help others?

Andrew Carnegie, 1835–1919

 Read the following article. Pay special attention to infinitives.

Andrew Carnegie was one of the world's richest men. He made a fortune in the oil and steel industries but spent most of his life giving his money away.

Carnegie was born in Scotland in 1835. When he was 13 years old, his family immigrated to the United States. A year later, he started **to work** for $1.20 a week. He was intelligent and hardworking, and it didn't take him long **to become** rich. But he always remembered the day he wanted **to use** a library in Pittsburgh but was not permitted **to enter.** He was disappointed **to learn** that the library was for members only.

---

[1] A *philanthropist* is a person who gives away money to help other people.

As Carnegie's fortunes grew, he started **to give** his money away. One of his biggest desires was **to build** free public libraries. He wanted everyone **to have** access to libraries and education. He believed that education was the key to a successful life. In 1881, there were only a few public libraries. Carnegie started to build free libraries for the people. Over the doors of the Carnegie Library of Pittsburgh, carved in stone, are his own words, "Free to the People." By the time Carnegie died, there were more than 2,500 public libraries in the English-speaking world.

But building libraries was not his only contribution. In his book, *The Gospel of Wealth*, he tried **to persuade** other wealthy people **to give** away their money. These are some of the ideas he wrote about in his book:

- **To give** away money is the best thing rich people can do.
- It is the moral obligation of the wealthy **to help** others.
- It is important for a rich person **to set** an example for others.
- It is not good **to have** money if your spirit is poor.
- It is the mind that makes the body rich.
- It is a disgrace[2] **to die** rich.

By the time he died in 1919, Carnegie had given away more than $350 million.

Did You Know?

$350 million in 1919 would be equivalent to $3.7 billion today.

[2] A *disgrace* is something that brings shame or dishonor.

7.2 | Verbs Followed by an Infinitive

Examples	Explanation
Carnegie wanted **to build** libraries. He started **to work** when he was 14. He decided **to give** away money. Everyone deserves **to have** an education.	Some verbs are followed by an infinitive.
I want **to make** money and **help** others.	In a sentence with two infinitives connected by *and*, the second *to* is usually omitted.
Everyone wants **to be given** an opportunity to succeed.	To make an infinitive passive, use *to be* + past participle.

Language Note:
The verbs below can be followed by an infinitive.

agree	deserve	love*	seem
appear	expect	manage	start*
attempt	forget	need	try*
begin*	hate*	offer	want
can('t) afford	hope	plan	wish
can't stand*	intend	prefer*	would like
choose	know how	prepare	refuse
continue*	learn	pretend	
decide	like*	promise	

* These verbs can also be followed by a gerund with little or no change in meaning. See Section 7.14.

EXERCISE 1   Fill in the blanks with an infinitive based on the story you just read.

EXAMPLE   Andrew Carnegie started _____*to work*_____ when he was very young.

1. He tried _____ a library when he was young, but he wasn't allowed inside.

2. He wanted _____ free public libraries.

3. He thought it was important for rich people _____ poor people.

4. He thought it was better _____ a rich spirit than a big bank account.

5. He thought that rich people needed _____ an example for others.

6. He decided _____ a lot of money to help others.

7. He thought it was a terrible thing _____ rich.

EXERCISE 2 ABOUT YOU Fill in the blanks with an infinitive. Share your answers with the class.

EXAMPLE I like _____ *to eat Chinese food* _____.

1. I don't like _____, but I have to do it anyway.

2. I can't afford _____.

3. I've decided _____.

4. I want _____, but I don't have enough time.

5. I don't want _____, but I have to do it.

6. I sometimes forget _____.

7. I love _____.

8. I need _____ and _____ every day.

9. I don't know how _____, but I'd like to learn.

10. I would like _____.

EXERCISE 3 ABOUT YOU Answer these questions. You may discuss your answers.

EXAMPLE Why did you decide to come to this city?
I decided to come here because I wanted to go to this school.

1. Why did you decide to come to this school?

2. What did you need to do to get into this school?

3. When did you start to study English?

4. What do you expect to have five years from now (that you don't have now)?

5. What do you hope to accomplish in your lifetime?

6. Do you want to learn any other languages? Which ones? Why?

7. Do you plan to get a college degree? In what field?

8. Do you plan to transfer to a different school?

9. What do you plan to do after you graduate?

EXERCISE 4 Fill in the blanks with the passive form of the verb in parentheses ( ).

EXAMPLE Children like _____*to be given*_____ toys.
                          (give)

1. Children have _____ about giving, not just taking.
                      (teach)

2. My elderly neighbor needs _____ to the hospital
                                  (drive)
   because he can't drive. I'm going to offer to drive him.

3. Some people who make donations don't want their names

   _____.
        (know)

4. Money for a charity needs _____.
                                (collect)

5. There are many ways to help. Parks need _____.
                                              (clean)

6. There are many ways of helping children. Children need

   _____ and _____.
        (love)   *(respect)*

7. Carnegie thought that libraries needed _____ for
                                              (build)
   the public.

8. Everyone wants _____ a chance to succeed in life.
                      (give)

7.3 | Object Before Infinitive

After the verb, we can use an object + an infinitive.

Example	Explanation
a. Carnegie wanted **everyone to have** educational opportunities. b. He encouraged **rich people to help** others. c. He wanted **them to donate** money. d. Our parents want **us to help** others.	The object can be a noun (a and b) or a pronoun (c and d).
Carnegie encouraged people **not** to be selfish. The teacher advised us **not** to talk during an exam.	Put *not* before an infinitive to make a negative.

Language Note:
The verbs below can be followed by a noun or object pronoun + an infinitive.

advise	expect	persuade
allow	forbid	remind
appoint	force	teach*
ask	invite	tell
beg	need	urge
convince	order	want
encourage	permit	would like

*After *teach*, *how* is sometimes used: He taught me *how to ski*.

EXERCISE **5** ABOUT YOU Tell if you want or don't want the teacher to do the following.

EXAMPLES speak fast
I don't want the teacher to speak fast.

answer my questions
I want him to answer my questions.

1. explain the grammar
2. review modals
3. give us a lot of homework
4. give us a test on gerunds and infinitives
5. give a lot of examples
6. speak slowly
7. correct my pronunciation
8. teach us idioms

EXERCISE 6 Tell if the teacher expects or doesn't expect you to do the following.

come on time
The teacher expects us to come on time.

wear a suit to class
The teacher doesn't expect us to wear a suit to class.

1. write perfect compositions
2. learn English in six months
3. do the homework
4. stand up to answer a question
5. raise our hands to answer a question

6. ask questions
7. study on Saturdays
8. practice English every day
9. speak English without an accent
10. use the Internet

EXERCISE 7 Change the following imperative statements to statements with an object pronoun plus an infinitive.

EXAMPLE A woman says to her husband, "Teach the children good values."
She wants him to teach the children good values.

1. My parents always said to me, "Help others."

   My parents expected _____

2. A mother says to her children, "Be kind to others."

   She wants _____

3. The father said to his children, "Give to charity."

   The father advised _____

4. Parents say to their children, "Study hard."

   Parents want _____

5. I said to you, "Work hard."

   I would like _____

6. My parents said to us, "Give money to the poor."

   My parents reminded _____

7. A father says to his daughter, "Be generous."

   He wants _____

8. My parents said to me, "Don't be selfish."

   My parents encouraged _____

9. Parents say to their children, "Be polite."

   They expect _____

EXERCISE 8 ABOUT YOU Use the words given to tell what your family wanted from you when you were growing up.

EXAMPLES want / move away
My parents didn't want me to move away.

expect / get married
My mother expected me to get married when I graduated from college.

1. expect / respect older people
2. allow / stay out late at night
3. want / help them financially
4. expect / get good grades in school
5. encourage / have a lot of friends
6. want / be obedient
7. want / be independent
8. permit / choose my own friends
9. expect / get married
10. encourage / save money
11. advise / be honest
12. encourage / go to college

CHARITY AND VOLUNTEERING

Before You Read

1. Do you ever receive address labels in the mail with your name and address printed on them?
2. Do you ever watch a TV channel that asks you to send money to support it?

Read the following article. Pay special attention to verbs followed by infinitives and base forms.

There are more than 600,000 charities in the U.S. that you can give to. In addition, there are thousands of volunteer organizations. But it isn't always easy to **get** people **to give** willingly.

One way charities **get** people **to contribute** is by offering a payroll deduction at work. An employee can have a certain amount of each paycheck deducted, so the money goes to charity before the employee even sees it. If you are asked to give at your job, keep in mind that it is voluntary; no one can **make** you **give.**

Another way to **get** you **to give** is to send you something free in the mail, such as address labels with your name and address printed on them. Some people feel guilty about accepting the gift without giving something. Also some charities **have** volunteers **stand** at intersections with a can or box, asking passing drivers for donations. Often they give you something, such as candy, for your donation.

Public TV and radio stations have fundraisers. Several days out of the year, they ask for your money to support the programs you like. The station **has** volunteers **answer** phones to take your credit card number.

Besides giving money, people can volunteer their time. Some volunteers **help** kids **learn** to read; others help feed the homeless; others **help** elderly people **get** meals.

Helping others **makes** us **feel** good. To encourage us to give, the government **lets** us **deduct** our contribution, which lowers our taxes.

7.4 | Causative Verbs

Some verbs are often called *causative* verbs because one person causes, enables, or allows another to do something.

Examples	Explanation
Carnegie **persuaded** wealthy people **to give** away their money. You **convinced** me **to help** the poor. They **got** us **to contribute** to charity.	*Get, persuade, convince* are followed by an object + infinitive. *Get*, in the example on the left, means persuade.
Carnegie **helped** people **to get** an education. Volunteers **help** kids **learn** to read.	After *help* + object, either the infinitive or the base form can be used. The base form is more common.
The government **lets** you **deduct** your contribution to charity. The teacher doesn't **let** us **talk** during a test.	*Let* means permit. *Let* is followed by an object + base form. (*Permit* and *allow* are followed by an infinitive.) **Compare:** The teacher doesn't **let** us **talk.** The teacher doesn't **permit** us **to talk.**
a. No one can **make** you **give** to charity. b. Volunteering my time **makes** me **feel** good. c. A sad movie **makes** me **cry.**	*Make* is followed by an object + base form. In sentence (a), *make* means force. In sentences (b) and (c), *make* means to cause something to happen.
Public TV stations **have** volunteers **answer** the phones and take donations. The teacher **had** us **write** a composition about charity.	*Have* means to give a job or task to someone. *Have*, in this case, is followed by an object + base form.

EXERCISE **9** Fill in the blanks with the base form or the complete infinitive of the verb in parentheses ( ).

I volunteer for my local public radio station. Several times a year the

station tries to persuade listeners ___*to give*___ money to the station.
(example: give)

Without listener support, the radio station could not exist. The station

managers have us _____ the phones when listeners
(1 answer)

call to contribute. We let callers _____ by check or
(2 pay)

credit card. To get listeners _____, the station offers
(3 contribute)

Public Radio

some prizes. For example, for a $60 contribution, you can get a coffee mug. For a $100 contribution, you can get a book. Everyone can listen to public radio for free. No one makes you _____ for it.
(4 pay)

But listeners should pay for this service, if they can. They should help the station _____ for its excellent programming.
(5 pay)

EXERCISE 10 ABOUT YOU Fill in the blanks with the base form and finish the sentence.

EXAMPLE The teacher lets us ____*talk in groups when we work on a problem.*____

1. When I was a child, my parents didn't let me _____

_____

2. When I was a child, my parents made me _____

_____

3. During a test, the teacher doesn't let us _____

_____

4. The teacher often has us _____

5. My parents helped me _____

7.5 | Adjective Plus Infinitive

Certain adjectives can be followed by an infinitive.

Examples	Explanation
Some people are happy **to help** others. Are you willing **to donate** your time? I am proud **to be** a volunteer. I am sad **to see** so many needy people in the world. We are pleased to be able **to help.**	Certain adjectives can be followed by an infinitive. Many of these adjectives describe a person's emotional or mental state.

Language Note:
The following adjectives can be followed by an infinitive.

afraid	eager	pleased*	sad
ashamed*	glad	prepared*	sorry
delighted*	happy	proud	surprised*
disappointed*	lucky	ready	willing

*Note: Many *-ed* words are adjectives.

EXERCISE 11 **ABOUT YOU** Fill in the blanks with an infinitive (phrase).

EXAMPLE Before I came here, I was afraid _____ *to speak English.* _____

1. When I left my parents' house, I was eager _____
   _____

2. When I started college or high school, I was surprised (to see, learn, find out) _____

3. When I was a child, I was afraid _____
   _____

4. Now I'm afraid _____

5. I'm happy _____

6. I'm lucky _____

7. When I left my hometown, I was sorry _____
   _____

8. When I was _____ years old, I was ready _____
   _____

EXERCISE 12 *Combination Exercise.* Fill in the blanks with an infinitive or a base form in this conversation between an uncle (U) and his nephew (N). Answers may vary.

U: What do you plan ___to do___ this summer?
(example)

N: I wanted _____ (1) a summer job, but I couldn't find one. It's going to be boring. I'm ready _____ (2), but no one wants _____ (3) me. And my parents expect me _____ (4) a job. My mom won't let me _____ (5) home all day and watch TV or hang out with my friends at the swimming pool.

U: Are you trying _____ (6) money for your college education?

N: Not really. I haven't even thought about saving for college yet. I want a job because I'm planning _____ (7) a car.

U: You need _____ (8) about college too. You're going to graduate next year.

N: I'm planning _____ (9) to a community college, so it won't be so expensive. And my parents are willing _____ (10) for my college tuition.

U: Have you thought about volunteering your time this summer?

N: Not really. I just want _____ (11) money.

U: Don't just think about money. Try _____ (12) about how you can help other people. You can help little kids _____ (13) to read. Or you can help _____ (14) the parks by picking up garbage.

N: I keep telling you. I just want _____ (15) money. What will I get if I do those things? I won't get my car.

U: You'll get satisfaction. Helping others will make you

_____ good. And you will learn
(16)

_____ responsible. After you finish community
(17)
college and go to a four-year college, it will look good on your
application if you say you volunteered. It will help you

_____ into a good college.
(18)

A: Why are you trying so hard to get me _____ a
(19)
volunteer?

B: I volunteered when I was your age, and I found that it was more
valuable than money.

A: OK. I'll volunteer if you're willing _____ me the
(20)
money for the car.

BICYCLING TO RAISE MONEY FOR AIDS

Before You **Read**

1. How can one person help solve a big problem like AIDS or cancer?
2. Can you imagine riding a bike over 500 miles?

Read the following article.* Pay special attention to *in order to*
and *to*.

San Francisco

Los Angeles

California

Since the early 1980s, more than 25 million people have died of AIDS
worldwide and more than 40 million people are now infected. How can one
person do his or her part **to help** fight this deadly disease? Dan Pallotta
decided to try. In 1994, at the age of 32, he organized a bike ride from San
Francisco to Los Angeles **in order to call** attention to the AIDS epidemic. He
found 471 people willing to bike the 525 miles (845 km) in seven days. **To
raise** money, each rider asked friends and relatives to give donations in
support of the ride. Since 1994, more than 124,000 people have taken part in
the rides and more than $222 million have been raised for AIDS research.

*Statistics are as of May 2003.

(*continued*)

Infinitives; Gerunds **287**

These rides take place in many locations in the U.S. (Alaska, Minneapolis to Chicago, Boston to New York, San Francisco to Los Angeles). Of course, **to ride** such a long distance, a rider has to be in good shape. Many riders prepare for months ahead **in order to be** ready for the ride. But even riders in good shape sometimes need a break. Vans ride along with the cyclists **in order to pick up** anyone who needs to rest for a while.

At the end of the ride, cyclists are tired, but they have the satisfaction of having finished the ride and of raising money **to fight** the problem of AIDS.

7.6 | Using the Infinitive to Show Purpose

Example	Explanation
Dan organized the bike ride **in order to** raise money for AIDS. Vans ride along with the cyclists **in order to** pick up tired riders. **In order to** ride a long distance, you have to be in good shape.	*In order to* shows purpose. It answers the question "Why?" or "What for?"
Dan organized the bike ride **to** raise money for AIDS. Vans ride along with the cyclists **to** pick up tired riders. **To** ride a long distance, you have to be in good shape.	*In order to* can be shortened. We can simply use *to*.
a. **In order to help others,** Carnegie gave away his money.	a. The purpose clause can precede the main clause. Use a comma to separate the two clauses.
b. Carnegie gave away his money **in order to help others.**	b. The purpose clause can follow the main clause. Don't use a comma.

EXERCISE 13 Fill in the blanks to complete the sentences. Answers may vary.

EXAMPLE In order to _learn more about volunteering_, you can use the Internet. You can find lots of information there.

1. Carnegie donated his money to _____ libraries.

2. You can volunteer in order to _____ job experience.

   But in order to _____ money, you need a paying job.

3. To _____ a job, you need experience. To

   _____ experience, you need a job.

4. You can volunteer your time in order to _____ people. There are many people who need help.

5. Dan Pallotta organized bike rides in order to _____.

EXERCISE 14   Complete each sentence. Answers may vary.

EXAMPLE   Many students have jobs in order ____to pay for their education____ .

1. I want to learn English in order to _____ .

2. I came to this school to _____ .

3. We're studying this lesson to _____ .

4. I use my dictionary to _____ .

5. Many people use spell-check in order to _____ .

6. Many people use Caller ID to _____ .

7. I _____ in order to relax.

8. I _____ to learn new words.

9. You should register early to _____ .

10. Many students apply for financial aid to _____ .

11. If you aren't satisfied with your score on the TOEFL test, you can take it a second time in order to _____ your score.

12. If you're absent, you can call a classmate to _____ .

13. You need a password in order to _____ .

14. You can use the Web site "weather.com" to _____ .

15. Many people use e-mail to _____ .

7.7 | Infinitive as Subject

Examples	Explanation
It's good **to help** other people. **It** was Carnegie's dream **to build** libraries. **It**'s hard **to ride** a bike 500 miles.	An infinitive phrase can be the subject of a sentence. We usually begin the sentence with *it* and put the infinitive phrase at the end of the sentence.
It is important **for rich people** to set an example. It is necessary **for bike riders** to train for the long ride.	*For* + an object can give the infinitive a specific subject.
It costs a lot of money **to build** a library. **It takes** many days **to ride** from Los Angeles to San Francisco.	An infinitive is often used after *cost* + money and *take* + time.
Carnegie was a poor immigrant, but it didn't take **him** long **to become** rich. How much did it cost **him to build** a library?	An indirect object can follow *take* and *cost*.
To build libraries was Carnegie's dream. **To give** money away is the best thing rich people can do. **To help** others gives a person satisfaction.	Sometimes we begin a sentence with an infinitive phrase. A sentence that begins with an infinitive is very formal.

EXERCISE 15 Complete each statement with an infinitive phrase.

EXAMPLE It isn't polite _____ *to interrupt a conversation.* _____

1. It's dangerous _____

2. It isn't healthy _____

3. It isn't polite _____

4. It's illegal _____

5. It's a good idea _____

6. It's the teacher's responsibility _____

7. It costs a lot of money _____

8. It's important for me _____

9. It's boring for the students _____

10. It's fun for children _____

11. It's easy for Americans _____

12. It took me a long time _____

13. It cost me a lot of money _____

14. It will probably take me a long time _____

EXERCISE ■16 Make sentences with the words given.

EXAMPLE dangerous / children
It's dangerous for children to play with matches. _____

1. fun / children

   _____

2. necessary / children

   _____

3. important / a family

   _____

4. difficult / a large family

   _____

5. necessary / working parents

   _____

6. difficult / women in my native culture

   _____

7. hard / single parents

   _____

8. difficult / the teacher

   _____

EXERCISE 17 Complete each statement. Begin with *it*.

EXAMPLES   _It's impossible_____ to be perfect.

It costs me 30¢ a minute to make a long-distance phone call to my hometown.

1. _____ to work hard.

2. _____ to fall in love.

3. _____ to get married.

4. _____ to make a mistake in English.

5. _____ to be lonely.

6. _____ to help other people.

7. _____ to take a taxi from this school to my house.

8. _____ to eat lunch in a restaurant.

9. _____ to go to college.

10. _____ to buy my textbooks.

11. _____ to learn English.

12. _____ to give away money.

13. _____ to have a lot of friends.

14. _____ to travel.

15. _____ to ride your bike from New York to Boston.

EXERCISE 18 Change these statements to make them less formal by starting them with *it*.

EXAMPLE To raise money for charity is a good thing.

_____ It's a good thing to raise money for charity. _____

1. To ride a bike 500 miles is not easy.

_____

2. To fight disease takes a lot of money.

_____

3. To give away money is the responsibility of the rich.

_____

4. To produce high quality public radio takes a lot of money.

_____

5. To build libraries was Carnegie's dream.

6. To raise money for AIDS was Dan Pallotta's goal.

7.8 | Infinitive with *Too* and *Enough*

Too shows that the adjective or adverb is excessive for a specific purpose. *Enough* shows that an adjective, adverb, or noun is sufficient for a specific purpose.

Examples	Explanation
Young Carnegie was **too poor to enter** the library. You drive **too slowly to drive** on the highway. She's **too old to cook** for herself. A volunteer delivers her meals.	Word Order: *too* + adjective / adverb + infinitive
I have **too much work to do,** so I have no time to volunteer. There are **too many problems** in the world **to solve** in one day.	Word Order: *too much* + noncount noun + infinitive *too many* + plural count noun + infinitive
Are you **strong enough to ride** a bike for 500 miles? She trained **hard enough to finish** the AIDS ride.	Word Order: Adjective / adverb + *enough* + infinitive
Carnegie had **enough money to build** libraries. I don't have **enough time to volunteer** this summer.	Word Order: *enough* + noun + infinitive
There is enough volunteer work **for everyone** to do. The bike ride is too hard **for me** to do.	The infinitive phrase can be preceded by *for* + object.
a. I can't volunteer this summer because I'm **too busy.** b. Carnegie could build libraries because he had **enough money.**	Sometimes the infinitive phrase can be omitted. It is understood from the context. a. too busy to volunteer b. enough money to build libraries

EXERCISE 19 Fill in the blanks with *too* + adjective or adverb, or *too many / much* + noun. Answers may vary.

EXAMPLE It's ___*too late*___ for a student to register for this semester.

1. This lesson is _____ to finish in one class period.

2. The cafeteria is _____ for me to study there.

3. Some Americans speak English _____ for me to understand.

4. The bus is sometimes _____ for me to get a seat.

5. It's _____ to go swimming today.

6. It's _____ to predict next week's weather.

7. She earns _____ to qualify for a scholarship.

8. I can't go out with you. I have _____ to do this afternoon.

EXERCISE 20 Fill in the blanks with *enough* + noun, or adjective / adverb + *enough*. Answers may vary.

EXAMPLE I don't speak English ___*well enough*___ to be in a college-credit writing course.

1. This exercise is _____ to finish in a few minutes.

2. I don't type _____ to write my compositions by computer.

3. He doesn't have _____ to do all the things he wants to do.

4. She's only 16 years old. She's not _____ to get married.

5. You didn't run _____ to win the race.

6. He doesn't have _____ to buy new computer.

7.9 | Gerunds—An Overview

To form a gerund, put an *-ing* ending on a verb. A gerund is used as a noun (subject or object).

Examples	Explanation
Subject a. **Tennis** is fun. b. **Swimming** is fun. *Object* a. I enjoy **summer.** b. I enjoy **helping** people.	You can use a gerund in the same place you use any subject or object.
Contributing money is one way to help. **Volunteering** can give you a lot of satisfaction.	A gerund (phrase) can be used as the subject of a sentence.
I enjoy **volunteering my time**. I can't imagine **riding a bike** for 500 miles.	A gerund (phrase) can be used as the object of a sentence.
I'm excited *about* **going on a bike trip.** Let's volunteer this summer instead *of* **wasting our time at the beach.**	A gerund (phrase) can be used as the object of a preposition.
Carnegie accused rich people of **not helping** others. **Not being** able to enter a library made Carnegie feel bad.	To make a gerund negative, put *not* before the gerund.
I appreciate **being corrected** when I make a mistake. She enjoys **being treated** like a queen.	A gerund can be passive: *being* + past participle.

HELPING OTHERS GET AN EDUCATION

Before You Read
1. Do you think that all rich people like to live in luxury?
2. Do you know anyone who is very generous?

Read the following article. Pay special attention to gerunds.

When we think of philanthropists, we usually think of the very rich and famous, like Andrew Carnegie. However, Matel Dawson, who was a forklift driver in Michigan, was an ordinary man who did extraordinary things.

Dawson started **working** at Ford Motor Company in 1940 for $1.15 an hour. By **working** hard, **saving** carefully, and **investing** his money wisely, he became rich. But he didn't care about **owning** expensive cars or **taking** fancy vacations. Instead of **spending** his money on himself, he enjoyed **giving** it away. Since 1995, he donated more than $1 million for college scholarships to help poor students who want to get an education.

Matel Dawson, 1921–2002

Why did Dawson insist on **giving** his money away to college students? One reason was that he did not have the opportunity to finish school. He had to drop out of school after the seventh grade to help support his poor family. He realized the importance of **having** an education and regretted not **having** the opportunity. Also, he learned about **giving** from his parents. He watched them work hard, save their money, and help others less fortunate. His mother made Dawson promise to always give something back. He was grateful to his parents for **teaching** him the importance of **helping** others.

When he became rich, he didn't change his lifestyle. He continued **driving** his old car and **living** in a one-bedroom apartment. And he didn't stop **working** until shortly before he died at the age of 81. When asked why he worked long past the time when most people retire, he replied, "It keeps me **going**, **knowing** I'm helping somebody."

7.10 | Gerund as Subject

Examples	Explanation
Working gave Dawson satisfaction. **Giving away money** made Dawson feel good.	A gerund or a gerund phrase can be the subject of the sentence.
Helping others *gives* a person pleasure.	A gerund subject takes a singular verb.
Not finishing school can affect your whole life.	To make a gerund negative, put *not* before the gerund.

EXERCISE 21   Fill in the blanks with a gerund.

EXAMPLE   ____*Helping*____ others made Dawson feel good.

1. _____ in a factory was not an easy job.

2. Not _____ an education always bothered Dawson.

3. _____ an education is expensive in the U.S.

4. _____ money didn't give Dawson satisfaction.

5. _____ an old car was not a problem for Dawson.

6. _____ a vacation wasn't important for Dawson.

7. _____ that he was helping people was very important to Dawson.

EXERCISE 22   Complete each statement.

EXAMPLE   Leaving home ____*was the most difficult decision I have ever made.*____

1. Making new friends _____

2. Changing old habits _____

3. Finding an apartment _____

4. Thinking about my future _____

5. Getting a job _____

EXERCISE 23   Complete each statement with a gerund (phrase) as the subject.

EXAMPLE   ____*Taking a warm bath*____ relaxes me at the end of the day.

1. _____ is difficult for people who don't speak English.

2. _____ is an important decision in a person's life.

3. _____ is a healthy activity.

4. _____ isn't good for you (is an unhealthy activity).

5. _____ makes me feel proud.

7.11 | Gerund After Prepositions and Nouns

Examples	Pattern
Dawson **didn't care about owning** fancy things. He **believed in helping** others.	Verb + preposition + gerund
Carnegie was **famous for building** libraries. Dawson was **concerned about helping** poor college students. Dan Pallotta was **successful at raising** money for AIDS.	Adjective + preposition + gerund
Dawson **thanked his parents for teaching** him to save money.	Verb + object + preposition + gerund
Dawson didn't **spend money going** on vacations or **eating** in expensive restaurants. He didn't **have a hard time saving** money.	A gerund is used directly after the noun in the following expressions: *have a difficult time, have difficulty, have experience, have fun, have a good time, have a hard time, have a problem, have trouble, spend time, spend money*

EXERCISE 24 Complete the questions with a gerund (phrase). Then ask another student these questions.

EXAMPLE   Are you lazy about _____ *writing compositions?* _____

1. Are you worried about _____
2. Are you interested in _____
3. Do you ever think about _____
4. Were you excited about _____
5. Do you ever dream about _____

EXERCISE 25 ABOUT YOU Fill in the blanks with a gerund phrase.

EXAMPLE   I had problems _____ *getting a student loan.* _____

1. I had a hard time _____
2. I have a lot of experience _____
3. I don't have much experience _____
4. I spent a lot of money _____
5. I don't like to spend my time _____

6. I have a lot of fun _____

7. I don't have a good time _____

8. I don't have a problem _____

7.12 | Using the Correct Preposition

It is important to choose the correct preposition after a verb, adjective, or noun.

Preposition Combinations		Common Phrases	Examples
Verb + Preposition	verb + *about*	care about complain about dream about forget about talk about think about worry about	I **care about helping** people. Carnegie **dreamed about opening** public libraries.
	verb + *to*	adjust to look forward to object to	I am **looking forward to volunteering.**
	verb + *on*	depend on insist on plan on	I **insist on helping** my grandmother.
	verb + *in*	believe in succeed in	Does he **believe in giving** to those in need?
Verb + Object + Preposition	verb + object + *of*	accuse . . . of suspect . . . of	He **accused me of leaving** work early.
	verb + object + *for*	apologize to . . . for blame . . . for forgive . . . for thank . . . for	They **thanked me for taking** care of their children.
	verb + object + *from*	keep . . . from prevent . . . from prohibit . . . from stop . . . from	Don't let him **keep you from getting** to your job.
	verb + object + *about*	warn . . . about	The teacher **warned the students about talking** in the library.

(*continued*)

Preposition Combinations		Common Phrases	Examples
Adjective + Preposition	adjective + *of*	afraid of capable of guilty of proud of tired of	I'm **afraid of going** out at night.
	adjective + *about*	concerned about excited about upset about worried about	The students are **worried about passing** the exam.
	adjective + *for*	responsible for famous for grateful . . . to . . . for	The victims are **grateful to the** volunteers **for helping.**
	adjective + *at*	good at successful at	Bill Gates is very **good at giving** a lot of money away.
	adjective + *to*	accustomed to used to	I'm not **accustomed to wearing** glasses.
	adjective + *in*	interested in	Are you **interested in getting** a volunteer job?
Noun + Preposition	noun + *of*	in danger of in favor of the purpose of	The students are all **in favor of having** class outside.
	noun + *for*	a need for a reason for an excuse for technique for	What is your **reason for going** home early?

Language Notes:

1. *Plan, afraid,* and *proud* can be followed by an infinitive too.

    I plan **on buying** a laptop. / I plan **to buy** a laptop.

    I'm afraid **of going** out at night. / I'm afraid **to go** out at night.

    He's proud **of being** a volunteer. / He's proud **to be** a volunteer.

2. Notice that in some expressions, *to* is a preposition followed by a gerund, not part of an infinitive.

    Compare:

    I need *to wear* glasses. (infinitive)

    I'm not accustomed *to wearing* glasses. (*to* + gerund)

EXERCISE 26 Fill in the blanks with a preposition (if necessary) and the gerund of the verb in parentheses ( ). In some cases, no preposition is necessary.

A: My father's going to retire next month. He's worried ___*about having*___
    (example: have)

  nothing to do.

B: I don't blame him _____ worried. For a lot of people,
                  (1 be)

  their self-worth depends _____, and when they
                      (2 work)

  retire, they feel worthless.

A: My mother is afraid that he'll spend all his time _____
                              (3 watch)

  TV. Besides, she's not accustomed _____ him home
                        (4 have)

  all day.

B: Doesn't he have any interests?

A: Well, he's interested _____, but he lives in an apartment
                  (5 garden)

  now so he doesn't have a garden. When he had a house, he was always

  proud _____ the nicest garden on the block.
      (6 have)

B: Has he thought _____ at the Botanical Gardens?
                (7 volunteer)

A: Do they use volunteers?

B: I think so. He would have a great time _____ there.
                            (8 work)

A: You're right. He would be good _____ tours because
                        (9 give)

  he knows so much about flowers. This would give him a reason

  _____ up in the morning. I'm grateful to you
      (10 get)

  _____ me this idea. I can't wait to tell him.
      (11 give)

B: I'm sure your mother will be grateful too.

EXERCISE 27 ABOUT YOU Ask a question with the words given. Use the correct preposition (if necessary) and a gerund. Another student will answer.

EXAMPLES fond / read

  A: Are you fond of reading?
  B: Yes, I am.

care / get a good grade

A: Do you care about getting a good grade?

B: Of course I do.

1. have trouble / understand spoken English

2. lazy / do the homework

3. have a technique / learn new words

4. afraid / fail this course

5. good / spell English words

6. interested / study computer programming

7. have experience / work with computers

8. think / buy a house some day

7.13 | Verbs Followed by Gerunds

Examples	Explanation
Dawson enjoyed **giving** money away. He couldn't imagine not **helping** others. Students appreciate **receiving** financial aid.	Many verbs are followed by a gerund.

The following verbs take a gerund.

admit	delay	finish	permit	recommend
advise	deny	imagine	postpone	resent
appreciate	discuss	keep (on)	practice	risk
avoid	dislike	mind[2]	put off[3]	stop
can't help[1]	enjoy	miss	quit	suggest
consider				

Do you **go shopping** every day? Do you like to **go fishing**?	Go + gerund is used in many idiomatic expressions of sport and recreation.

Below are expressions with go + gerund.

go boating	go fishing	go sailing	go skiing
go bowling	go hiking	go shopping	go swimming
go camping	go hunting	go sightseeing	
go dancing	go jogging	go skating	

Language Notes:

[1] Can't help means to have no control: When I see a sad movie, I can't help crying.

[2] I mind means that something bothers me. I don't mind means that something is OK with me; it doesn't bother me: Do you mind living with your parents? No, I don't mind.

[3] Put off means postpone: I can't put off buying a car. I need one now.

EXERCISE 28 Fill in the blanks to complete these statements about the reading on Matel Dawson. Answers may vary.

EXAMPLE Matel Dawson liked _____*helping students.*_____

1. He regretted not _____

2. Students appreciated _____ from Dawson.

3. He didn't mind _____ an old car.

4. He couldn't imagine not _____, so he didn't retire.

5. He didn't mind _____ in a small apartment.

6. He kept on _____ until shortly before he died at the age of 81.

EXERCISE 29 ABOUT YOU Complete the sentences with a gerund (phrase).

EXAMPLE I avoid _____*walking alone at night.*_____

1. The teacher doesn't permit _____

2. I don't mind _____

3. It's difficult to quit _____

4. I enjoy _____

5. I don't enjoy _____

6. I can't imagine _____

7. I don't like to go _____

8. I avoid _____

9. I appreciate _____

10. I often put off _____

7.14 | Verbs Followed by Gerund or Infinitive

Examples	Explanation
Dawson liked **giving** money away. He liked **to give** money away. He started **working** in 1940. He started **to work** in 1940.	Some verbs can be followed by either a gerund or an infinitive with no difference in meaning.

Language Note:
The verbs below can be followed by either a gerund or an infinitive with no difference in meaning.

begin	continue	like	prefer
can't stand*	hate	love	start

* *Can't stand* means can't tolerate: I *can't stand* living in a cold climate.

EXERCISE 30 In the following sentences, change gerunds to infinitives and infinitives to gerunds.

EXAMPLES He began to work at 4:30.
He began working at 4:30.

I love sleeping on the beach.
I love to sleep on the beach.

1. Do you prefer to study in the morning?

2. She hates washing the dishes.

3. When did you begin studying English?

4. If you continue talking about politics, I'm going to leave.

5. They can't stand to watch violent movies.

6. I love to get letters, don't you?

EXERCISE 31 This is a conversation between a teenager and his older brother.
 Fill in the blanks with an appropriate gerund or infinitive. It doesn't matter which one you use.

A: I want to work this summer, but I can't decide what to do.

B: How about volunteering in a museum?

A: I can't stand _____*being*_____ indoors all day. I prefer
    (example)

_____ outdoors.
    (1)

B: You're a great swimmer. Why don't you volunteer to teach kids how to swim?

A: I hate _____ with kids. It's hard work.
    (2)

B: Well, what do you like?

A: I love _____ at the beach.
(3)

B: Maybe you should get a job as a lifeguard.

A: Great idea! I'll start _____ for a job tomorrow.
(4)

B: That's what you said yesterday.

A: I guess I'm lazy. I just don't like _____.
(5)

7.15 | Infinitive and Gerund as Subject

Examples	Explanation
It is expensive **to go** to college. **It** is important **to have** a college education. **It** makes me feel good **to give** money to poor people.	An infinitive phrase can be the subject of a sentence. We usually begin the sentence with *it* and put the infinitive phrase at the end of the sentence.
Going to college is expensive. **Having** a college education is important. **Giving** money to poor people makes me feel good.	A gerund phrase can be used as the subject.
To pay for college is difficult for most families. **To build** libraries was Carnegie's dream. **To give** money away is the best thing rich people can do, according to Carnegie.	Sometimes we begin a sentence with an infinitive phrase. A sentence that begins with an infinitive is very formal.

EXERCISE 32 Change these statements. Change the subject to a gerund form.

EXAMPLE It is wonderful to help others.

Helping others is wonderful.

1. It costs a lot of money to go to college.

   _____

2. It is hard to work and study at the same time.

   _____

3. It is important to invest your money wisely.

   _____

4. It is difficult to work in a factory.

   _____

5. It can be boring to do the same thing every day.

   _____

6. It is satisfying to help others.

_____

7. It is a challenge to ride a bike for 500 miles.

_____

8. It is necessary to ask viewers to contribute to public TV.

_____

7.16 | Gerund or Infinitive After a Verb: Differences in Meaning

After *stop, remember,* and *try*, the meaning of the sentence depends on whether you follow the verb with a gerund or an infinitive.

Examples	Explanation
a. Dawson loved to work. He didn't **stop working** until he was 80. b. Dawson wanted to finish school, but he **stopped to get** a job.	a. *Stop* + gerund = Quit or discontinue an activity b. *Stop* + infinitive = Quit one activity in order to start another activity
a. Do you **remember reading** about Carnegie? b. Dawson's mother said, "Always **remember to help** other people."	a. *Remember* + gerund = Remember that something happened earlier b. *Remember* + infinitive = Remember something and then do it
a. Dawson has always had a simple lifestyle. When he became rich, he **tried living** a fancier lifestyle, but it didn't bring him satisfaction. a. I always write my compositions by hand. I **tried writing** them on a computer, but I don't type fast enough. b. Carnegie **tried to enter** a library when he was young, but he was told it was for members only. b. Mary **tried to ride** her bike 500 miles, but she couldn't.	a. *Try* + gerund = Experiment with something new. You do something one way, and then, if that doesn't work, you try a different method. b. *Try* + infinitive = Make an effort or an attempt

EXERCISE 33 Fill in the blanks with the gerund or infinitive of the verb in parentheses ( ).

EXAMPLES   Stop ___*bothering*___ me. I'm trying to study.
                         (bother)

The teacher always says, "Remember ___*to do*___ your homework."
                                                              (do)

1. When the teacher came in, the students stopped _____.
                                                                                  (talk)

2. When you learn more English, you will stop _____ your
                                                                          (use)

   dictionary so much.

3. When you're tired of studying, stop _____ a break.
                                                                  (take)

4. I saw my friend in the hall, and I stopped _____ to her.
   (speak)

5. My sister and I had a fight, and we stopped _____
   (speak)

   to each other. We haven't spoken to each other for two weeks.

6. Cyclists in the AIDS ride often stop _____.
   (rest)

7. If they are tired, they can stop _____ their bicycles.
   (ride)

8. There's a van that will stop _____ up tired cyclists.
   (pick)

9. The teacher usually remembers _____ the homework papers.
   (return)

10. You should remember _____ an infinitive after certain verbs.
    (use)

11. Will you remember _____ the homework during spring break?
    (do)

12. Do you remember _____ the passive voice last month?
    (learn)

13. Remember _____ the passive voice when the subject does
    (use)

    not perform the action of the verb.

14. I remember not _____ much English a few years ago.
    (understand)

15. I remember _____ the present perfect tense even
    (study)

    though I don't always use it correctly.

16. I always try _____ a few new words every day.
    (learn)

17. I need more money. I'm going to try _____ a part-time job.
    (find)

18. Susan tried _____ her bike 100 miles, but she couldn't
    (ride)

    because she was out of shape.

19. I need to find out information about a new bike. I went to the
    company's Web site, but I couldn't find the information I needed. I

    tried _____ the Webmaster, but I got no answer. I tried
    (e-mail)

    _____ the phone number on the Web site, but I didn't get a
    (call)

    person to talk to. I tried _____ a letter by postal mail. I'm
    (send)

    still waiting for an answer.

EXERCISE **34**   Read the following conversation between a son (S) and his mother (M). Fill in the blanks with the gerund or infinitive of the word in parentheses ( ).

S: Hi, Mom. I'm calling to say good-bye. I'm leaving tomorrow.

M: Where are you going?

S: To California.

M: You didn't tell me.

S: Of course, I did. I remember ___*telling*___ you about it when I was at
        (example: tell)

    your house for dinner last week.

M: Oh, yes. Now I remember _____ you say something about it.
                         (1 hear)

    Why are you going?

S: I have a good friend there, and I'm going to do an AIDS ride with

    him. We're going to try _____ it together.
                       (2 finish)

M: Have I met your friend?

S: He was here last year at my birthday party. You met him then.

M: I don't remember _____ him. Anyway, how are you
                      (3 meet)

    getting to California?

S: I'm driving.

M: Alone?

S: Yes.

M: If you get tired, you should stop _____ at a rest area.
                            (4 rest)

    And you can stop _____ a cup of coffee every few hours.
                 (5 get)

S: I will.

M: Don't stop _____ strangers. It could be dangerous.
              (6 pick up)

S: Of course, I won't.

M: And remember _____ your cell phone on in case
                   (7 leave)

    I want to call you.

S: I will. Mom, stop _____ so much. And stop
                   (8 worry)

    _____ me so much advice. I'm 24 years old!
       (9 give)

M: Try _____. I'm your mother. Of course, I worry.
      (10 understand)

Before You Read

1. After reading the articles in this lesson, can you think of ways you'd like to volunteer to help others?

2. What do you think motivates people to volunteer?

 Read the following personal account of Mimi, a woman who went on several AIDS rides. Pay special attention to *used to*, *be used to*, and *get used to*.

Anchorage

Fairbanks

Alaska

Before I went on my AIDS ride, I **used to think** that one person's contribution is not very important. But I was wrong. In 1998, I went on my first AIDS ride in California, from San Francisco to Los Angeles.

Even though I bike to and from work every day (20 miles round trip), I **wasn't used to riding** long distances. Also, I live in Chicago, where the land is flat so I **wasn't used to riding** in hills and mountains. I trained for about six months before the ride, riding at least 150 miles a week.

I **used to own** a ten-speed road bike, but I realized that I would need something better for the long, hilly ride. I bought a new 24-speed mountain bike. This new bicycle helped me a lot in the California trip. It was so satisfying to complete the ride. I raised almost $5,000 for AIDS research. I felt so good about it that I started looking for more rides to do.

In 2001, I did the Alaska ride, which was especially difficult. It was much colder than expected. Some of the riders **couldn't get used to** the cold and had to quit. But I'm proud to say that I finished it and went on to do four more AIDS rides.

7.17 | *Used To / Be Used To / Get Used To*

Used to + base form and *be used to* + gerund have completely different meanings.

Examples	Explanation
Mimi **used to** own a ten-speed bike. Now she owns a 24-speed bike. She **used to** think that one person couldn't make a difference. Now she knows that every person's contribution counts. Libraries **used to be** for rich people only. Now anyone can use the library. I didn't **use to** speak English at all. Now I speak it fairly well.	*Used to* + base form shows that an activity was repeated or habitual in the past. This activity has been discontinued. For the negative, use *didn't use to.* **Note:** Omit the *d* in the negative.
Mimi **is used to riding** her bike in Chicago, which is flat. She **is used to riding** in nice weather. She **isn't used to** cold wind in August.	*Be used to* + gerund or noun means "be accustomed to." The sentences to the left describe a person's habits. They show what is normal and comfortable. For the negative, use *be + not + used to.*
Some of the riders **couldn't get used to** the cold and wind and had to quit. Dawson **couldn't get used to spending** money on himself. I'm from Arizona. I **can't get used to** the cold Chicago winters. My friend comes from India, where they drive on the left side of the street. He had to **get used to driving** on the right side in the U.S.	*Get used to* + gerund or noun means "become accustomed to." Often we use *can, can't, could,* or *couldn't* before *get used to.* For the negative, use *can't* or *couldn't get used to.* **Note:** Do not omit the *d* in the negative.

Pronunciation Note:
The *d* in *used to* is not pronounced.

EXERCISE 35 Finish these statements. Answers may vary.

EXAMPLE I used to ___*go everywhere by bus*___, but now I have a car and drive everywhere.

1. My uncle used to _____, but now he's rich.

2. I used to _____ a stick shift car, but now I drive an automatic.

3. They used to _____ an apartment, but now they have a house.

4. When she was younger, she used to _____, but now she stays home on Saturday nights.

5. He used to _____ money on foolish things, but now he saves his money.

6. My college used to _____ Northeast College, but they changed the name. Now it's called Kennedy College.

EXERCISE 36 ABOUT YOU Write sentences comparing the way you used to live with the way you live now.

EXAMPLES *I used to live with my whole family. Now I live alone.*

I used to work in a restaurant. Now I'm a full-time student.

I didn't use to speak English at all. Now I speak English pretty well.

Ideas for sentences:

| school | job | hobbies | fashions |
| apartment / house | family life | friends | |

1. _____
2. _____
3. _____
4. _____
5. _____

EXERCISE 37 A student wrote about things that are new for her in the U.S. Fill in the blanks with a gerund or a noun.

EXAMPLE I'm not used to *shopping in large supermarkets*. In my native country, I shopped in small stores.

1. I'm not used to _____ a small apartment. In my native country, we lived in a big house.

2. I'm not used to _____. In my native country, it's warm all year round.

3. I'm not used to _____ a student. I'm 35 years old, and I've been out of school for 15 years.

4. I'm not used to _____. I studied British English in my native country.

5. I'm not used to _____ on Sundays. In my native country, Sunday is a day when people rest, not shop and do laundry.

6. I'm not used to _____ in class. In my native country, the teacher talks and the students only listen and write.

7. I'm not used to _____ on the right side of the road. In my native country, we drive on the left side of the road.

EXERCISE 38 ABOUT YOU Fill in the blanks to make three different sentences beginning with "I'm not used to . . ."

EXAMPLE *I'm not used to wearing a coat in the winter.*

1. _____

2. _____

3. _____

EXERCISE 39 ABOUT YOU Fill in the blanks with three different answers.

EXAMPLES When I came to this city, it was hard for me to get used to:

living in a small apartment.

American pronunciation.

When I came to this city, it was hard for me to get used to:

1. _____

2. _____

3. _____

EXERCISE 40 Here is a story of a San Francisco woman who did the Alaska AIDS ride. Circle the correct words in parentheses ( ) to complete the story.

In 2000 I went on the AIDS bike ride in Alaska. My friends told me about it and asked me to join them. At first I was afraid. My friends are good bike riders. They (*used to / are used to*) (*ride / riding*) long
                     (1)   (2)
distances because they do it all the time. They persuaded me to try it because it was for such a good cause.

To get ready for the ride, I had to make some lifestyle changes. (*I'm / I*) used to be a little overweight, so I had to slim down and get in
 (3)
shape. First, I went on a diet. (*I / I'm*) used to a lot of meat, but now I
 (4)
try to eat mostly vegetables and fish. Also, I decided to get more exercise. I used to (*take / taking*) the bus to work every day, but I
 (5)
decided to start riding my bike to work. I work ten miles from home, so it was hard for me at first. But little by little, I (*got used to / used to*) it.
 (6)
On the weekends, I started to take longer rides. Eventually I got used to (*ride / riding*) about 45–50 miles a day.
 (7)

When the time came for the AIDS ride, I thought I was prepared. I live in San Francisco, which is hilly, so I was used to (*ride / riding*) up and down hills. But it's not cold in San Francisco. On some days the temperature in Alaska was only 25 degrees (F) with strong winds. At first I (*wasn't / couldn't*) get used to the cold and sometimes had to ride in the van. It was especially hard to (*used / get used*) to the strong winds. But little by little, I got (*use / used*) to it.

I am proud to say I was one of the 1,600 riders who finished the ride. I didn't (*use / used*) to think that one person could make a difference, but I raised close to $4,000. As a group we raised $4 million. And I've become a much healthier person because of this experience.

GLOBAL VOLUNTEERS

Before You Read

1. Do you ever think about all the poor people in the world?

2. How can we help poor people in other countries?

 Read the following article. Pay special attention to base forms and *-ing* forms after sense-perception verbs (*see, listen, hear,* etc.).

When Michele Gran and Bud Philbrook were planning to get married in 1979, they were planning to take a relaxing honeymoon cruise. But whenever Michele turned on the world news, she **saw** people **living** in poverty. She **saw** children **go** without proper nutrition and education. Instead of their planned honeymoon, Michele suggested that they spend a week helping poor people in Guatemala.

When their friends and relatives **listened** to them **tell** about their unusual honeymoon, they became interested in how they could also help. In 1984, Bud and Michele established Global Volunteers, an organization that helps people throughout the world. Since then, they have sent almost 13,000 volunteers to 25 countries. Volunteers work together with the local people on projects, such as building schools in Ghana or taking care of orphans in Romania.

Bud used to practice law and Michele used to work in state government, but in the early '90s, they quit their jobs to spend all their time with Global Volunteers.

7.18 | Sense-Perception Verbs

After sense-perception verbs (*hear, listen to, feel, smell, see, watch, observe*), we can use either the *-ing* form or the base form with only a slight difference in meaning.

a. Their friends **listened to** them **tell** about their unusual honeymoon. b. Matel Dawson **saw** his mother **work** hard.	The base form shows that a person sensed (*saw, heard,* etc.) something from start to finish. a. They listened to Bud and Michele tell the whole story. b. All his life, Dawson saw his mother's work habits.
a. Michele **saw** people **living** in poverty. b. When I entered the classroom, I **heard** the teacher **talking** about volunteer programs.	The *-ing* form shows that something is sensed while it is in progress. a. Michele saw people while they were living in poverty. b. I heard the teacher while she was talking about volunteer programs.

EXERCISE 41 Fill in the blanks with the base form or *-ing* form of the verb in parentheses ( ). In many cases, both forms are possible.

By their example, my parents always taught me to help others. One time when I was a child going to a birthday party with my father, we saw a small boy ___*walking*___ alone on the street. As we approached him, we

(example: walk)

heard him _____. My father went up to him and asked him

(1 cry)

what was wrong. The boy said that he was lost. I saw my father

_____ his hand and heard him _____ the boy

(2 take) (3 tell)

that he would help him find his parents. My father called the police on his cell phone. Even though we were in a hurry to go to the party, my father insisted on staying with the boy until the police arrived. I really wanted to go to the party and started to cry. I felt my father

_____ my hand and talk to me softly. He said, "We

(4 take)

can't enjoy the party while this little boy is alone and helpless." Before

the police arrived, I saw a woman _____ frantically in

(5 run)

our direction. It was the boy's mother. She was so grateful to my father for helping her son that she offered to give him money. I heard my father

_____ her, "I can't take money from you. I'm happy to

(6 tell)

be of help to your son."

Another time we saw new neighbors _____ into
(7 move)
the house next door. We saw them _____ to move a piano
(8 struggle)
into the apartment. We had planned a picnic that day, but my parents
suggested that we help them. I heard my mother _____
(9 tell)
my father, "We can have a picnic another day. But these people need to
move in today. Let's offer them a hand." There are many other cases
where I saw my parents _____ their own pleasure to
(10 sacrifice)
help others.

I hear so many children today _____, "I want" or
(11 say)
"Buy me" or "Give me." I think it's important to teach children to think
of others before they think of themselves. If they see their parents

_____ others, they will probably grow up to be
(12 help)
charitable people.

EXERCISE 42 *Combination Exercise.* Read the true story of a young woman,
Charity Bell, who became a foster mother (a person who gives
temporary care to a child in her home). Fill in the blanks with the
correct form of the verb in parentheses ( ) and add prepositions
to complete the story.

It's difficult ___*for*___ a college student ___*to have*___ time for
(example)   (example: have)
anything else but studying. But Charity Bell, a student at Harvard, made

time in her busy schedule _____ babies in need. Bell, a single
(1 help)
woman, became a foster mother.

Bell became interested in _____ needy babies when she was 23
(2 help)
years old. At that time, she volunteered at a hospital for very sick

children. The volunteer organization wanted her _____ to the kids
(3 read)
and _____ games with them. The parents of these very sick
(4 play)
children were there too, but they were often too tired _____ or
(5 read)
_____ with their kids. They were grateful to her _____
(6 play)   (7 help)
them. One day she went to the hospital and heard a baby _____
(8 cry)
so loudly in the next room. She went into that room and picked up the
baby; the baby immediately stopped _____. She stayed with the
(9 cry)

baby for a few hours. When she began _____, the baby started
(10 leave)

_____ again. Bell asked the nurse about this baby, and the nurse
(11 cry)

told her that the baby was taken away from her parents and they couldn't
find a temporary home for her.

The next day, Bell made some phone calls and started _____
(12 learn)

about how to be a foster parent. She made herself available to help on

nights and weekends. Her phone started _____ immediately.
(13 ring)

She got used to _____ up the phone in the middle of the night.
(14 pick)

She became accustomed _____ in children that
(15 take)

no one else wanted. Before she started taking care of babies, she used

_____ seven or eight hours a night. Now she sometimes gets as
(16 sleep)

little as three or four hours of sleep a night.

By the time she was 28 years old and in graduate school, Bell had

been foster mother to 50 children. _____ order _____
(17)   (18)

complete her studies, she had _____ take "her" babies to class
(19)

with her. Her professors let her _____ this. They understood that it
(20 do)

was necessary _____ her _____ and _____ care
(21)   (22 study)   (23 take)

of the babies at the same time. And her classmates didn't complain

_____ a baby crying in the back of the class.
(24 have)

Everyone understood how important it was _____ her
(25)

_____ these babies.
(26 help)

Usually, she takes in babies for a few days, but one time she had a
baby for six months. Even though she is sometimes tired, she is never

too tired _____ in a child that needs her. Incredibly, she only
(27 take)

gets $12 a day for _____ care of these children. However, she
(28 take)

gets great satisfaction watching a baby _____. Bell has had
(29 grow)

as many as eight children at a time. It is hard _____ her

_____ "her babies" _____, but there are more babies
　(31 see)　　　　　　　　　　　(32 leave)

waiting for her. _____ love to an unwanted child is her
　　　　　　　　　(33 bring)

greatest joy.

SUMMARY OF LESSON 7

Infinitives and Base Forms

Examples	Explanation
Dawson wanted **to help** others.	An infinitive is used after certain verbs.
His mother wanted him **to help** others.	An object can be added before an infinitive.
He was happy **to give** away his money.	An infinitive can follow certain adjectives.
Public TV stations have fundraisers **in order to get** money. Matel Dawson gave his money **to help** students get an education.	An infinitive is used to show purpose.
It's important **to help** others. **To help** others is our moral obligation.	*It* can introduce an infinitive subject. (INFORMAL) The infinitive can be in the subject position. (FORMAL)
It's important **for rich people to help** others. It's fun **for me to volunteer**.	*For* + noun or object pronoun is used to give the infinitive a subject.
Carnegie had enough money **to build** libraries. Dawson was too poor **to finish** school.	An infinitive can be used with *too* and *enough*.
Dawson heard his mother **talk** about helping others. I hear a baby **crying**.	After the sense perception verbs, a base form or an *-ing* form is used.
It is important **to be loved**.	An infinitive can be used in the passive voice.
She let me **work**. She made me **work**. She had me **work**.	After causative verbs *let, make,* and *have*, use the base form.
She got me **to work**. She convinced me **to work**. She persuaded me **to work**.	After causative verbs *get, convince,* and *persuade*, use the infinitive.
Dawson helped students **to get** an education. He helped them **pay** their tuition.	After *help*, either the infinitive or the base form can be used.

Gerunds

Examples	Explanation
Going to college is expensive in the U.S.	A gerund can be the subject of the sentence.
Dawson enjoyed **giving** money away.	A gerund follows certain verbs.
Dawson learned about **giving** from his parents.	A gerund is used after a preposition.
He had a hard time **supporting** his family.	A gerund is used after certain nouns.
He doesn't like to **go shopping**.	A gerund is used in many idiomatic expressions with *go*.
I dislike **being told** a lie.	A gerund can be used in the passive voice.

Gerund or Infinitive—Differences in Meaning

Examples	Explanation
My father **used to be** a lawyer. Now he is retired. I **used to be** overweight. Now I'm in great shape.	Discontinued past habit
She has six children. She **is used to being** around kids. I ride my bike to work every day. I **am used to riding** my bike in all kinds of weather.	Present custom
I have never lived alone before and it's hard for me. I can't **get used to living** alone.	Change of custom
I met a friend at the library, and I **stopped to talk** to her.	Stop one activity in order to do something else
I had a fight with my neighbor, and we **stopped talking** to each other.	Stop something completely
I **try to give** a little money to charity each year. Mimi **tries to ride** her bike to work a few times a week.	*Try* = make an attempt or effort
I put 85¢ in the soda machine and nothing came out. I **tried hitting** the machine, but still nothing happened.	*Try* = experiment with a different method
You must **remember to turn off** the stove before you leave the house.	Remember and then do
My grandmother repeats herself a lot. She didn't **remember telling** the story, so she told it again.	Remember something about the past

For a list of words followed by gerunds or infinitives, see Appendix D.

1. Don't forget *to* when introducing an infinitive.

   to
   He needs ∧ leave.

   to
   It's necessary ∧ have a job.

2. Don't omit *it* when introducing an infinitive.

   It's
   ~~Is~~ important to know a second language.

   It c
   ~~C~~osts a lot of money to get a college education.

3. With a compound infinitive, use the base form after *and*.

   go
   He needed to finish the letter and ~~went~~ to the post office.

4. After *want*, *need*, and *expect*, use the object pronoun, not the subject pronoun, before the infinitive.

   me to
   She wants ~~that I~~ speak English all the time.

5. Don't use *to* between *cost* or *take* and the indirect object.

   It cost ~~to~~ me $500 to fly to Puerto Rico.

   It took ~~to~~ him three months to find a job.

6. Use *for*, not *to*, when you give a subject to the infinitive.

   for
   It is easy ~~to~~ me to speak Spanish.

7. Use *to* + base form, not *for*, to show purpose.

   to
   He exercises every day ~~for~~ improve his health.

8. Use a gerund or an infinitive, not a base form as a subject.

   ing
   Find ∧ a good job takes time. **OR** *It takes time to find a good job.*

9. Be careful with *used to* and *be used to*.

> My brother ~~is~~ used to live in New York. Now he lives in Boston.

> I've lived alone all my life and I love it. I ^'m^ used to ~~live~~ *living* alone.

10. Be careful to use the correct form after *stop*.

> She told her son to stop ~~to watch~~ *watch*^ing^ TV and go to bed.

11. Use a gerund, not an infinitive, after a preposition.

> I thought about ~~to return~~ *return*^ing^ to my hometown.

12. Make sure to choose a gerund after certain verbs and an infinitive after others.

> I enjoy ~~to walk~~ *walk*^ing^ in the park.

> I like to walk in the park. *Correct*

13. Use *not* to make the negative of a gerund.

> He's worried about ~~don't~~ *not* finding a job.

14. Use a base form or an *-ing* form after a sense-perception verb.

> I saw the accident ~~to~~ happen.

> I can smell the soup ~~to~~ cook^ing^.

15. Use a gerund, not the infinitive, with *go* + a recreational activity.

> I like to go ~~to~~ fish^ing^ at the river.

16. Use the base form, not the infinitive, after causative verbs *let*, *make*, and *have*.

> He let me ~~to~~ borrow his car.

> The teacher made me ~~to~~ rewrite my composition.

PART 1 Find the mistakes with the underlined words, and correct them. Not every sentence has a mistake. If the sentence is correct, write *C*.

EXAMPLES   He was surprised ∧get the job.
            to

To help other people is our moral obligation.   **C**

1. She let me to use her cell phone.

2. My daughter is out of town. I want that she call me.

3. Do you like to watch TV?

4. She's old enough get married.

5. She wanted me to help her with her homework.

6. He decided to rent a car and drove to San Francisco.

7. It took me five minutes finish the job.

8. My friend helped me move the piano.

9. Live in a foreign country is difficult.

10. The teacher had us come to her office to discuss our grades.

11. It will cost to me a lot of money to replace my old computer.

12. She needs speak with you.

13. She got me to tell her the secret.

14. The teacher made the student take the test a second time.

15. It was hard to me to find a job.

16. She persuaded her son to wash the dishes.

17. Costs a lot of money to buy a house.

18. He turned on the TV for watch the news.

19. He stopped to work at 4:30 and went home.

20. I met my friend in the cafeteria, and I stopped to talk to her for a few minutes.

21. I like to cook, but I dislike to wash the dishes.

22. I had a good time talking with my friends.

23. Do you go shop for groceries every week?

24. I used to living with my parents, but now I live alone.

25. My sister couldn't get used to live in the U.S., so she went back to our native country.

26. When I came into the room, I heard the teacher <u>talking</u> about the final exam.

27. The walls of my apartment are thin, and I can hear my neighbors <u>to fight</u>.

28. I can smell my neighbors' dinner <u>cooking</u>.

29. She thanked me <u>for take</u> care of her dog while she was on vacation.

30. Did you have trouble <u>to find</u> my apartment?

31. Please remember <u>to turn</u> off the lights before you go to bed.

32. I started <u>learning</u> English when I was a child.

33. I thought about <u>don't coming</u> back to this school next semester.

34. She complained about <u>being disturbed</u> while she was trying to study.

35. Your dress needs <u>to be cleaned</u> before you can use it again.

36. He tried <u>to repair</u> the car by himself, but he couldn't.

37. Did you see the boy <u>fell</u> from the tree?

PART 2 Fill in the blanks with the gerund, the infinitive, or the base form of the verb in parentheses ( ). In some cases, more than one answer is possible.

EXAMPLE _____<u>Answering</u>_____ the phone during dinner really bothers me.
  (answer)

1. I started _____ dinner last night and the phone rang.
  (eat)

2. Someone was trying _____ me something.
  (sell)

3. I don't enjoy _____ during dinner.
  (passive: interrupt)

4. Sometimes they want me _____ money to charity, but I
  (donate)

   don't like _____ my credit card number to strangers on
  (give)

   the phone.

5. I tell them I'm not interested in _____ their product.
  (buy)

6. _____ them you're not interested doesn't stop them.
  (tell)
   They don't let you _____ their sales pitch.
  (interrupt)

7. I used to _____ to the caller politely, but I don't do it
  (listen)

   anymore.

8. I've told them politely that I don't want to _____,
    (passive: bother)

but they don't listen.

9. I keep _____ these phone calls.
    (get)

10. I've thought about _____ my phone number, but I
    (change)

heard that they'll get my new number.

11. _____ my phone number is not the answer to the
    (change)

problem.

12. It's impossible _____ them from _____ you.
    (stop)   *(call)*

13. I finally decided _____ Caller ID.
    (get)

14. It's better _____ who's calling before you pick up the
    (see)

phone.

15. Now I have the choice of _____ up or
    (pick)

_____ up the phone when it rings.
    (not pick)

PART 3 Fill in the blanks with the correct preposition.

> **EXAMPLE** We must concentrate ___*on*___ learning English.

1. What is the reason _____ doing this exercise?

2. Your grade in this course depends _____ passing the tests and doing the homework.

3. I dreamed _____ climbing a mountain.

4. The teacher insists _____ giving tests.

5. The Wright brothers are famous _____ inventing the airplane.

6. I hope I succeed _____ passing this course.

7. Most students care _____ getting good grades.

8. I'm not accustomed _____ wearing jeans to school.

9. Students are interested _____ improving their pronunciation.

10. Are you afraid _____ getting a bad grade?

11. Are you worried _____ getting a bad grade?

12. I'm not used _____ speaking English all the time.

PART 4 Tell if these pairs of sentences mean about the same thing or have completely different meanings. Write *same* or *different*.

EXAMPLES It's important to spell correctly.
To spell correctly is important. _____*same*_____

I used to live in New York.
I'm used to living in New York. _____*different*_____

1. I can't remember to brush my teeth.
   I can't remember brushing my teeth. _____

2. I like to cook.
   I like cooking. _____

3. Going to college is expensive.
   It's expensive to go to college. _____

4. I plan to buy a computer.
   I plan on buying a computer. _____

5. I stopped watching TV.
   I stopped to watch TV. _____

6. She started to lose weight.
   She started losing weight. _____

EXPANSION ACTIVITIES

Classroom Activities

1. Tell about teachers and students in your school. What do students expect from teachers? What do teachers expect from students? Find a partner, and compare your lists.

Teachers (don't) expect students to:	Students (don't) expect teachers to:
Teachers expect students to come to class on time.	Students don't expect teachers to be friendly.

2. Fill in the blanks. Discuss your answers in a small group.

   a. I used to worry about _____

   b. Now I worry about _____

   c. I used to have difficulty _____

   d. Now I have difficulty _____.

   e. People in my family are not used to _____

   f. Americans are not used to _____

   g. I'm used to _____ because I've done it all my life.

   h. I'm not used to _____

      because _____

   i. I often used to _____,
      but I don't do it anymore. (OR I rarely do it.)

Talk About it

1. These words are written on Andrew Carnegie's tombstone: "Here lies a man who was able to surround himself with men far cleverer than himself." What do you think this means?

2. In your native culture, do rich people help poor people?

3. Do you ever give money to people on the street who collect money for charity? Why or why not?

4. If a homeless person asks you for money, do you help this person? Why or why not? Are there a lot of homeless people or beggars in your hometown? Do other people help them?

5. Would you like to volunteer your time to help a cause? What would you like to do?

Write About it

1. Write a paragraph telling if you agree or disagree with the following statements by Andrew Carnegie:

   • It is not good to have money if your spirit is poor.
   • It is the mind that makes the body rich.
   • It is a disgrace to die rich.

2. Write about a belief you used to have that you no longer have. What made you change your belief?

3. Write a paragraph or short essay telling how your lifestyle or habits have changed over the last ten years.

4. Write about an expectation that your parents had for you that you did not meet. Explain why you did not do what they expected.

5. Write about an expectation you have for your children (or future children).

Outside Activities

1. Ask a friend or neighbor to fill in the blanks in these statements. Report this person's answers to the class.

   - I'm worried about _____

   - I'm grateful to my parents for _____

   - I have a good time _____

   - I used to _____, but I don't do it anymore.

2. Rent the movie *Pay It Forward*. Write a summary of the movie.

Internet Activities

1. At a search engine, type in *charity*. Find the names of charitable organizations. What do these organizations do to help people?

2. Type in *volunteer*. Find the names of volunteer organizations. Write down three ways people can volunteer to help others.

3. Find the name of a volunteer organization near you. What kind of volunteers are needed?

4. At a search engine, type in *AIDS bike ride*. Print an article about someone's personal account of a specific ride.

Additional Activities at **http://elt.thomson.com/gic**

LESSON

8

GRAMMAR

Adverbial Clauses and Phrases
Sentence Connectors
So / Such . . . That

CONTEXT: Coming to America

A Nation of Immigrants
New Immigrants: The Lost Boys of Sudan
Slavery—An American Paradox
The Changing Face of America
Adopting a Baby from Abroad

8.1 | Adverbial Clauses—An Overview

An adverbial clause gives more information about the main clause. It is also called a *dependent clause.*

Main clause	*Dependent clause*
I like living in the U.S.	even though I miss my country.

Example	Type of Clause
She went to Canada **before she came to the U.S.**	Time clause
She went to Canada first **because she couldn't get a visa for the U.S.**	Reason clause
She came to the U.S. **so that she could be with her relatives.**	Purpose clause
She came to the U.S. **even though she didn't know English.**	Contrast clause
She will go back to her country **if she saves enough money.**	Condition clause

Language Notes:

1. An adverbial clause is dependent on the main clause for its meaning. It must be attached to the main clause.

   Wrong: She came to America. Because she wanted to study English.

   Right: She came to America because she wanted to study English.

2. The dependent clause can come before or after the main clause. If it comes before, it is usually separated from the main clause with a comma.

   Compare:

   I went to Canada before I came to the United States. (No comma)

   Before I came to the United States, I went to Canada. (Comma)

A NATION OF IMMIGRANTS

Before You Read

1. Why do many people leave one country and move to another?

2. What do immigrants have to give up? What do they gain?

Read the following article. Pay special attention to different ways of giving reasons.

The United States is unique in that it is a nation of immigrants, old and new. The U.S. takes in more immigrants than the rest of the world combined, about 1.3 million a year. In 2003, 32.5 million people, or 11.5 percent of the population, was foreign born. Between 1995 and 1998, three million immigrants entered the U.S. legally. Why have so many people from other countries left family and friends, jobs, and traditions to start life in a new country? The answer to that question is as diverse as the people who have come to America.

Between 1820 and 1840, many Germans came **because of** political unrest and economic problems. Between 1840 and 1860, many Irish people came **because of** famine.[1] The potato crop, which they depended on, had failed. Between 1850 and 1882, many Chinese people came to America **because of** famine.

The early group of immigrants came from Northern and Western Europe. In 1881, a large group started arriving from Eastern and Southern Europe. Jews from Eastern Europe came **to** escape religious persecution; Italians came **for** work. Most came **to** find freedom and a better life. The number of immigrants grew; between 1881 and 1920, more than 23.4 million immigrants came. In 1910, 15 percent of the population was foreign born.

In 1924, Congress passed a law restricting the number of immigrants, and immigration slowed. In 1965, Congress opened the doors again and immigration started to rise. In the 1960s and 1970s, Cubans and Vietnamese people came **to** escape communism. In the 1980s, Jews from the former Soviet Union came **because of** anti-Semitism,[2] and in the 1990s, Bosnians came **because of** war. Many people came **so that** they could be reunited with their families who had come before.

In addition to legal immigration, about 300,000 come to the U.S. each year illegally. **Since** the U.S. Census cannot count these people, this number is only an estimate.

[1] *Famine* means extreme hunger because of a shortage of food.
[2] *Anti-Semitism* means prejudice or discrimination against Jews.

8.2 | Reason and Purpose

There are several ways to show reason and purpose.

Examples	Explanation
We came to the U.S. *because* **our relatives are here.** *Because* **he couldn't find a job in his country,** he came to the U.S.	*Because* introduces a clause of reason.
Many Irish immigrants came to the U.S. *because of* **hunger.** *Because of* **war in their country,** many people left Ethiopia.	*Because of* introduces a noun (phrase).
Since **the U.S. Census cannot count illegal immigrants,** their number is only an estimate. *Since* **the U.S. limits the number of immigrants it will accept,** many people cannot get an immigrant visa.	*Since* means *because*. It is used to introduce a fact. The main clause is the result of this fact. Remember: *Since* can also be used to show time. **Example:** He has been in the U.S. *since* 2003. The context tells you the meaning of *since*.
In order to **make money,** my family came to the U.S. Many people come to America *to* **escape economic hardship.**	*In order to* shows purpose. The short form is *to*. We follow *to* with the base form of the verb.
Many people come to the U.S. *so that* **they** *can* **be reunited with family members.** Many people come to the U.S. *so* **they** *can* **be reunited with family members.** *So that* **I** *would* **learn English,** I came to the U.S. *So* **I** *would* **learn English,** I came to the U.S.	*So that* shows purpose. The short form is *so*. The purpose clause usually contains a modal: *can, will,* or *may* for future; *could, would,* or *might* for past.
People come to America *for* **freedom.** Some people come to America *for* **better jobs.**	*For* + noun or noun phrase shows purpose.
Compare: a. She came here **to** be with her family. b. They came here **for** a better life.	a. Use *to* before a verb. b. Use *for* before a noun.
Compare: a. He came to the U.S. **because he wanted to be** reunited with his brother. b. He came to the U.S. **so that he could be** reunited with his brother.	a. **Because** can be followed with **want.** b. Do not follow *so that* with *want*. *Wrong:* He came to the U.S. *so that he wanted to be* reunited with his brother.

EXERCISE 1 Fill in the blanks with *because, because of, since, for, (in order) to,* or *so (that)*.

EXAMPLE Many immigrants came to America ____*to*____ escape famine.

1. Many immigrants came _____ they didn't have enough to eat.

2. Many immigrants came _____ they could feed their families.

3. Many immigrants came _____ they could escape religious persecution.

4. Many immigrants came _____ the political situation was unstable in their countries.

5. Many immigrants came _____ the poor economy in their countries.

6. Many immigrants came _____ be reunited with their relatives.

7. _____ war destroyed many of their homes and towns, many people had to leave their countries.

8. Many immigrants came _____ escape poverty.

9. Many immigrants came _____ freedom.

10. Often immigrants come _____ they can make more money.

11. Often immigrants come _____ make more money.

12. Often immigrants come _____ they see a better future for their children here.

13. Most immigrants come to America _____ a better life.

EXERCISE 2 Fill in the blanks with a reason or purpose. Answers will vary.

EXAMPLE   Some immigrants come to the U.S. because ___their native country___
has an unstable government.

1. Some immigrants come to the U.S. because _____

_____

2. Some immigrants come to the U.S. so that _____

_____

3. Some immigrants come to the U.S. for _____

_____

4. Since _____, many
immigrants choose not to return to their country of origin.

5. Life in the U.S. is sometimes difficult because of _____

_____

6. I chose to live in this city because _____

7. I chose to study at this school because _____

8. I come to this school for _____

9. I use my dictionary to _____

10. I'm saving my money because _____

11. I'm saving my money so that _____

12. I'm saving my money for _____

13. I'm saving my money in order to _____

14. Since _____, many
immigrants go to big cities.

EXERCISE 3 Fill in the blanks with *because, because of, since, so (that),* or
(in order) to. Answers may vary.

Two women are talking.

A: I heard you moved.

B: Yes. We moved last month. We bought a big house

_____so that_____ we would have room for my parents. They're
        (example)

coming to the U.S. next month _____ they want to be
                                        (1)

near their children and grandchildren.

A: Don't you mind having your parents live with you?

B: Not at all. It'll be good for them and good for us.

_____ our jobs, we don't get home until after 6 p.m.
(2)

A: Aren't your parents going to work?

B: No. They're not coming here _____ jobs. They're in
(3)

their late 60s and are both retired. They just want to be grandparents.

A: It's great for kids to be near their grandparents.

B: I agree. Grandparents are the best babysitters. We want the kids

to stay with their grandparents _____ they won't
(4)

forget our language. Also, we want them to learn about our native

culture _____ they have never been to our country.
(5)

Our son, who's five, is already starting to speak more English than

Spanish. He prefers English _____ all his friends in
(6)

kindergarten speak English.

A: That's how kids are in America. They don't want to speak their

native language _____ they want to be just like
(7)

their friends. Do your parents speak English?

B: Just a little. When we get home after work, we hope they'll take

classes at a nearby college _____ improve their
(8)

English. What about your parents? Where do they live?

A: They live a few blocks away from me.

B: That's great! You can see them any time.

A: Yes, but we almost never see each other _____ we
(9)

don't have time. _____ they work in the
(10)

day and I work in the evening, it's hard for us to get together.

1. Was your trip to America difficult? In what ways?

2. Was there anything that surprised you about life in America?

 Read the following article. Pay special attention to time words: *when, while, until, during, for,* and *whenever.*

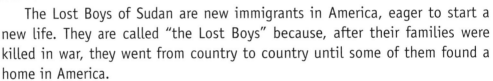

Africa

The Lost Boys of Sudan are new immigrants in America, eager to start a new life. They are called "the Lost Boys" because, after their families were killed in war, they went from country to country until some of them found a home in America.

The Lost Boys were just children living in southern Sudan **when** their long journey to America began in the late 1980s. **While** these young boys were in the field taking care of their cattle, their villages were bombed. These boys, mostly between the ages of 4 and 12 years old, ran for their lives. **For** three months, they walked hundreds of miles **until** they reached Ethiopia. They survived by eating leaves, roots, and wild fruit. **During** that time, many died of starvation and disease or were eaten by lions. They finally reached Ethiopia, where they stayed in refugee camps **until** 1991, **when** a war started in Ethiopia and the camps were closed. They ran again, back to Sudan and then to Kenya, where they stayed in a refugee camp **for** almost ten years. Of the approximately 27,000 boys who left Sudan, only 11,000 of them survived.

During their time in the refugee camp, they got some schooling and learned basic English. In 1999, the United Nations and the U.S. government agreed to resettle 3,700 lost boys in the U.S. **As** they were coming to America, they were thinking about the new and uncertain life ahead. Things in the U.S. would certainly be different.

Now in their twenties and early thirties, the Lost Boys living in America have had to learn a completely new way of life. **When** they moved to their new homes, they had to learn about new foods, different appliances, and new technologies. They had not even seen a refrigerator or stove or telephone **until** they came to America. In addition to their home surroundings, their world around them was completely different. **When** John Bol of Chicago saw an American supermarket for the first time, he was amazed at the amount of food. He asked if it was the palace of a king.

Agencies helped them with money for food and rent for a short time **until** they found jobs. Most of them have been studying English and working full time **since** they arrived. Although their future in the U.S. looks bright, **whenever** they think about their homeland, they are sad because so many of their family members and friends have died.

8.3 | Time Expressions

Examples	Explanation
When their villages were bombed, the Lost Boys ran. Some Sudanese boys think they will go home **when** their country *is* at peace.	*When* means "at that time" or "immediately after that time." In a future sentence, use the present tense in the time clause.
Whenever they think about their country, they are sad. **Whenever** they tell their story, Americans are amazed.	*Whenever* means "any time" or "every time."
They walked **until** they reached Ethiopia. They received money for a short time **until** they got jobs.	*Until* means "up to that time."
Some of them have had no news of their families **since** they left Sudan. They have been studying English **ever since** they came to the U.S.	*Since* or *ever since* means "from that time in the past to the present." Use the present perfect or present perfect continuous in the main clause.
They walked **for** three months. They stayed in a refugee camp **for** many years.	Use *for* with the amount of time.
During the day, they walked. **During** their time in the refugee camp, they studied English.	Use *during* with a time such as *day, night, summer* or a specific time period (*the time they were in Ethiopia, the month of August, the week of March 2*) or an event (*the class, the trip, the movie, the meeting*).
While they were taking care of their cattle, their villages were bombed. **As** they were coming to America, they were thinking about their new life ahead.	Use *while* or *as* with a continuous action.
Compare: a. They walked **for** three months. b. They walked **during** the day. They lived in refugee camps **during** their childhood.	a. Use *for* with the amount of time. b. Use *during* with a named period of time (such as *the day, their childhood, the class, the month of May*).
Compare: a. They were taking care of their cattle **when** their villages were bombed. b. **While** they were taking care of their cattle, their villages were bombed.	a. Use *when* with a simple past action. b. Use *while* with a continuous action.

EXERCISE 4   Fill in the blanks with *since, until, while, when, as, during, for,* or *whenever.* In some cases, more than one answer is possible.

EXAMPLE   The Lost Boys were very young _____*when*_____ they left Sudan.

1. They had never seen a gas stove _____ they came to the U.S.

2. Some of them have not heard anything about their families _____ they left Sudan.

3. _____ they were traveling to the U.S., they were wondering about their future.

4. _____ their march to Ethiopia, many of them died.

5. _____ they came to the U.S., they saw modern appliances for the first time.

6. They walked _____ many months.

7. They crossed the river _____ the rainy season.

8. Some died _____ they were marching to Ethiopia.

9. They studied English _____ they were living in Kenya.

10. _____ they came to the U.S., they have been studying English.

11. _____ they think about their families, they feel sad.

12. In the U.S. many of them work _____ they are going to school.

13. They lived in Ethiopia _____ about four years.

14. They had very little to eat _____ they came to America.

EXERCISE 5   Fill in the blanks with an appropriate time word. In some cases, more than one answer is possible.

_____*When*_____ I was a child, I had heard many stories about life in
(example)

America. _____ I saw American movies, I imagined that
(1)

one day I would be in a place like the one I saw. My uncle had lived in

the U.S. _____ many years, and he often came back to
(2)

visit. _____ he came back, he used to tell me stories and
                (3)

show me pictures of the U.S. _____ I was a teenager, I
                                      (4)

asked my mother if she would let me visit my uncle _____
                                                              (5)

my summer vacation, but she said I was too young and the trip was too

expensive. _____ I was 20, I finally decided to come to the
                  (6)

U.S. _____ I was traveling to the U.S., I thought about all
          (7)

the stories my uncle had told me. But I really knew nothing about the

U.S. _____ I came here.
          (8)

_____ I came to the U.S., I've been working hard and
       (9)

trying to learn English. I haven't had time to meet Americans or have

much fun _____ I started my job. I've been here
                (10)

_____ five months now, and I just work and go to
       (11)

school. _____ I'm at school, I talk to my classmates
              (12)

_____ our break, but on the weekends I'm alone most of
       (13)

the time. I won't be able to make American friends _____
                                                            (14)

I learn more English.

 The American movies I had seen showed me beautiful places, but I
never imagined how much I would miss my family and friends.

EXERCISE 6   Fill in the blanks with an appropriate expression.

EXAMPLES   For _____*many years*_____, she has been living in the U.S.

       Since _____*1997*_____, she has been living in the U.S.

       1. During _____, she lived in Poland.

       2. For _____, she lived in Poland.

       3. Since _____, she has been working in the U.S.

       4. While _____, she met her future husband.

       5. When _____, she was living in Poland.

6. Until _____, she lived with her parents.

7. Whenever _____, she visits her parents.

EXERCISE 7 ABOUT YOU Complete the statements that apply to you. If the time expression is at the beginning of the sentence, add a comma before the main clause.

EXAMPLES Whenever I have a job interview , *I feel nervous.* _____

Ever since I found a job , *I haven't had much time to study.* _____

1. Ever since I was a child _____

2. When I was a child _____

3. _____ ever since I started attending this school.

4. _____ when I started attending this school.

5. _____ until I started attending this school.

6. When the semester began _____

7. Since the semester began _____

8. _____ when I was _____ years old.

9. _____ until I was _____ years old.

10. _____ ever since I was _____ years old.

11. When I graduated _____

12. Since I graduated _____

13. Until I graduated _____

14. _____ when I found a job.

15. _____ since I found a job.

16. _____ until I found a job.

17. When I bought my car _____

18. Until I bought my car _____

19. Since I bought my car _____

20. Whenever I drive _____

8.4 | Using the -*ing* Form After Time Words

If the subject of a time clause and the subject of the main clause are the same, the time clause can be changed to a participle phrase. The subject is omitted, and the present participle (-*ing* form) is used.

Examples

Subject   *Subject*
a. The Lost Boys went to Ethiopia after **they left** Sudan.

b. The Lost Boys went to Ethiopia after **leaving** Sudan.

Subject   *Subject*
a. While **they were crossing** the river, some of the Lost Boys drowned.

b. While **crossing** the river, some of the Lost Boys drowned.

In sentences (a), the subject of the main clause and the subject of the time clause are the same.

In sentences (b), we delete the subject after the time word (*after, while*) and use a present participle (-*ing*).

EXERCISE 8   Change the time clause to a participle phrase.

EXAMPLE   While they were crossing a river, many boys drowned.
While crossing a river, many boys drowned.

1. The Lost Boys went to Kenya before they came to America.

2. While they were living in Kenya, they studied English.

3. Before they came to America, the Lost Boys had never used electricity before.

4. Santino learned how to use a computer after he came to America.

5. Until he found a job, Daniel got help from the U.S. government.

6. Peter wants to go back to Sudan after he graduates from college.

Before You Read

1. What do you know about the history of slavery in the U.S.?
2. Do you think everyone is equal in the U.S. today?

 Read the following article. Pay special attention to *even though, although,* and *in spite of (the fact that)*.

For the first three centuries after Columbus came to America in 1492, the largest group of immigrants arrived in America—unwillingly. Ten to twelve million Africans were brought to work as slaves in the rice, sugar, tobacco, and cotton fields of the agricultural south.

In 1776, when America declared its independence from England, Thomas Jefferson, one of the founding fathers of the United States, wrote, "All men are created equal" and that every person has a right to "life, liberty, and the pursuit of happiness." **In spite of** these great words, Jefferson owned 200 slaves at that time.

Even though the importation of slaves finally ended in 1808, the slave population continued to grow as children were born to slave mothers. The country became divided over the issue of slavery. The North wanted to end slavery; the South wanted to continue it. In 1861, civil war broke out between the North and the South. In 1865, when the North won, slavery was ended. **In spite of the fact that** African-Americans were freed, it took another 100 years for Congress to pass a law prohibiting discrimination because of race, color, religion, sex, or national origin.

Although many new arrivals see the U.S. as the land of equality, it is important to remember this dark period of American history.

[3] A *paradox* is a situation that has contradictory aspects.

8.5 | Contrast

Examples	Explanation
Even though slavery ended, African-Americans did not get equality.	For an unexpected result or contrast of ideas, use a clause beginning with *even though, although,* and *in spite of the fact that.*
Although life in the refugee camps was hard, the Lost Boys learned English.	
In spite of the fact that Jefferson wrote about equality for everyone, he owned 200 slaves.	A clause has a subject and a verb.
In spite of Jefferson's declaration of liberty for all, he owned slaves.	Use *in spite of* + noun or noun phrase to show contrast.
In spite of their hard lives, the Lost Boys are hopeful about their future.	A clause doesn't follow *in spite of.*
Even though the Lost Boys are happy in the U.S., they **still** miss their families in Sudan.	*Still* and *anyway* can be used in the main clause to emphasize the contrast.
Even though it's hard for an immigrant to work and go to school, they have to do it **anyway.**	

EXERCISE **9** Fill in the blanks with *in spite of* or *in spite of the fact that.*

EXAMPLES   _____*In spite of the fact that*_____ the law says everyone has equal rights, some people are still suffering.

The Sudanese boys have not lost their hopes for a bright future, _____*in spite of their hard lives*_____.

1. _____ slavery ended in 1865, African-Americans did not receive equal treatment under the law.

2. The slave population continued to grow _____ Americans stopped importing slaves from Africa.

3. _____ Thomas Jefferson's belief in equality for all, he owned slaves.

4. Many immigrants come to America _____ the difficulty of starting a new life.

5. _____ their busy work schedules, the Sudanese boys go to school.

6. _____ everything in America is new for them, the Sudanese boys are adapting to American life.

7. _____ life is not perfect in the U.S., many immigrants want to come here.

EXERCISE 10 Complete each statement with an unexpected result.

EXAMPLE I like the teacher even though _____*he gives a lot of homework.*_____

1. I like my apartment even though _____

2. I like this city even though _____

3. I like this country even though _____

4. I like this school even though _____

5. I have to study even though _____

6. I like my job in spite of (the fact that) _____

7. Some students fail tests in spite of (the fact that) _____

8. My uncle passed the citizenship test even though _____

9. The U.S. is a great country in spite of (the fact that) _____

10. Many people want to come to the U.S. even though _____

11. There are many poor people in the U.S. in spite of (the fact that)

_____

EXERCISE 11 Complete each statement by making a contrast.

EXAMPLE Even though many students have jobs, _they manage to come to class and do their homework._

1. Even though the U.S. is a rich country, _____

2. In spite of the fact that Thomas Jefferson wrote "All men are created equal," _____

3. Even though I don't speak English perfectly, _____

4. In spite of the fact that my teacher doesn't speak my language, _____

5. Even though I miss my friends and family, _____

6. In spite of my accent, _____

THE CHANGING FACE OF AMERICA

Before You Read

1. What do you think is the largest ethnic minority in the U.S.?

2. Do you ever see signs in public places in Spanish or any other language?

Read the following article. Pay special attention to condition clauses beginning with *if*, *even if*, and *unless*.

The U.S. population is over 295 million. This number is expected to rise to more than 400 million by 2050. **Unless** there are changes in immigration patterns, 80 million new immigrants will enter the U.S. in the next 50 years.

For most of the nineteenth and twentieth centuries, the majority of immigrants to the U.S. were Europeans. However, since 1970, this trend has changed dramatically. Today most immigrants are Hispanics.[4] In 2003, Hispanics passed African-Americans as the largest minority. The Hispanic population increased more than 50% between 1990 and 2000. **If** current patterns of immigration continue and **if** the birth rate remains the same, Hispanics, who are now 13% of the total population, will be 24% of the population by 2050. Hispanics are already about 32% of the population of California and Texas. More than 50% of the people who have arrived since 1970 are Spanish speakers. The largest group of Hispanic immigrants comes from Mexico.

Because of their large numbers, Hispanic voters will have political power. **If** they vote as a group, they will have a great influence on the choice of our nation's leaders.

There are many questions about the future of America. One thing is certain: the face of America is changing and will continue to change.

Estimated and Projected U.S. Population, White and Hispanic Origin, 2000 and 2050.

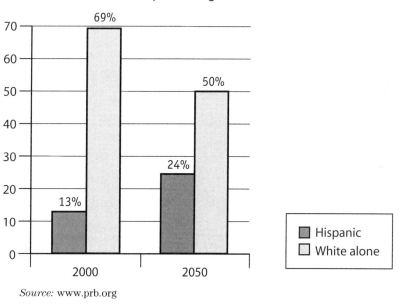

Source: www.prb.org

---

[4] A *Hispanic* is an American whose origin is a Spanish-speaking country, such as Mexico or Cuba.

8.6 | Condition

If, *even if*, and *unless* are used to show that a condition is needed for something to happen.	
If current immigration patterns and birth rates **remain** the same, Hispanics **will be** 25 percent of the population by 2050. *If* Hispanics **vote** together, they **will have** a lot of political power. *If* my brother **comes** to the U.S., he **will live** with me.	Use *if* to show that the condition affects the result. In a future sentence, use the simple present tense in the condition clause.
Even if the immigration of Hispanics **slows** down, their number **will increase** because of their present birth rate. *Even if* the economy of my country **improves**, I **won't go** back.	Use *even if* to show that the condition doesn't affect the result.

Unless immigration laws **change**, 80 million new immigrants **will come** here in the next 50 years.
 	
 My brother **won't come** to the U.S. *unless* he **gets** a scholarship at an American university.
 	
 I **won't go** back to my country *unless* my parents **need** me.
	Use *unless* to mean *if not*.
	 Compare:
	     I won't go **unless** you **go.**
	     I won't go **if** you **don't go.**

a. *If* I **think** about my native country, I **get** homesick. b. *Whenever* I **think** about my native country, I **get** homesick. c. Children in America **learn** English *even if* their parents **speak** another language at home. d. You **can't come** to the U.S. *unless* you **have** a visa.	Sentences with *if*, *even if*, and *unless* can also be about the general **present.** In that case, the present tense is used in both clauses. **Note:** Sentences (a) and (b) have the same meaning.

EXERCISE 12   Fill in the blanks with the correct form of the verb in parentheses ( ).

EXAMPLE   If the Hispanic population _____*continues*_____ to grow, 24% of the
                                                      (continue)

           U.S. population _____*will be*_____ Hispanic by the year 2050.
                                    (be)

     1. If the U.S. _____ almost 80 million people
                            (add)

       to the population in the next 50 years, it _____
                                                        (have to)

       build 30 million more housing units.

2. Even if the number of immigrants _____ down,
   ___(go)___

   the population _____ because of the high birth
   ___(increase)___

   rates of immigrants.

3. If more children _____ born in the next 50 years,
   ___(be)___

   more schools _____.
   ___(passive: need)___

4. The class size _____ if the number of school-age
   ___(increase)___

   children _____.
   ___(grow)___

5. The U.S. population _____ over 400 million by
   ___(be)___

   2050 if immigration _____ at the same rate.
   ___(continue)___

6. Immigrants _____ to come to the U.S. unless
   ___(continue)___

   there _____ a change in immigration policy.
   ___(be)___

7. Children of immigrants _____ their native
   ___(forget)___

   language unless their parents _____ them to
   ___(encourage)___

   speak, read, and write it.

8. If immigrant parents _____ their children about
   ___(not/educate)___

   their former country, their children _____ about
   ___(not/know)___

   their family history.

EXERCISE 13 ABOUT YOU Complete each statement.

EXAMPLE If I speak my native language all the time, __*I won't learn English.*__

1. If I make a lot of long distance calls, _____

2. I'll get a good grade if _____

3. If I don't pass this course, _____

4. My English will improve if _____

5. I'll go back to my native country if _____

6. I will become a citizen if _____

7. If I can't come to class next week, _____

EXERCISE 14   Change the *if* clause in the sentences below to an *unless* clause.

EXAMPLE   You can't get on an airplane if you don't have a photo ID. *You can't get on an airplane unless you have a photo ID.*

1. You can't enter the U.S. if you don't have a passport. _____
_____

2. Children of immigrants will forget their language if they don't use it.
_____

3. Immigrants will continue to come to the U.S. if conditions in their native countries don't improve. _____
_____

4. An American citizen can't be president of the U.S. if he or she was not born in the U.S. _____
_____

5. If the increase in the Hispanic population doesn't change, Hispanics will be 24% of the U.S. population by the middle of the century. _____
_____
_____

EXERCISE 15   ABOUT YOU Complete each statement.

EXAMPLE   I don't usually eat fast food *unless I'm in a hurry.*

1. I work / study every day unless _____

2. I'm usually in a good mood unless _____

3. I usually answer the phone unless _____

4. I'm going to stay in this city unless _____

5. I will continue to study at this school unless _____
_____

6. I can't afford to go to college / school unless _____
_____

7. I won't be able to take the next course unless _____

_____

EXERCISE 16 Complete each statement. Answers will vary.

EXAMPLE Coffee doesn't affect me. I can sleep even if _*I drink a cup of coffee*_ *at night.*

1. Cold weather doesn't bother me. I go out even if _____

_____

2. Making grammar mistakes is OK. People will understand you even if

_____

3. A lot of people in the U.S. have a foreign accent. People will understand you even if _____

4. Will they call off the football game for bad weather? No. They will play football even if _____

5. He will fail the course because he never does his homework and he's absent a lot. Even if _____, he will fail the course.

6. I always do my homework. I may be absent next week, but I'll do my homework even if _____

7. I may move to a suburb. I will continue to study in the city even if

_____

8. Children of immigrants learn English even if _____

_____

EXERCISE 17 Fill in the blanks in this conversation between two Hispanic mothers.

A: My youngest daughter is seven years old, and she doesn't speak Spanish anymore. _____*If*_____ I say something to
(example)
her in Spanish, she understands, but she answers in English.

B: _____ all her friends speak English, of course she's
_(1)_
going to speak English.

A: My mother lives with us. She doesn't speak English. She can't understand what my daughter is saying _____ (2) I translate it for her.

B: I have the same problem. My son is 14 and he won't speak Spanish _____ (3) he has to. Last month he had to because my parents came to visit from Guatemala. But he mixes Spanish with English. My parents had a hard time understanding him. There are a lot of Spanish words he doesn't remember _____ (4) I remind him.

A: We can't fight it. Our kids won't speak Spanish well _____ (5) we go back to live in our native countries. And we're not going to do that. We came to the U.S. as immigrants.

ADOPTING A BABY FROM ABROAD

Before You Read

1. Do you know anyone who has adopted a baby?

2. Is it important for parents to teach their children about their ancestors?

Read the following article. Pay special attention to sentence connectors: *however, in addition, furthermore,* and *as a result.*

Many American couples want to adopt children. **However,** there is such a long waiting list and there are so few babies available that people often have to wait years for a child. **In addition,** the process has become so complicated and slow that people often get discouraged with American adoptions. **As a result,** many Americans are turning to foreign countries for adoption. Americans bring home babies from countries such as China, Russia, Ukraine, South Korea, Guatemala, and the Philippines. In 2002, 20,000 foreign babies were adopted by American families.

However, the process of foreign adoption is not easy or cheap. First, it can cost from $10,000 to $25,000. **In addition,** the Immigration and Naturalization Service (INS) often takes six weeks to four months to process the paperwork. **Furthermore,** parents usually have to travel to the country for a one- to four-week stay.

In spite of all these difficulties, these tiny immigrants bring joy to many American families.

8.7 | Sentence Connectors

Ideas can be connected by sentence connectors. These connectors show the relationship between ideas.

Examples	Explanation
Many couples want to adopt American children. **However,** there are very few babies available. The U.S. is not a perfect country. **Nevertheless,** many people want to immigrate to this country.	Sentence connectors that show contrast are *however* and *nevertheless*. These words are similar in meaning to *but*.
Foreign adoption is not for everyone. It can be expensive. **In addition,** it can take a long time. My sister came to the U.S. to earn more money. **Furthermore,** she wanted to be reunited with our family.	Sentence connectors that add more information to the same idea are *in addition, furthermore,* and *moreover*. These words are similar in meaning to *and*.
The Hispanic population is growing for several reasons. **First,** immigration brings in a large number. **In addition,** the birth rate among Hispanics is high.	Sometimes people order their thoughts using *first, second, third,* etc. These ordinal numbers can be substituted with *in addition, furthermore,* and *moreover*.
Many couples are frustrated with the adoption process in the U.S. **Therefore,** they go to other countries to adopt. Many couples in China prefer sons. **As a result,** the majority of adoptions from China are girls.	Sentence connectors that show result or conclusion are *therefore, as a result,* and *for this reason*. These words are similar in meaning to *so*.

Punctuation Note:
Use either a period or a semicolon (;) before a sentence connector. Use a comma after a sentence connector.

My friends couldn't adopt a baby here. **Therefore,** they went to another country to adopt.

My friends couldn't adopt a baby here; **therefore,** they went to another country to adopt.

EXERCISE 18 Fill in the blanks with an appropriate connecting word.

EXAMPLE The Lost Boys were happy living with their families in Sudan. _However_, a war forced them to leave.

1. The Lost Boys faced many problems when they left Sudan. They didn't know where to go. _____, they didn't have enough to eat.

2. Some of them couldn't swim. _____, some drowned when they had to cross a river in their escape.

3. Finally they found safety in a refugee camp in Kenya. _____, conditions in the camp were very poor.

4. Many of the boys had never seen a gas stove before they came to the U.S. _____, they did not understand how to cook at first.

5. They faced problems in the U.S. They had to find jobs quickly. _____, they had to go to school to improve their English.

6. They are happy that they came to the U.S. _____, they still miss their family and friends back home.

7. Many immigrants came to America at the beginning of the twentieth century. _____, immigration slowed down during World War I.

8. Jews had a hard life in Russia and Poland. Many lived in poor conditions. _____, they were the victims of anti-Semitism.

9. My grandfather immigrated to the U.S. to find a job and make more money. _____, he wanted to be reunited with his relatives.

10. There was a big famine in Ireland. _____, many Irish people left and came to America.

11. In 1924, Congress passed a law restricting the number of immigrants. _____, many people who wanted to come here couldn't.

12. Many Cubans wanted to escape communism in the 1960s. _____, many of them couldn't get permission to leave Cuba.

13. Many Cubans tried to get permission to leave Cuba legally but couldn't. _____, many people found other ways of leaving. Some built or bought small boats and tried to reach Florida by sea.

14. More than a million legal immigrants came to the U.S. in 2001. _____, about 400,000 illegal immigrants came that year.

15. A war broke out in Yugoslavia in 1992. _____, many people died or lost their homes.

16. Most immigrants came to the U.S. because they wanted to. _____, Africans were brought here against their will to work as slaves.

17. In 1776, Thomas Jefferson wrote, "All men are created equal." _____, Jefferson had 200 slaves at the time he wrote these words.

18. Africans were brought to the U.S. to work as slaves in different areas of the U.S. _____, many African families were destroyed.

19. Slavery officially ended in 1865. _____, many African-Americans continued to suffer.

20. African-Americans had been the largest minority for many years. _____, this changed in 2003 when the Hispanic population became the largest minority.

21. Adopting a foreign baby is complicated. People have to pay a lot of money. _____, they have to travel to the foreign country to fill out forms and pick up the baby.

EXERCISE 19 Complete each statement. Answers will vary.

EXAMPLE The U.S. is a rich country. However, _____*it has many poor people.*_____

1. It is important for me to learn English. Therefore, _____

_____

2. It is important for me to learn English. However, _____

_____

3. Living in another country is difficult. Immigrants have to adjust to a new language. In addition, _____

_____

4. Some children speak one language at home and another at school. As a result, _____

5. To learn a new language, you must master the grammar. In addition,

_____

6. No one wants to leave friends and family. However, _____

_____

7. If someone wants to come to the U.S. to visit, he or she must have a passport. In addition, _____

_____

8. It's important for a new immigrant to know English. Therefore,

_____

9. I wanted to study English when I was young. However, _____

_____

10. I may not speak English perfectly. However, _____

_____

EXERCISE 20

Combination Exercise. Circle the correct words to complete this story.

Many people have come to America (*because* /(*for*)) freedom. But Africans lost their freedom and were brought to America against their will (*for / to*) work in the fields. Africans were taken from their homes
(1)
and put on slave ships (*for / to*) cross the Atlantic. (*Because of / Since*)
(2)   (3)
hard conditions, many died along the way.

(*In spite of / In spite of the fact that*) they worked hard from morning
(4)
till night, they received no money. In fact, they were often beaten if they didn't obey. They were forced to work hard (*so that / in order to*) white
(5)
plantation owners could become rich. (*Although / Unless*) many people
(6)
in the North were against slavery, slavery continued in the South

(*because of / since*) Southern slave owners did not want to give up their
(7)
cheap labor supply.

(*Even though / However,*) the law prohibited the importation of slaves,
(8)
slavery continued to increase. (*In spite of / In spite of the fact that*) the
(9)
difficulties of living under slavery, slaves formed strong communities. They tried to keep their African cultural practices, which included music and dance. (*Because / For*) people from the same regions in Africa
(10)
were separated from each other, they lost their native languages, used English, and were given biblical names rather than African names.

Most of the African-Americans in the North were free.
(*In addition / However*), they didn't have an easy life. They couldn't
(11)
attend public schools. (*Furthermore / However*), they weren't allowed
(12)
to vote. Many slaves from the South tried to run away to the North.
(*However, / Although*) some were caught and sent back to their "owners."
(13)

(*Unless / Until*) the slaves were finally freed in 1865, they
(14)
faced many difficulties. (*In spite of the fact that / In spite of*) the
(15)
majority of Africans by that time were born in America, they suffered
discrimination (*because / because of*) the color of their skin.
(16)
Discrimination was still legal (*when / until*) 1965, when Congress
(17)
passed a law prohibiting discrimination in jobs and education.
(*Although / In spite of*) there has been progress toward equality for
(18)
all, there are still many inequalities in American life.

8.8 | *So ... That / Such ... That*

We can show result with *so ... that* and *such (a) ... that*.

Examples	Explanation
Americans have to wait **such a long time** to adopt an American baby **that** many are turning to foreign adoptions. The Sudanese Boys had **such an awful trip that** many of them died along the way.	We use: *Such* + adjective + noun + *that* **Note:** Use *a* or *an* before a singular count noun.

Foreign adoption is **so expensive that** many people cannot afford it.
 Small children learn English **so easily that** they become fluent in a short time.
	We use:
	    So + adjective + *that*
	    So + adverb + *that*

There are **so many** Spanish-speaking people in Miami **that** you can hear Spanish wherever you go.
 There are **so few** babies available for adoption in the U.S. **that** many Americans adopt foreign babies.
	We use:
	    So many + plural count noun + *that*
	    So few + plural count noun + *that*

There was **so much** poverty in Ireland in the 1800s **that** Irish people were forced to leave.
 The Sudanese Boys had **so little** to eat **that** many of them died.
	We use:
	    So much + noncount noun + *that*
	    So little + noncount noun + *that*

Language Note:
That is often omitted in informal speech.
    John works **so hard** (*that*) he doesn't have time to rest.
    American life is **so strange** for him (*that*) it will take him time to understand it.

EXERCISE 21 Fill in the blanks with *so, so much, so many, so few, so little,* or *such (a / an).*

EXAMPLE We had __*so many*__ problems in our country that we decided to leave.

1. I waited _____ long time that I thought I would never get permission.

2. When I got to the Miami airport, the security lines were

   _____ long that I had to wait for almost two hours.

   There were _____ people arriving at the same time.

3. I came to the U.S. by winning the Green Card Lottery. I was

   _____ happy when I got my letter that I started to cry.

4. The U.S. is _____ rich and powerful country that people from all over the world want to come here.

5. I come from Mexico. There is _____ unemployment in Mexico that many people try to come to the U.S. for jobs.

6. Before I got my visa, I had to fill out _____ papers and

   answer _____ questions that I thought I would never be able to do it.

7. Our family has been in the U.S. for _____ long time that we hardly even speak our native language anymore.

8. My neighbor's baby was _____ young when she arrived from China that she doesn't remember anything about China at all.

9. There are _____ American babies to adopt that many families adopt babies from China, Russia, and other countries.

10. My uncle earned _____ money in Guatemala that he couldn't support his family, so he came to the U.S.

EXERCISE **22**   Fill in the blanks with *so, so much / many / little / few,* or *such (a / an)*. Then complete each statement with a result.

EXAMPLES   Michael is _such a_ good student _that he gets 100% on all his tests._

Learning another language is _so_ hard _it can take a lifetime to do it._

1. My math class is _____ easy _____

   _____

2. Peter is taking _____ classes this semester

   _____

3. The teacher gives _____ homework _____

   _____

4. Sometimes the teacher talks _____ fast _____

   _____

5. My roommate is from India. She speaks English _____ well

   _____

6. My biology class is _____ boring _____

   _____

7. Ms. Stevens is _____ good teacher _____

   _____

8. English has _____ irregular verbs _____

   _____

9. We had _____ long test _____

   _____

10. I had _____ mistakes on my test _____

    _____

11. The teacher gave _____ confusing explanation

    _____

12. I was _____ tired in class yesterday _____

    _____

Abbreviations: C   = Clause
NP = Noun Phrase
VP = Verb Phrase

1.

Words that connect a dependent clause or phrase to an independent clause:		
Function	**Connectors**	**Examples**
Reason	*because* + C *since* + C *because of* + NP	**Because** he doesn't understand English, he can't find a job. **Since** he doesn't understand English, he can't find a job. **Because of** his poor English, he can't find a job.
Time	*when* *whenever* *until* *while* *for* *during* *since*	**When** I find a job, I'll buy a car. **Whenever** I work overtime, I make extra money. I worked **until** 8 p.m. I worked **until** the store closed. **While** I was slicing the bread, I cut my finger. I've been working **for** three hours. I worked **during** my summer vacation. I've been working **since** 9 a.m. I've been working **since** I woke up this morning.
Purpose	*(in order) to* + VP *so (that)* + C *for* + NP	He exercises **(in order) to** lose weight. He exercises **so (that)** he can lose weight. He exercises **for** his health.
Contrast	*even though* + C *although* + C *in spite of the fact that* + C *in spite of* + NP	**Even though** he's rich, he's not happy. **Although** he's rich, he's not happy. **In spite of the fact that** he's rich, he's not happy. **In spite of** his wealth, he's not happy.
Condition	*if* *even if* *unless*	**If** it snows, we won't drive. We'll drive **even if** it rains. I won't go **unless** you go with me. I don't want to go alone.

2.

Words that connect two independent clauses:		
Function	**Connectors**	**Examples**
To add more to the same idea	*in addition* *furthermore* *moreover*	Adopting a baby from another country is not easy. Parents have to pay a lot of money. **In addition,** they have to get permission from the INS.
To add a contrasting idea	*however* *nevertheless*	The law says that everyone is equal. **However,** inequalities still exist.
To show a result	*therefore* *as a result* *for this reason*	It is difficult for an uneducated person to find a job that pays well. **Therefore,** I've decided to educate myself and get a degree. There was a war in Sudan. **For this reason,** many people left.

3.

Words that introduce result clauses:		
Function	**Connectors**	**Examples**
Result with adjectives and adverbs	*so* + adjective + *that* *so* + adverb + *that*	I was **so tired that** I fell asleep in front of the TV. She speaks English **so fluently that** everyone thinks it's her first language.
Result with quantity words	*so many* + plural noun + *that* *so much* + noncount noun + *that* *so few* + plural noun + *that* *so little* + noncount noun + *that*	I received **so many letters that** I didn't have time to read them all. I received **so much mail that** I didn't have time to read it all. He has **so few friends that** he's lonely. She has **so little time that** she rarely takes a vacation.
Result with nouns	*such (a)* + adjective + noun + *that*	It was **such a good movie that** I watched it three times. These are **such good grapes that** I can't stop eating them.

Punctuation Note:

Compare:

He went home from work early because he was sick. (No comma)

Because he was sick, he went home from work early. (Comma)

He was sick. Therefore, he went home from work early. (Period before the connecting word, comma after *therefore*)

He had such a bad headache that he had to go to bed. (No comma)

1. Use *to*, not *for*, with a verb when showing purpose.

   She went to the doctor ~~for~~ get a checkup.
   (to)

2. Don't combine *so* with *because*, or *but* with *even though*.

   Because he was late, ~~so~~ he didn't hear the explanation.

   Even though she speaks English well, ~~but~~ she can't write it.

3. Use *because of* when a noun phrase follows.

   He came late because ᵒᶠ bad traffic.

4. Don't use *even* without *though* or *if* to introduce a clause.

   Even ᵗʰᵒᵘᵍʰ he's a poor man, he's happy.

   I won't call you even ⁱᶠ I need your help.

5. Use the *-ing* form, not the base form, after a time word if the subject is deleted.

   Before ᵍᵒⁱⁿᵍ ~~go~~ home, he bought some groceries.

6. Don't confuse *so that* with *because*.

   He came to the U.S. ~~so that~~ he wanted freedom.
   (because)

7. After *so that*, use a modal before the verb.

   I bought a DVD player so that I ᶜᵒᵘˡᵈ watch all my favorite movies at home.

8. Always follow a sentence connector with a complete sentence.

   He came to the U.S. because he wanted more freedom. In addition, ʰᵉ ʷᵃⁿᵗᵉᵈ ᵗᵒ ᵍᵉᵗ ᵃ ᵇᵉᵗᵗᵉʳ education.

9. In a future sentence, use the simple present tense in the *if* clause or time clause.

   If I ~~will~~ go back to my hometown, I will visit my best friend.

10. *However* connects two sentences. *Although* connects two parts of the same sentence.

> *However,*
> She was absent for three weeks. ~~Although~~ she did all the homework.

11. Use *so* + adjective / adverb. Use *such* when you include a noun.

> *such a*
> My grandfather is ~~so~~ wise person that everyone goes to him for advice.

LESSON 8 TEST/REVIEW

PART 1 Find the mistakes with the underlined words, and correct them. Not every sentence has a mistake. If the sentence is correct, write *C*. Do not look for punctuation mistakes.

EXAMPLES

> *could be*
> I came here so that I <u>am</u> with my family.

> <u>After leaving</u> Greece, I went to Turkey.   **C**

1. <u>Even</u> he is a rich man, he isn't very happy.

2. <u>Since</u> she came to the U.S., she has been living with her sister.

3. She can't go to the party <u>unless</u> she gets a babysitter for her baby.

4. Because he can't find a job, <u>so</u> he doesn't have much money.

5. If I <u>will go</u> to the library today, I'll return your books for you.

6. Even though she has good qualifications and speaks English well, <u>but</u> she can't find a job.

7. I'm saving my money <u>for buy</u> a new car.

8. <u>Because</u> her health is bad, she is going to quit her job.

9. The children couldn't go out and play <u>because</u> the rain.

10. <u>In spite of</u> she has a big family, she feels lonely.

11. The weather won't stop me. I'll drive to New York <u>even</u> it rains.

12. Before <u>prepare</u> dinner, she washed her hands.

13. <u>Since</u> the stores are very crowded on the weekends, I like to shop during the week.

14. He's going to buy a digital camera <u>so that he can</u> take pictures of his children.

15. He sent his mother a picture of his children <u>so that she sees</u> her grandchildren.

16. Alex left his country <u>so that</u> he didn't like the political situation there.

17. You shouldn't open the door <u>unless</u> you know who's there.

18. He uses spell-check <u>to</u> check the spelling on his compositions.

19. She is <u>so a bad cook</u> that no one wants to eat dinner at her house.

20. I have <u>so much</u> homework that I don't have time for my family and friends.

21. I use e-mail <u>for stay</u> in touch with my friends.

22. I need to get some credits before I enter the university. In addition, <u>the TOEFL test.</u>

PART 2   Punctuate the following sentences. Some sentences are already complete and need no more punctuation. If the sentence is correct, write *C*.

EXAMPLES   When he met her, he fell in love with her immediately.

I'll help you if you need me.   **C**

1. The teacher will help you if you go to her office.

2. She always gets good grades because she studies hard.

3. Even though owning a dog has some disadvantages there are more advantages.

4. Because he didn't study he failed the test.

5. Before he got married his friends made a party for him.

6. She did all the homework and wrote all the compositions however she didn't pass the course.

7. Although I didn't do the homework I understood everything that the teacher said.

8. Even though he worked hard all weekend he wasn't tired.

9. I stayed home last night so that I wouldn't miss a call from my parents.

10. I am unhappy with my job because I don't get paid enough furthermore my boss is an unpleasant person.

11. She was so emotional at her daughter's wedding that she started to cry.

12. My boss never showed any respect for the workers as a result many people quit.

PART 3 Fill in the blanks with an appropriate time word: *when, whenever, while, for, during, since,* or *until.*

> **EXAMPLE** My friends were talking <u>*during*</u> the whole movie. Everyone around them was annoyed.

1. They talk _____ they go to the movies. This happens every time.

2. They were talking _____ everyone else was trying to watch the movie.

3. They started talking _____ they sat down at the beginning of the movie.

4. They talked _____ two hours.

5. They didn't stop talking _____ they left.

6. _____ the movie was over, they left and went their separate ways.

7. I haven't seen them _____ we went to the movies last week.

8. I hate it when people talk to each other _____ a movie.

PART 4 Fill in the blanks with *because, because of, since, for, so that, in order to,* or *therefore.* In some cases, more than one answer is possible.

> **EXAMPLE** I came to this school <u>*in order to*</u> learn English.

1. He came to the U.S. _____ he could learn English.

2. He came to the U.S. _____ find a better job.

3. He came to the U.S. _____ economic problems in his country.

4. He came to the U.S. _____ be with his family.

5. He came to the U.S. _____ a better future.

6. _____ the U.S. is a land of opportunity, many immigrants want to come here.

7. The U.S. is a land of opportunity. _____, many people from other countries want to immigrate here.

8. Irish people came to America in the 1800s _____ they didn't have enough to eat.

PART 5 Fill in the blanks with *even though, in spite of the fact that, in spite of,* or *however.* In some cases, more than one answer is possible.

EXAMPLE ____Even though____ there are many opportunities in the U.S., my cousin can't find a job.

1. _____ his fluency in English, he can't find a job.

2. He's fluent in English. _____, he can't find a job.

3. _____ he has lived here all his life, he can't find a job.

4. He can't find a job _____ he has good job skills.

PART 6 Fill in the blanks with *if, unless,* or *even if.*

EXAMPLE _____If_____ you're absent, you should call the teacher to let him know.

1. You must do the homework _____ you're absent. Absence is no excuse for not doing the homework.

2. You should come to every class _____ you're sick. If you're sick, stay home.

3. _____ can't come to class, you need to call the teacher.

4. Some people go to work _____ they have a cold. They don't want to lose a day's pay.

PART 7 Fill in the blanks with *so, so many, so much,* or *such.*

EXAMPLE I was _____so_____ late that I missed the meeting.

1. There were _____ people at the party that there wasn't anywhere to sit down.

2. The food was _____ delicious that I didn't want to stop eating.

3. I had _____ a hard day at work yesterday that I didn't have time for lunch.

4. My son is _____ intelligent that he graduated from high school at the age of 15.

5. She spent _____ a long time on her composition that she didn't have time to do the grammar exercises.

PART 8 Complete each sentence.

EXAMPLE I didn't learn to drive until _____*I was 25 years old.*_____

1. I come to this school for _____

2. I come to this school so that _____

3. People sometimes don't understand me because of _____

_____

4. Since _____, it is necessary for
   immigrants to learn it.

5. She came to the U.S. to _____

6. I don't watch much TV because _____

7. I like to watch movies even though _____

8. Many people like to live in big cities in spite of the fact that _____

_____

9. Please don't call me after midnight unless _____

10. I can usually understand the general meaning of a movie even if __

_____

11. I didn't speak much English until _____

12. I fell asleep during _____

13. Some students didn't study for the last test. As a result, _____

_____

14. The teacher expects us to study before a test. However, _____

_____

15. When applying for a job, you need to write a good résumé. In

    addition, _____

16. My mother has such a hard job that _____

17. There are so many opportunities in the U.S. that _____

_____

18. It was so cold outside last night that _____

Classroom Activities

1. Write the following sentence on a card, filling in the blank with one of your good qualities. The teacher will collect the cards and read them one by one. Other students will guess who wrote the card.

   My friends like me because _____

2. Form a small group. Tell which one of each pair you think is better and why. Practice reason and contrast words.

   - owning a dog or owning a cat
   - driving a big car or driving a small sports car
   - sending an e-mail or writing a letter by hand
   - watching a movie at home on a DVD player or watching a movie in a theater
   - writing your compositions by hand or writing them on a computer
   - studying at a small community college or studying at a large university
   - living in the city or living in a suburb

3. For each of the categories listed below, write a sentence with *even though* in the following pattern:

   I like _____ even though _____.

   Categories: food, exercise, movies, people, places, restaurants, hobbies, or animals

   EXAMPLES I like to travel even though it's expensive.
   I like to eat fast food even though I know it's not good for me.

   Find a partner and compare your answers to your partner's answers.

4. Write three sentences to complain about this city. Work with a small group. Practice *so / such . . . that*.

   EXAMPLE There is so much traffic in the morning that it takes me over an hour to get to work.

5. Write three sentences about this school. Try to convince someone that this is a good school.

   EXAMPLE The teachers are so friendly that you can go to them whenever you need help.

Talk About it

1. Frederick Douglass was an ex-slave who became a leader against slavery. In 1852, at a celebration of American Independence Day, Frederick Douglass gave a speech. He said, "This Fourth of July is yours, not mine. You may rejoice, I must mourn." Look up the words *rejoice* and *mourn*. Then tell what you think he meant by this.

2. In what ways will the U.S. be different when Hispanics make up 25 percent of the population?

3. What are the major reasons people immigrate to the U.S. from your native country?

4. Do you think the U.S. is richer or poorer because of its immigrant population?

5. Besides the U.S., what other countries have large numbers of immigrants? Is the immigrant population accepted by the native population?

6. When American parents adopt babies from other countries, should they try to teach them about their native countries? Why or why not?

Write About it

1. Write about how an agency or people have helped you and your family since you came to the U.S.

2. Do you think a country is richer or poorer if it has a large number of immigrants? Write a short composition to explain your point of view.

Outside Activities

1. Interview an African-American. Ask him to tell you how slavery has affected his life today. Ask him to tell you about discrimination in America today. Tell the class what you learned about this person.

2. Interview a Hispanic who has been in the U.S. for a long time. Ask him to tell you if Spanish is still used in the home. Ask him if he feels discrimination as a Hispanic-American. Tell the class what you learned about this person.

3. Interview an American-born person. Tell him or her some of the facts you learned in this lesson about immigration. Ask this person to tell you his or her opinion about immigration.

4. Ask an American-born person where his ancestors were originally from. How many generations of his family have lived in the U.S.? Does he have any desire to visit his family's country of origin?

Internet Activities

1. The following people came to America as immigrants. Find information about one of them on the Internet. Who is this person? What country did he / she come from? Print out a page about one of these people.

Madeleine Albright	David Ho	Carlos Santana
Mario Andretti	Henry Kissinger	Sammy Sosa
Liz Claiborne	Yo-Yo Ma	Arnold Schwarzenegger
Gloria Estefan	Zubin Mehta	Elizabeth Taylor
Andy Garcia	Martina Navratilova	Elie Wiesel

2. Type in *Ellis Island* at a search engine. What is Ellis Island and why is it important in the history of immigration? Where is it?

3. Find information about one of the following African-Americans: Frederick Douglass, Harriet Tubman, John Brown, Martin Luther King, Jr. Write a summary of an article you found on the Internet.

4. Find the Declaration of Independence on the Internet. Print it out and read it.

5. Type in *Lost Boys of Sudan* at a search engine. Print an article and bring it to class. Write a short summary of the article.

6. Type in *Foreign Adoption* or *International Adoption* at a search engine. Find a Web site that gives information about adopting a baby abroad. Find out the costs, where the babies come from, how long a family has to wait to get a baby, or any other interesting information. Report your information to the class.

7. Go to About.com. Type in *Immigration Policies* or *Immigration Affairs* or *Immigration 9/11*. Find an article about pre- and post-9/11 immigration guidelines. Did the events of September 11, 2001, change immigration policies? If so, how?

Additional Activities at **http://elt.thomson.com/gic**

LESSON

9

GRAMMAR: Noun Clauses

Noun Clauses After Verbs and Adjectives
Noun Clauses as Included Questions
Noun Clauses as Direct Quotes
Noun Clauses in Reported Speech

CONTEXT: Caring for Children

Bringing Up Baby
Pediatricians' Recommendations
Day Care
Dr. Benjamin Spock
A Folk Tale
Being an Au Pair

9.1 | Noun Clauses—An Overview

A **clause** is a group of words that has a subject and verb. A **noun clause** functions as a noun in a sentence.

Compare:

noun
He said hello.

noun clause
He said that **he wanted to see the baby.**

Examples	Explanation
I think **that babies are cute.** It's important **that children get a good education.** She didn't realize **that the baby was sick.**	We use a noun clause to include a *statement* within a statement.
I don't know **how old the child is.** I don't remember **if I had a babysitter when I was a child.**	We use a noun clause to include a *question* within a statement.
She said, "**I will pick up my son at 4:30.**" I asked, "**Where will you pick him up?**"	We use a noun clause to *repeat* someone's exact words.
She said **that she would pick up her son at 4:30.** I asked her **where she would pick him up.**	We use a noun clause to *report* what someone has said or asked.

BRINGING UP BABY

Before You Read

1. Should employers provide maternity leave for new mothers? Why or why not?

2. Do you think grandparents should have a big part in raising children? Why or why not?

Read the following article. Pay special attention to noun clauses.

Research shows **that a baby's early experiences influence his brain development.** What happens in the first three years of a baby's life affects his emotional development and learning abilities for the rest of his life. It is a well-known fact **that talking to infants increases their language ability** and **that reading to them is the most important thing parents can do to raise a good reader.** Some parents even think **that it's important to play Mozart to babies and show them famous works of art.** However, there is no scientific evidence to support this. It is known, however, **that babies whose parents rarely talk to them or hold them can be damaged for life.** One study shows **that kids who hardly play or who aren't touched very much develop brains 20 to 50 percent smaller than normal.**

Educators have known for a long time **that kids raised in poverty enter school at a disadvantage.** To prevent a gap[1] between the rich and the poor, they recommend early childhood education. A recent study at the University of North Carolina followed children from preschool to young adulthood. The results showed **that children who got high quality preschool education from the time they were infants benefited in later life.** In this study, 35 percent of children who had preschool education graduated from college, compared with only 14 percent of children who did not have preschool education.

While it is important to give babies stimulating activities, experts warn **that parents shouldn't overstimulate them.**

[1]A *gap*, in this case, means a difference.

9.2 | Noun Clauses After Verbs and Adjectives

Examples	Explanation
Parents know **(that) kids need a lot of attention.** Some parents think **(that) babies should listen to Mozart.** Studies show **(that) early childhood education is important.**	A noun clause can follow certain **verbs.** *That* introduces a noun clause. *That* is often omitted, especially in conversation.

A noun clause often follows one of these verbs:

believe	find out	notice	remember
complain	forget	predict	show
decide	hope	pretend	suppose
dream	know	realize	think
expect	learn	regret	understand
feel*			

Feel followed by a noun clause means "believe" or "think." I *feel* that it's important for a mother to stay home with her baby. = I *believe / think* that it's important for a mother to stay home with her baby.

Examples	Explanation
I am sure **(that) children need a lot of attention.** Are you surprised **(that) some parents read to babies?** Parents are worried **(that) they don't spend enough time with their kids.**	A noun clause can be the complement of the sentence after certain **adjectives.**

A noun clause often follows *be* + an adjective:

be afraid	be clear	be obvious
be amazed	be disappointed	be sure
be aware	be glad	be surprised
be certain	be happy	be worried

Examples	Explanation
It has been said **that it takes a village to raise a child.**	A noun clause can be used after certain verbs in the passive voice.
A: I hope **that our children will be successful.** B: I hope **so** too. A: Do you think **that the children are learning something?** B: Yes, I think **so.**	Noun clauses can be replaced by *so* after *think, hope, believe, suppose, expect,* and *know.* Do not include *so* if you include the noun clause. *Wrong:* I think **so** the children are learning something.
I realize that the child is tired **and that** he hasn't eaten lunch. I know that you are a loving parent **but that** you can't spend much time with your child.	Connect two noun clauses in the same sentence with *and that* or *but that.*

EXERCISE 1 Underline the noun clauses in the conversation below between two mothers.

EXAMPLE
A: Do you know <u>that it's good to read to children when they're very young?</u>

B: Yes, I do. But I didn't realize that playing music was important too.

A: I'm not so sure that music is beneficial, but I suppose it can't hurt.

B: I think that it's good to give kids as much education as possible before they go to school.

A: I'm sure that's a good idea. But don't forget that they're just kids. They need to play too.

B: Of course they do. I hope my children will be successful one day.

A: I predict they will be very successful and happy.

EXERCISE 2 Fill in the blanks to complete the noun clause. Answers may vary.

EXAMPLE Research shows that _____*a baby's early experiences*_____ influence his brain development.

1. Educators know that _____ enter school at a disadvantage.

2. Some parents think that _____ classical music for babies.

3. We all know that _____ to babies increases their language ability.

4. A study shows that _____ have smaller brains.

EXERCISE 3 Respond to each statistic about American families by beginning with *"I'm surprised that . . ."* or *"I'm not surprised that . . ."*

EXAMPLE Fifty percent of marriages in the U.S. end in divorce.
I'm not surprised that 50 percent of marriages end in divorce.

1. Only 26 percent of American households are made up of a mother, a father, and children.

2. About 7 million American children are home alone after school.

3. About 12 percent of American children don't have health insurance.

4. About 20 percent of American children live in poverty.

5. Sixty-eight percent of married mothers work outside the home.

6. In families where both parents work, women do most of the housework and child care.

7. Thirty-two percent of working wives with full-time jobs earn more than their husbands.

8. Fifty-six percent of adults are married.

9. About ten percent of adults live alone.

10. Sixty-five percent of families own their homes.

11. The average size of new American homes has increased as the size of the American family has decreased.

12. Twenty-five percent of households have only one person.

13. Twenty-seven percent of kids live in single-parent families.

EXERCISE 4 ABOUT YOU Fill in the blanks with a noun clause to talk about your knowledge and impressions of the U.S.

EXAMPLES I know *that there are fifty states in the U.S.*

I'm surprised that *so many people live alone.*

1. I think _____

2. I'm disappointed _____

3. I know _____

4. I'm afraid _____

5. It's unfortunate _____

6. I'm surprised _____

7. I've noticed _____

8. Many people think _____

EXERCISE 5 What's your opinion? Answer the questions using *I think* and a noun clause. Discuss your answers.

EXAMPLE Should mothers of small kids stay home to raise them?

I think mothers of small kids should stay home if their husbands can make enough money. But if they need the money, I think they should work.

1. Should the government pay for child care for all children?

2. Can children get the care and attention they need in day care?

3. Should fathers take a greater part in raising their kids?

4. Should grandparents help more in raising their grandchildren?

5. Should the government give new mothers maternity leave? For how long?

6. Should parents read books to babies before they learn to talk?

7. Should parents buy a lot of toys for their children?

PEDIATRICIANS' RECOMMENDATIONS

Before You Read

1. What are some good habits that children should develop? How can their parents encourage these habits?

2. Is television a bad influence on children? Why or why not?

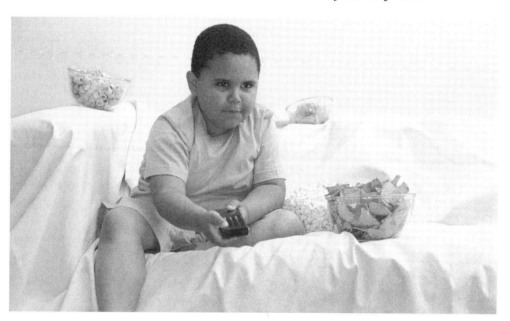

 Read the following article. Pay special attention to noun clauses.

The American Academy of Pediatrics (AAP) is worried that American children spend too much time in front of the TV. The AAP suggests **that pediatricians help parents evaluate their children's entertainment habits.** Doctors are concerned that children who spend too much time in front of the TV don't get enough exercise. At least one in five children is overweight. In the last 20 years, this number has increased more than 50 percent.

The AAP recommends **that children under two not watch any TV at all.** It is essential **that small children have direct interactions with parents for healthy brain growth.** The AAP advises **that parents offer children stimulating activities.**

The AAP recommends **that pediatricians be good role models** by not having TVs in their waiting rooms.

9.3 | Noun Clauses After Expressions of Importance

Examples	Explanation
The AAP *recommends* **that pediatricians be good role models.** The pediatrician *suggested* **that she read to her kids.**	A noun clause is used after verbs that show importance or urgency. The base form is used in the noun clause. The subject pronoun is used before the base form. **Compare Pronouns:** He wants *her* to read. He suggested that *she* read.

Some verbs that express importance or urgency are:

advise*	forbid*	request
ask*	insist	require*
beg*	order*	suggest
demand	recommend	urge*

*The starred verbs can also be followed by an object + infinitive.
I advise *that she stay* home with her small children.
I advise *her to stay* home with her small children.

Examples	Explanation
It is essential **that a baby have stimulation.** *It is important* **that parents spend time with their children.**	A noun clause is used after expressions of importance beginning with *it*. The base form is used in the noun clause.

Some expressions that show importance or urgency are:

It is advisable	It is important
It is essential	It is necessary
It is imperative	It is urgent

The above expressions can also be followed by *for* + object + infinitive.
It is essential *that they play* with their children. =
It is essential *for them to play* with their children.

Examples	Explanation
The AAP advises that children under two **not watch** any TV at all.	For negatives, put *not* before the base form.

EXERCISE 6   Rewrite these sentences as noun clauses.

EXAMPLE   Kids should see a doctor regularly.

It is important that _kids see a doctor regularly._

    1. Kids should eat a healthy diet.

    It is essential that _____

    2. A child should exercise regularly.

    It is important that _____

3. A child must receive love.

It is essential that _____

4. Children shouldn't watch a lot of TV.

Doctors recommend that _____

5. Doctors want parents to give their children a healthy diet.

Doctors suggest that _____

6. Parents should talk to their babies and hold them.

It is essential that _____

7. Some parents tell their children to turn off the TV.

Some parents insist that _____

8. Children shouldn't eat a lot of candy.

Dentists recommend that _____

9. Parents should be good role models.

It is essential that _____

DAY CARE

Before You Read

1. Do you think it's OK for mothers of small babies to work outside the home?

2. In your native culture, do women with babies work outside the home? Who takes care of the children?

Read the following article. Pay special attention to noun clauses.

Working parents often put their children in day care. While most parents interviewed say they are satisfied with the day care they use, experts believe that only about 12 percent of children receive high quality care. Many parents really don't know **how good their day care service is.**

When choosing a day care center, of course parents want to know **how much it costs.** But there are many other questions parents should ask and observations they should make. Parents need to know **if the caregiver is loving and responds to the child's needs.** Does the caregiver hug the child, talk to the child, smile at the child, play with the child?

It is also important to know **if the day care center is clean and safe.** A parent should find out **how the caregiver takes care of sick children.** Is there a nurse or doctor available to help with medical care? Do caregivers know first aid?

Parents should ask **how many children there are per caregiver.** One caregiver for a group of eight four- or five-year-olds may be enough, but babies need much more attention; one caregiver for three babies is recommended.

Experts believe that parents should not put their babies in child care for the first four months. During this time, it is important for babies to form an attachment to their mothers.

9.4 | Noun Clauses as Included Questions

A noun clause is used to include a question in a statement or another question.

Examples	Explanation
Wh- Questions with auxiliaries or *be*	
Where is the mother? I don't know **where the mother is**. What should she do? I'm not sure **what she should do**. When will the children go home? Do you know **when the children will go home?**	Use statement word order in an included question—put the subject before the verb.
Wh- Questions with *do / does / did*	
When do the children go home? I don't know **when the children go home**. What does the child want? Do you know **what the child wants?** Where did the child go? I wonder **where the child went**.	Remove *do / does / did* in the noun clause. The verb will show the *-s* ending or the past tense.
Wh- Questions About the subject	
Who takes care of the kids? I'd like to know **who takes care of the kids**. How many teachers work there? Please tell me **how many teachers work there**.	There is no change in word order in questions about the subject.
Yes / No Questions with auxiliaries or *be*	
Will the children be safe? I don't know **if the children will be safe**. Is the center clean? I'd like to know **if the center is clean or not**. Can the child play outside? I'm not sure **whether the child can play outside or not**.	Add the word *if* or *whether* before including a *yes / no* question. You can add *or not* at the end. Use statement word order—put the subject before the verb.
Yes / No Questions with *do / does / did*	
Do the kids like their teacher? Can you tell me **whether the kids like their teacher?** Does the child want to go home? I don't know **if the child wants to go home**. Did your parents give you toys? I can't remember **if my parents gave me toys or not**.	Remove *do / does / did* in the included question. Add *if* or *whether* (. . . *or not*). The verb in the included question will show the *-s* ending or the past tense.

(continued)

An included question is used after phrases such as these:	
I don't know	Do you remember
Please tell me	Do you know
I have no idea	Can you tell me
I wonder	Are you sure
I don't remember	Do you understand
You need to decide	Would you like to know
It's important to ask	Does anyone know
I'm not sure	
Nobody knows	
I can't understand	
I'd like to know	
I can't tell you	

Punctuation Note: Use a period at the end of the included question if the sentence is a statement. Use a question mark if the sentence begins with a question.

> I don't know what time it is.
> Do you know what time it is?

Usage Note: When asking for information, especially from a stranger, an included question sounds more polite than a direct question.

> **Direct Question:** Who is the director of the day care center?
> **More Polite:** Can you tell me who the director of the day care center is?

EXERCISE 7 Fill in the blanks with an appropriate question word or phrase *(who, what, where, when, why, how, how many, or how much)* or *if* or *whether.*

EXAMPLE Can you tell me ___how much___ time the children spend watching TV?

I'd like to know ___if___ the day care center is expensive.

1. I don't know _____ my child's teacher's name is.

2. I can't remember _____ the class begins at seven o'clock or eight o'clock.

3. You should ask _____ people take care of the children. It's good to have a lot of teachers.

4. I would like to know _____ the day care center is clean or not.

5. I would like to know _____ the day care center is expensive.

6. I would like to know _____ the caregivers do if the child gets sick.

7. Can you tell me _____ the director of the program is? I've never met her.

8. I have no idea _____ the day care center costs.

9. Please tell me _____ the day care center is located.

EXERCISE 8 Circle the correct words to complete the statement or question.

EXAMPLE Please tell me how old (*is your child /* (*your child is*)).

    1. I'd like to know when (*I have to / do I have to*) pick my child up.

    2. Do you know what (*is the teacher's name / the teacher's name is*)?

    3. Do you know (*is the center open / if the center is open*) on Saturday?

    4. Can you tell me how much (*you paid / did you pay*) for the service?

    5. I don't know where (*the day care center is located / is located the day care center*).

    6. I want to know how old (*your son is / is your son*).

    7. I'd like to know how much (*the service costs / does the service cost / costs the service*).

    8. Can you tell me when (*the center closes / closes the center*)?

    9. I'd like to know (*the children watch TV / do the children watch TV / if the children watch TV*) at the center.

    10. Please tell me (*if works a nurse / whether a nurse works / does a nurse work*) at the center.

    11. I'd like to know (*the center has / has the center / whether the center has*) an outdoor playground or not.

    12. I wonder (*if the teacher loves / does the teacher love / if loves the teacher*) small children.

EXERCISE 9 Write these questions as included questions. (These are questions about the subject.)

EXAMPLE Who wants to leave now?

I don't know *who wants to leave now.*

1. How many students in this class come from South America?

   I don't know _____

2. Who read the article about working mothers?

   I'd like to know _____

3. What happened in the last class?

   Can you tell me _____

4. Who brought a dictionary today?

   I don't know _____

5. Who failed the test?

   I wonder _____

EXERCISE 10 Write these questions as included questions. (These are *wh-* questions with *be* or an auxiliary verb.)

EXAMPLE How many tests have we had?

I don't remember *how many tests we have had.*

1. When will we have the final exam?

   I need to know _____

2. How many lessons are we going to finish?

   Can you tell me _____

3. Where is the teacher from?

   I wonder _____

4. Where will the final exam be?

   You should ask _____

5. When can the teacher see me?

   I need to know _____

EXERCISE 11 Write these questions as included questions. (These are *wh-* questions with *do, does,* or *did.*)

EXAMPLE Where did you buy your books?

Can you tell me *where you bought your books?*

1. When does the class begin?

   Can you tell me _____

2. What grade did I get on the last test?

   Can you tell me _____

3. How many mistakes did I make?

   I'd like to know _____

4. How many questions does the test have?

   It's not important to know _____

5. How many compositions does the teacher want?

   You should ask the teacher _____

EXERCISE 12 Write these questions as included questions. (These are *yes / no* questions with an auxiliary verb or *be.*)

EXAMPLE Is the teacher American?

I'd like to know *if the teacher is American.*

1. Is the test going to be hard?

   I don't know _____

2. Will you be our teacher next semester?

   I'd like to know _____

3. Can you help us with registration?

   I'd like to know _____

4. Have you been teaching here for a long time?

   Can you tell me _____

5. Are the students confused?

   I have no idea _____

EXERCISE 13 Write these questions as included questions. (These are *yes / no* questions with *do*, *does*, or *did*.)

EXAMPLE Does your teacher give a lot of homework?

Can you tell me *if your teacher gives a lot of homework?*

1. Does the school have a cafeteria?

   You should ask _____

2. Did everyone pass the last test?

   I don't know _____

3. Did you buy a used book?

   Please tell me _____

4. Does the teacher speak Spanish?

   I'm not sure _____

5. Do I need to write a composition?

   Can you tell me _____

EXERCISE 14 These are some questions parents can ask before choosing day care for their children. Include each question after "I'd like to know."

EXAMPLE How much does it cost?

I'd like to know *how much it costs.*

1. Do the caregivers have a lot of experience?

   I'd like to know _____

2. How does the caregiver discipline the children?

   I'd like to know _____

3. Can the caregiver handle problems without getting angry or impatient?

   I'd like to know _____

4. Am I welcome to drop in and visit?

   I'd like to know _____

5. How does the caregiver take care of sick children?

   I'd like to know _____

6. Is there a nurse or doctor to help with medical care?

   I'd like to know _____

7. Are there smoke alarms in the building?

   I'd like to know _____

8. How many caregivers are there?

   I'd like to know _____

9. Does the caregiver hug the children?

   I'd like to know _____

10. How many children are there for each caregiver?

    I'd like to know _____

11. Are the toys clean?

    I'd like to know _____

12. Is the day care center licensed by the state?

    I'd like to know _____

13. Do the children have stimulating activities?

    I'd like to know _____

9.5 | Question Words Followed by an Infinitive

Examples	Explanation
What should I do? a. I don't know **what I should do.** b. I don't know **what to do.** Where can I find information? a. Please tell me **where I can find information.** b. Please tell me **where to find information.**	Some noun clauses with *can*, *could*, and *should* can be shortened to an infinitive phrase. Sentences (a) use a noun clause. Sentences (b) use an infinitive.
Should she work or stay home with her children? a. She can't decide **if she should work or stay home with her children.** b. She can't decide **whether to work or stay home with her children.**	Sentence (a) uses a noun clause. Sentence (b) uses an infinitive. Use *whether*, not *if*, to introduce an infinitive. *Wrong:* She can't decide *if* to work or stay home with her children.
How can I find a good day care center? I don't know **how to find a good day care center.**	An infinitive is used after *know how*.

EXERCISE ⬛**15** Complete these sentences with an infinitive phrase.

EXAMPLE What should I do about my problem?

I don't know _what to do about my problem._

1. Where can I buy textbooks?

I don't know _____

2. What classes should I register for?

I can't decide _____

3. Should I take morning classes or evening classes?

I don't know _____

4. What else should I do?

I don't know _____

5. How can I use the computer in the library?

I don't know _____

6. What can I do about cancelled classes?

I don't know _____

7. Should I take biology or physics?

I can't decide _____ _____

8. Should I buy new textbooks or used books?

I'm not sure _____

EXERCISE ⬛**16** ABOUT YOU Complete each statement with an infinitive phrase. Discuss your answers in a small group or with the entire class.

EXAMPLE I can't decide _whether to stay in this city or move to another city._

1. When I came to this school, I didn't know _____

_____

2. I can't decide _____

3. When I came to this city, I had to decide _____

_____

4. A new student at this college needs to know _____

_____

5. There are so many choices of products in the stores. Sometimes I

can't decide _____

EXERCISE Two students are talking. Fill in the blanks to complete the included questions. Use correct punctuation (period or question mark). Answers may vary.

A: Hi. Where are you going in such a hurry?

B: I need to get to the library before it closes. What time does it close?

A: I'm not sure what time _____it closes_____.
                                      (example)

B: What time is it now?

A: I don't have my watch, so I don't know what time _____.
                                                          (1)

   But I'm sure it must be after six. Why do you need to use the library?

B: The teacher told us to write a paper. She told us to choose a topic.

   I don't know what topic _____.
                             (2)

A: You have small children. Why don't you write about child development?

B: That's a good topic. But I have to start somewhere. I don't even

   know where _____.
                  (3)

A: Try going to the Internet. Use a search engine and type in *child development*.

B: I don't know how _____ the Internet.
                          (4)

   And I don't have a computer at home.

A: You don't? Let's go to the library and use the computers there.

B: I don't know where _____.
                            (5)

A: They're in the back. Come. I'll show you.

   (Later)

B: Uh-oh. The library is closed. I wonder what time

   _____ tomorrow.
        (6)

A: The sign says, "Open 9 a.m. to 6 p.m."

B: Can you meet me at the library at 10 o'clock tomorrow and help me?

A: I'm not sure _____ or not. I have an appointment
                        (7)

   at 8:30, and I don't know _____
                                  (8)

   by 10 o'clock or not. But don't worry; the librarian can show you how
   to do a search.

Before You Read

1. Have you ever heard of Dr. Benjamin Spock? What do you know about him?

2. What are some differences in the ways that children are raised in different cultures?

Dr. Benjamin Spock, 1903–1998

 Read the following article. Pay special attention to the words in quotation marks ("...") and other noun clauses.

Did You Know?

Dr. Spock's book has been translated into 40 different languages.

New parents are always worried that they might be making a mistake with their new baby. The baby cries, and they don't know if they should let him cry or pick him up. The baby is sick, and they don't know what to do. **"Trust yourself. You know more than you think you do,"** wrote Benjamin Spock in his famous book *Dr. Spock's Baby and Child Care,* which first appeared in 1946. This book has sold over 50 million copies, making it the biggest-selling book after the Bible. In fact, many parents say **that it is the parents' bible for raising children.**

Before Dr. Spock's book appeared, John Watson was the leading child-care expert in the 1920s and 1930s. He wrote, **"Never hug or kiss your children; never let them sit in your lap."** He continued, **"If you must, kiss them once on the forehead when they say good night. Shake hands with them in the morning."** Also, he told parents **that it was necessary to feed children on a rigid schedule.** Dr. Spock disagreed with this strict manner of raising children and decided **that he would write a book. "I wanted to be supportive of parents rather than scold them,"** Dr. Spock said. **"Every baby needs to be smiled at, talked to, played with . . . gently and lovingly. Be natural and enjoy your baby."**

Dr. Spock never imagined **that his book would become so popular.** The last edition came out in 1998, a few months after his death at age 94. He will be remembered for his common-sense advice. **"Respect children because they deserve respect, and they'll grow up to be better people."**

9.6 | Noun Clauses as Exact Quotes of Notable Words

Dr. Spock said, **"Trust yourself."** John Watson said, **"Never hug or kiss your children."** Parents ask, **"What is the right way to take care of a baby?"**	An exact quote is used when the exact words are worth repeating and they are remembered because: • they have been recorded on video or audio. <p style="text-align:center">OR</p>• they are a quote from a book, newspaper, or magazine.
a. **Dr. Spock said,** "Every baby needs to be smiled at." b. "Every baby needs to be smiled at," **Dr. Spock said.** c. "Every baby needs to be smiled at," **said Dr. Spock.**	The *said* or *asked* phrase can come at the beginning (a) or the end of a quote (b and c). If it comes at the end, the subject and the verb can be inverted (c).
"More than anything else," **said Dr. Spock,** "children want to help."	An exact quote can be split, with the *said* or *asked* phrase in the middle, separated from the quote by commas.

Language Note:
Study the punctuation of sentences that contain an exact quote. Note that the first letter of an exact quote is a capital.

Dr. Spock said, "Trust yourself."

The mother asked, "Why is the baby crying?"

"Why is he crying?" asked the father.

"I'm going to feed him," said the mother.

"More than anything else," said Spock, "children want love."

EXERCISE 18   Read these quotes by Dr. Spock and Dr. Watson. Add quotation marks and capital letters where they are needed.

EXAMPLE   Watson said, "never kiss your child."

1. Spock said you know more than you think you do.

2. Spock said what good mothers and fathers instinctively feel like doing for their babies is usually best.

3. I wanted to be supportive of parents said Spock.

4. Watson said treat your children like small adults.

5. Too much love will harm your baby said Watson.

6. The most important value is to bring up children to help others, first in their family, and then other people said Spock.

7. To reduce violence in our society said Spock we must eliminate violence in the home and on television.

8. If children worship material success rather than truth or compassion Spock said it is because they have absorbed those values from others.

A FOLK TALE

Before You Read

1. What kinds of stories or folk tales are popular for children in your native culture?

2. What stories do you remember your parents telling you when you were a child?

Nasreddin is a character in many folk tales throughout the world. Read this story about Nasreddin. Pay special attention to exact quotes.

One day a neighbor passed Nasreddin's house and saw him outside his barn on his hands and knees. He appeared to be looking for something.

"What are you doing?" the neighbor asked.

"I'm looking for something," answered Nasreddin.

"What are you looking for?" the neighbor asked.

"I'm looking for my ring. It's very valuable," Nasreddin replied.

"I'll help you," said his neighbor. The neighbor got down on his hands and knees and started to help Nasreddin look for his ring. After searching for several hours, the neighbor finally asked, "Do you remember where you were when you lost it?"

"Of course," replied Nasreddin. "I was in the barn milking my cow."

"If you lost your ring inside the barn, then why are we looking for it outside the barn?" asked the neighbor.

"Don't be a fool," said Nasreddin. "It's too dark in the barn. But out here we have light."

9.7 | Exact Quotes in Telling a Story

Examples	Explanation
"What are you doing?" the neighbor asked. **"I'm looking for my ring,"** said Nasreddin.	Exact quotes are used in story telling to give words to the characters. Follow the same punctuation and word order rules as in Section 9.6.
"I will help you," said the neighbor, **"as soon as I can."**	An exact quote can be split, with the *said / asked* phrase in the middle.

EXERCISE 19 Read the following fable[2] by Aesop. Insert quotation marks and correct punctuation.

A hungry wolf was looking for food when he met a house dog that was passing by. Cousin said the dog. Your life is much harder than mine. Why don't you come to work with me and get your food given to you regularly?

I would like that said the wolf. Do you know where I can find such a job?

I will easily arrange that for you said the dog. Come with me to my master's house and we will share my work.

So the wolf and the dog went towards the town together. On the way there, the wolf noticed that the hair on a certain part of the dog's neck was very much worn away, so he asked him how that had come about.

Oh, it is nothing said the dog. That is only the place where the collar is put on me every night to keep me chained up. It hurts a bit at first, but you will soon get used to it.

Then good-bye to you said the wolf. I would rather starve than be a fat slave.

[2] A *fable* is a short story that teaches a lesson. Usually the characters of a fable are animals.

9.8 | Noun Clauses as Reported Speech

We use an **exact quote** when we want to write exactly what someone has said. The exact words are important. We use **reported speech** when we want to paraphrase what someone has said. The exact words are not important or not remembered. The idea is more important than the exact words.

Exact Quote	Reported Speech
Dr. Spock said, **"You know more than you think you do."**	Dr. Spock told parents that they should trust their own instincts.
The dog said to the wolf, **"I will take you to my master's house."**	The dog told the wolf that he **would** show him his way of life.
John Watson said, **"It is necessary to feed children on a rigid schedule."**	John Watson told parents that it **was** necessary to control their children's eating.
Nasreddin said, **"I lost my ring."**	Nasreddin told his neighbor that he **couldn't find** his ring.

EXERCISE 20 In the paragraph below, underline the noun clauses that show reported speech. Circle the verbs in the noun clauses. What tenses are used?

Last week my daughter's day care teacher called me at work and told me that my daughter had a fever and was resting in the nurse's office. I told my boss that I needed to leave work immediately. He said that it would be fine. As I was driving my car on the expressway to the school, a police officer stopped me. She said that I had been driving too fast. She said that I had been driving 10 miles per hour over the limit. I told her that I was in a hurry because my daughter was sick. I said I needed to get to her school quickly. I told the police officer that I was sorry, that I hadn't realized I had been driving so fast. She said she wouldn't give me a ticket that time, but that I should be more careful in the future, whether my daughter was sick or not.

9.9 | The Rule of Sequence of Tenses

After a past tense verb in the main clause (such as *said, told, reported,* etc.), the tense of the verb in the noun clause moves back one tense. This change in tense is called the **rule of sequence of tenses.** Observe the difference in verb tenses in the exact quotes on the left and the reported speech on the right.

Exact Quote	Reported Speech
He said, "I **know** you." (present)	He said (that) he **knew** me. (simple past)
He said, "I **am studying**." (present continuous)	He said (that) he **was studying**. (past continuous)
He said, "She **saw** me yesterday." (simple past)	He said (that) she **had seen** him the day before. (past perfect)
He said, "She **was helping** me." (past continuous)	He said (that) she **had been helping** him. (past perfect continuous)
He said, "I **have taken** the test." (present perfect)	He said (that) he **had taken** the test. (past perfect)
He said, "I **had** never **done** that." (past perfect)	He said (that) he **had** never **done** that. (past perfect)
	Note: There is no change for the past perfect.

Modals	
He said, "I **can** help you tomorrow."	He said (that) he **could** help me the next day.
He said, "She **may** leave early." (*may* = possibility)	He said (that) she **might** leave early.
He said, "You **may** go." (*may* = permission)	He said (that) **I could** go.
He said, "I **must** go."	He said (that) he **had to** go.
He said, "I **will** stay."	He said (that) he **would** stay.

Modals That Do Not Change Their Forms in Reported Speech	
He said, "You **should** leave."	He said (that) I **should** leave.
He said, "You **should have** left this morning."	He said (that) I **should have** left that morning.
He said, "You **could have** come."	He said (that) I **could have** come.
He said, "You **must have** known."	He said (that) I **must have** known.

Language Note:
We even change the tense in the following sentence:
     The teacher asked me what my name **was.**
Even though your name is still the same, the tense shows that the conversation took place at a different time and place.

(*continued*)

Observe all the differences between a sentence that has an exact quote and a sentence that uses reported speech.

Sentence with Exact Quote:	Sentence with Reported Speech:
She said, "I will help you tomorrow."	She said *that she would* help *me the next day*.
• quotation marks • comma after *said* • doesn't contain *that* • pronouns = *I, you* • verb = *will help* • time = *tomorrow*	• no quotation marks • no comma after *said* • contains *that* (optional) • pronouns = *she, me* • verb = *would help* • time = *the next day*

Language Note:
Time words change in reported speech.

today → that day

yesterday → the day before; the previous day

tomorrow → the next day; the following day

this morning → that morning

tonight → that night

now → at that time

EXERCISE 21 An adult is talking about things her parents and grandparents used to tell her when she was a little girl. Change to reported speech. Follow the rule of sequence of tenses.

EXAMPLE You are the love of my life.
My grandmother told me that ___*I was the love of her life.*___

1. You will always be my baby.

   My mother told me that _____

2. You have an easy life compared to mine.

   My father told me that _____

3. We had a much harder life.

   My grandparents told me that _____

4. We want you to be happy.

   My parents told me that _____

5. You don't understand life.

   My mother told me that _____

6. You have to listen to your teacher.

My father told me that _____

7. You can be anything you want if you study hard.

My parents told me that _____

8. We don't like to punish you, but sometimes it's necessary.

My parents told me that _____

9. Punishing you hurts me more than it hurts you.

My father told me that _____

10. We will always love you.

My grandparents told me that _____

11. You should wash your hands before meals.

My mother told me that _____

12. We will take you to the circus if your grades are good.

My grandparents promised me that _____

9.10 | Say vs. Tell

Examples	Explanation
a. She **said that** the children were happy. b. She **told me that** the children were happy.	a. In reported speech, we **say** that . . . . b. In reported speech, we **tell** <u>someone</u> that . . . . Tell is followed by an indirect object, but said is not.
c. She **added that** the day care had 15 staff members.	c. Other common verbs used in reported speech that *do not* have an indirect object are: add answer } that explain reply
d. She **informed the parents that** the day care center would be closed for the holiday.	d. Other common verbs used in reported speech that have an indirect object are: inform notify } someone that . . . remind promise
Compare: She **said,** "I love you." She **said to her daughter,** "I love you."	In an exact quote, we use say or say to someone. We do not usually use tell in an exact quote. *Wrong:* She *told,* "I love you."

EXERCISE **22** Fill in the blanks with *said* or *told*.

EXAMPLES He _____told_____ his children that they should study hard.

I _____said_____ that I was a very happy child.

1. I _____ that I wanted to learn more about raising children.

2. Dr. Spock _____ parents that they should trust their instincts.

3. John Watson _____ that parents should not hug their children.

4. Dr. Spock _____, "You know more than you think you do."

5. The mother _____ to her son, "Eat your vegetables."

6. The mother _____ her son that she would pick him up after school.

7. My parents _____ me that they wanted me to get a good education.

8. I called my parents last week and _____ them about my new roommate.

9. The little girl _____ to her mother, "I want to grow up to be just like you."

10. My parents _____ us to be honest.

EXERCISE **23** Change each sentence to reported speech. Follow the rule of sequence of tenses.

EXAMPLE Lisa said, "I need to put the kids to bed."

Lisa said that she needed to put the kids to bed.

1. Lisa said, "I have never read Dr. Spock's books."

_____

2. Lisa said to her friend, "I want to take my children to the zoo."

_____

3. Lisa said, "My children need to get exercise."

_____

4. Lisa and Paul said, "We will take our kids to the park tomorrow."

_____

5. Lisa said, "I forgot to give the kids their vitamins this morning."

_____

6. Lisa said, "The children went to bed early last night."

_____

7. Lisa said to her neighbor, "My son is in kindergarten."

_____

8. Lisa and Paul said, "Our son wants us to read him a story."

_____

9. Lisa said to Paul, "It's your turn to put the kids to bed."

_____

10. Lisa said to the teacher, "Our son's name is Tod."

_____

11. Tod said to his mother, "I don't want to go to bed."

_____

12. Tod said to his father, "I'm thirsty."

_____

13. Tod said to his friend, "I love my new bicycle."

_____

14. Tod said to his teacher, "I can write my name."

_____

15. Tod said to his friend, "My grandmother will buy me a toy."

_____

16. Lisa said to Tod, "You must go to bed."

_____

17. Tod said to his father, "I can't sleep."

_____

18. Tod said to his father, "I want to watch my favorite program on TV."

_____

19. Paul said to Tod, "You will not get enough sleep."

_____

20. Paul said to Tod, "I don't want to argue with you."

_____

9.11 | Exceptions to the Rule of Sequence of Tenses

Examples	Exceptions to the rule:
Parents **say** that Dr. Spock's book **is** their bible for raising children.	When the main verb is in the **present** tense, we do not change tenses.
Dr. Spock said that children **deserve** respect. Dr. Spock told parents that children **need** love.	In reporting a general truth, it is not necessary to follow the rule of sequence of tenses.
My brother has five children. He said that he **loves** (or **loved**) children. He said that he **wants** (or **wanted**) to have more children.	In reporting something that is still present, you can leave the tenses with no change or follow the rule of sequence of tenses.
Compare: a. Our teacher said that the test on Lesson 9 **will** (or **would**) be next week. b. My kindergarten teacher said that she **would** always remember me.	a. When the action has not happened yet, you can use *will* or *would*. b. When the action is past, use *would*.
A: I can't find my wallet. **B:** I didn't hear you. What did you say? **A:** I said I **can't** find my wallet.	When repeating speech immediately after it was said for someone who did not hear it, we do not usually follow the rule of sequence of tenses.
a. My mother said that she **was** born in 1948. b. My mother said that she **had** (or **had had**) a difficult childhood. c. She said that she lived (or had lived) in Poland when she was a child.	In reporting a statement about the past, it is not necessary to follow the rule of sequence of tenses if it is clear that the original verb was past. In sentence (a), it is clear that she said, "I **was** born in 1948" and not "I **am** born in 1948." It is rare to change *be* to past perfect if there is no confusion of time. In sentence (b), it is clear that she said, "I **had** a difficult childhood" not "I **have** a difficult childhood." In sentence (c), it is clear that she said, "I **lived** in Poland when I was a child."
Compare: a. She said that she **was** angry. b. She said that she **had been** angry, but that later she calmed down.	In sentence (a), she said, "I **am** angry." In sentence (b), she said, "I **was** angry." We change to past perfect in sentence (b) to show that the anger was gone by the time she said something about it.

EXERCISE 24 Circle the correct verb to complete these sentences. In a few cases, both answers are possible.

1. She said that she *will / would* come to the U.S. in 2001.

2. The teacher said that we *will / would* finish this lesson next week.

3. I always say that money *isn't / wasn't* as important as health.

4. She said that she *can't / couldn't* come to my party last week.

5. Pediatricians say that children *watch / watched* too much TV.

6. My little brother said that he *wants / wanted* to be president when he grows up.

7. Last semester our teacher said that we *will / would* have our final exam on Saturday, so all the students were unhappy. But they came anyway.

8. Our teacher last semester said that her name *is / was* Sandy and that she *wants / wanted* us to call her by her first name.

9. My doctor said that fatty food *is / was* bad for your health.

10. My boss said that he *lost / had lost* his keys.

11. Last Saturday, he said that he *needed / had needed* my help because he was moving that day.

9.12 | Reporting an Imperative

Examples	Explanation

"Trust yourself."
Spock **told** parents **to trust** themselves.
 	
"Sit down, please."
She **asked** me **to sit** down.
	To report an imperative, an infinitive is used. Use *ask* for an invitation or request. Use *tell* for a command or instruction. Don't use *say* to report an imperative.
	    Wrong: She *said me to sit* down.
	Use an object after *tell* or *ask*.
	    Wrong: He *told to close* the door.

"Don't hit your children." The doctor told us **not to hit** our children.	For a negative, put *not* before the infinitive.

Language Note:
Don't forget to change the pronouns and possessive forms in the infinitive phrase.
    "Show **your** children love."
He told us to show **our** children love.

    "Give **me your** book."
He asked me to give **him my** book.

EXERCISE 25 Change these imperatives to reported speech. Use *asked* or *told* + an object pronoun.

EXAMPLE The mother told her children, "Study for your test."

The mother told them to study for their test.

1. The son said to his mother, "Read me a story."

_____

2. She told the babysitter, "Don't let the kids watch TV all day."

_____

3. The girl said to her father, "Buy me a doll."

_____

4. The mother said to her child, "Eat your vegetables."

_____

5. The father said to his daughter, "Help me in the garage."

_____

6. The girl said to her parents, "Take me to the zoo."

_____

7. The dentist said to the boy, "Brush your teeth after every meal."

_____

8. I said to my parents, "Don't spoil your grandchildren."

_____

9. The girl said to her mother, "Comb my hair."

_____

10. The father said to his daughter, "Do your homework."

_____

11. The father said to his teenage daughter, "Don't come home late."

_____

12. The father said to his son, "Always be a gentleman."

_____

EXERCISE 26 Circle the correct word to complete this story about a babysitter.

Last month I babysat for a family that lives near me. It was my first

babysitting job. They (*said* / *told*) that the children (*would* / *will*) sleep
(example)   (1)

through the night and not cause any problems. But Danielle, the three-

year-old girl, woke up at 9 and (*said* / *told*) that (*I* / *she*) (*can't* / *couldn't*)
(2)   (3)   (4)

sleep. I (*said* / *told*) her that I (*will* / *would*) read (*her* / *you*) a story. Every
(5)   (6)   (7)

time I finished the story, she (*said* / *told*) me (*read* / *to read*) (*her* / *me*)
(8)   (9)   (10)

another one. She finally fell asleep at 10. Then Estelle, the five-year-old,

started crying. When I went to her room, she told me that (*I* / *she*)
(11)

(*has seen* / *had seen*) a monster in the closet. I tried to (*tell* / *say*) her that
(12)   (13)

there (*aren't* / *weren't*) any monsters in her closet, but she didn't stop
(14)

crying. I wanted to call the parents and tell them that Estelle (*is* / *was*)
(15)

upset and that she (*is* / *was*) crying. They had given me their cell phone
(16)

number and told me (*call* / *to call*) (*us* / *them*) in case of any problem,
(17)   (18)

but when I called, there was no answer. Later they told me that they

(*must* / *had to*) turn off their cell phone because they were at a concert.
(19)

They said (*we* / *they*) (*would* / *will*) be home by 11. But they
(20)   (21)

didn't come home till 1 a.m. They called and told me that the concert

(*has started* / *had started*) an hour late. I called my mother and told
(22)

her that I (*can't* / *couldn't*) leave because the parents hadn't come home.
(23)

She told me (*don't / not to*) worry. She said that it (*is / was*) my respon-
(24)   (25)

sibility to stay with the kids until the parents came home. When they

finally got home, they told me that (*we / they*) (*don't / didn't*) have any
(26)   (27)

money to pay (*you / me*) because they (*have forgotten / had forgotten*)
(28)   (29)

to stop at a cash machine. They said that (*they / we*) (*would / will*)
(30)   (31)

pay (*you / me*) (*next / the following*) week.
(32)   (33)

    When I got home, my mother was waiting up for me. I told her that I

(*don't / didn't*) ever want to have children. She laughed and told me that
(34)

the children's behavior (*wasn't / isn't*) unusual. She told me that (*you / I*)
(35)   (36)

(*will / would*) change (*my / your*) mind some day. I (*said / told*) her
(37)   (38)   (39)

that I (*don't / didn't*) want to babysit ever again. She told me that I
(40)

(*will / would*) get used to it.
(41)

Before You Read

1. Have you ever taken care of small children?

2. Do you know anyone who works in child care?

Read the following article. Pay special attention to reported questions.

Five years ago, when I was 18 years old and living in my native Estonia, I read an article about an "au pair" program in the U.S. This is a program where young people, mostly women between the ages of 18 and 25, go to live in the U.S. with an American family for a year to take care of their small children. In the process, these young people can improve their English, learn about American culture, and travel in the U.S.

When I heard about it, I became very excited and asked my mother **if I could join.** At first she said, "Absolutely not." She asked me **why I wanted to leave our family for a year.** I told her that it would be an opportunity for me to improve my English. I have always wanted to be an English teacher in Estonia, but my English was far from perfect. My mother said she would talk it over with Dad, and they finally agreed to let me go.

After filling out the application, I had an interview. The interviewer asked **why I wanted to be an au pair.** She also asked me **whether I knew how to drive.** Sometimes an au pair has to drive kids to school and to play dates. I told her that I had just gotten my license. I asked her **how many hours a week I would have to work,** and she said 45. I wanted to know **if I would get paid,** and she said I would be paid about $200 a week. I also wanted to know **if I would have the opportunity to go to school in the U.S.,** and she said, "Yes." She told me that the family would have to help pay for my schooling. I asked her **if I had to do housework,** and she said no, that my job was only to take care of the kids: wake them up, get them dressed, give them breakfast, take them to school, and help them with homework.

I was so excited when I was accepted.

My year in the U.S. (in Lansing, Michigan) was wonderful. The family treated me like a member of their family, taking me with them on trips and other family outings. I met other au pairs from around the world and have made many new friends. My English is 100 percent better now.

Friends often ask me **if I am happy that I spent a year in the U.S.,** and I say, "This was the opportunity of a lifetime."

9.13 | Noun Clauses as Reported Questions

When we report a question, we follow the rule of sequence of tenses if the main verb is in the **past tense** (*asked, wanted to know, tried to understand*, etc.). Remember: Reported speech is a paraphrase of what someone has said. The exact words are not important or not remembered. The idea is more important than the exact words.

Wh- Questions with auxiliaries or *be*	
"How old are you?" She asked me **how old I was.** "Where will I go to school?" I asked her **where I would go to school.** "What's your name?" She asked me **what my name was.**	Use statement word order—put the subject before the verb. Use a period at the end. An object (*me, him, her*, etc.) can be added after *asked*.

Wh- Questions with *do / does / did*	
"Why do you want to be an au pair?" She asked me **why I wanted to be an au pair.** "How did you hear about the program?" She asked me **how I had heard about the program.**	Remove *do / does / did* in the noun clause. Use statement word order—put the subject before the verb.

Wh- Questions about the subject	
"Who taught you to drive?" She asked me **who had taught me to drive.** "What happened?" She asked me **what had happened.**	There is no change in word order in questions about the subject.

Yes / No Questions with auxiliaries or *be*	
"Will I have time to go to school?" I asked her **if I would have time to go to school.** "Can I take classes?" I asked her **whether I could take classes or not.** "Am I responsible for housework?" I asked **whether I was responsible for housework.**	Add the word *if* or *whether* before reporting a *yes / no* question. You can add *or not* at the end. Use statement word order—put the subject before the verb.

Yes / No Questions with *do / does / did*	
"Do I have to do housework?" I asked her **whether I had to do housework.** "Does your mother approve?" She asked me **if my mother approved.** "Did you receive the application?" She asked me **if I had received the application.**	Remove *do / does / did*. Use statement word order—put the subject before the verb.

EXERCISE **27** These are some questions the interviewer asked the au pair candidate. Change these questions to reported speech.

EXAMPLE How old are you?

She asked me _how old I was._

1. Have you discussed this with your parents?

   She asked me _____

2. Do you have experience with small children?

   She asked me _____

3. When did you graduate from high school?

   She asked me _____

4. Do you have younger sisters and brothers?

   She asked me _____

5. Do you speak English?

   She asked me _____

6. Have you ever traveled to another country?

   She asked me _____

7. Do you have a driver's license?

   She asked me _____

8. How long have you had your driver's license?

   She asked me _____

9. Did you receive our brochure?

   She asked me _____

10. What are your plans for the future?

    She asked me _____

11. Have you ever left your parents before?

    She asked me _____

EXERCISE 28 These are some questions the au pair candidate asked the interviewer.

EXAMPLE   How much will I get paid?

She asked her _how much she would get paid._

1. Will I have my own room?

    She asked her _____

2. How many children does the family have?

    She asked her _____

3. How old are the children?

    She asked her _____

4. Are the children in school?

    She asked her _____

5. Should I get an international driver's license?

    She asked her _____

6. What is the climate like in Michigan?

    She asked her _____

7. Does the family have a computer?

    She asked her _____

8. Can I e-mail my own family every day?

    She asked her _____

9. When will I get a vacation?

    She asked her _____

10. How much is the airfare?

    She asked her _____

11. Who will pay for the airfare?

    She asked her _____

12. Where can I study English?

    She asked her _____

EXERCISE **29**   Change these questions to reported speech.

EXAMPLE   The babysitter asked the child, "Do you feel sick?"

The babysitter asked the child _if he felt sick._

1. The babysitter asked the parents, "What time will you be home?"

   The babysitter asked the parents _____

2. The babysitter asked the parents, "Where are you going?"

   The babysitter asked the parents _____

3. The children asked the babysitter, "What's your name?"

   The children asked the babysitter _____

4. The babysitter asked the little boy, "How old are you?"

   The babysitter asked the little boy _____

5. The babysitter asked the parents, "Have the kids eaten dinner yet?"

   The babysitter asked the parents _____

6. The children asked the babysitter, "Do we have to go to bed at 8 p.m.?"

   The children asked the babysitter _____

7. The babysitter asked the parents, "Should I give the kids a snack before bed?"

   The babysitter asked the parents _____

8. The children asked the babysitter, "Do you want to play a game with us?"

   The children asked the babysitter _____

9. The children asked the babysitter, "Can we watch TV?"

   The children asked the babysitter _____

10. The parents asked the babysitter, "Have you ever taken care of an infant before?"

    The parents asked the babysitter _____

11. The babysitter asked the parents, "Do you have a phone number where I can reach you?"

    The babysitter asked the parents _____

12. The babysitter asked the parents, "Can I use your telephone?"

    The babysitter asked the parents _____

9.14 | Noun Clauses After Other Past Tense Verbs

Examples	Explanation
Dr. Spock *decided* that **he would write a book.** He *thought* that **he could help parents feel more comfortable with their kids.** He *knew* **that he wanted to help parents.** The au pair *didn't know* **if she would be happy in the U.S.** She *wondered* **what her life would be like in the U.S.** Her mother *wasn't sure* **whether she should let her daughter to go the U.S. or not.**	If the verb in the main clause is past tense (*thought, knew, believed, wondered, realized, decided, imagined, understood, was sure,* etc.), follow the rule of sequence of tenses in Section 9.9.

EXERCISE **30** ABOUT YOU Fill in the blanks and discuss your answers. Follow the rule of sequence of tenses.

EXAMPLE Before I came to this city, I thought that *everybody here was unfriendly,* but it isn't true.

1. Before I came to this city (or the U.S.), I thought that _____ _____, but it isn't true.

2. Before I came to this city (or the U.S.), I didn't know that _____ _____

3. Before I came to this city (or the U.S.), I was worried that _____ _____

4. When I lived in my hometown, I was afraid that _____ _____

5. When I came to this school, I was surprised to learn that _____ _____

6. When I came to this school, I realized that _____ _____

7. When I was younger, I never imagined that _____ _____

8. Before I came to the U.S. (or this city), I wondered _____ _____

EXERCISE **31** ABOUT YOU Fill in the blanks to tell about you and your parents when you were a child.

EXAMPLE When I was a child, I dreamed that _____ *I would be a movie star.* _____

1. My parents told me that _____

2. My parents hoped that _____

3. My parents thought that _____

4. When I was a child, I dreamed that _____

5. When I was a child, I thought that _____

6. When I was a child, I didn't understand _____

7. When I was younger, I never imagined that _____

8. When I was younger, I wondered _____

9. When I was younger, I didn't know _____

10. When I was younger, I couldn't decide _____

EXERCISE **32** *Combination Exercise.* The author of this book remembers this true story from her childhood. Change the words in parentheses to reported speech.

When I was about 6 years old, I had the measles.[3] My mother told me

_____ *to stay in the bedroom* _____ because it was dark in there. She said
(example: "Stay in the bedroom.")

_____. My bedroom was near
(1 "I don't want the bright light to hurt your eyes.")

the dining room of the house. My mother told me _____

_____ because it was dark in
(2 "You can go into the dining room.")

there. She told me _____ because
(3 "Don't go into the living room.")

it was too light there. The TV was in the living room and she thought

_____.
(4 "The brightness of the TV can hurt your eyes.")

My sister Micki was three years older than I and liked to bully[4] me. She had already had the measles, so she wasn't afraid of getting

sick. She came to the door of my bedroom and asked me _____

_____. I told her
(5 "Do you know why you can't go into the living room?")

---

[3] *Measles* is an illness that children often get. The medical name is rubeola.
[4] To *bully* means to act cruel to someone who is smaller and more helpless.

_____. She said, "The living room is

(6 "I don't understand.")

for living people. The dining room is for dying people, and you're gonna die." Of course, I believed her because she was 9 years old and knew

much more than I did. I didn't understand that _____

_____ .

(7 " 'Dining' means 'eating,' not 'dying'.")

Today we can laugh about this story, but when I had the measles, I was

afraid that _____.

(8 "I will die.")

EXERCISE 33 *Combination Exercise.* This is a composition written by a former au pair. Change the words in parentheses ( ) to reported speech.

Two years ago, when I was 18 and living in my native Poland, I didn't

know exactly ___*what I should do*___ with my life. I had just graduated

(example: "What should I do?")

from high school and I couldn't decide _____.

(1 "Should I go to college or not?")

I was not sure _____. A neighbor

(2 "What do I want to do with my life?")

of mine told me _____ and

(3 "I had the same problem when I was your age.")

decided to go to the U.S. for a year to work as an "au pair." She asked me

_____. I told

(4 "Have you ever heard of the au pair program in America?")

her that _____. She told me that

(5 "I haven't.")

_____, helping them take care

(6 "I lived with an American family for a year.")

of their two small children. I asked her _____ :

(7 "How much will this program cost me?")

She laughed and told me _____

(8 "You will earn about $200 a week, get your own room, and

_____ . She also told me _____

get three meals a day.")   *(9 "You will have a chance to travel in the U.S.")*

I asked her _____, and she said

(10 "Was it a good experience for you?")

_____. She said _____

(11 "It has changed my life.")

412 Lesson **9**

_____and _____
(12 "I have gained a new understanding of people.")

_____. I asked her _____
(13 "My English has improved a lot.")   (14 "Is the work very hard?")

and she said _____ but that _____.
(15 "It is.")   (16 "It is very rewarding.")

I looked up *au pair* on the Internet and found out how to apply. I

told my parents that _____.
(17 "I am thinking about going to America for a year.")

At first they told me _____. They thought that
(18 "Don't go.")

_____ and that _____.
(19 "You are too young.")   (20 "You don't have any experience.")

I reminded them _____ _____
(21 "I have babysat many times for our neighbors' kids.")

and that by working in America _____.
(22 "I will get even more experience.")

I also told them that _____.
(23 "My English will improve if I live with an American family.")

My parents finally agreed to let me go. I filled out the application, had
an interview, and was accepted.

I told my parents _____. I promised them
(24 "Don't worry.")

_____.
(25 "I will keep in touch with you by e-mail almost every day.")

When I arrived, my American family explained to me _____

_____. They had two small kids, and I had to wake them
(26 "What do I have to do?")

up, make them breakfast, and take them to school in the morning. I asked

them _____, and they laughed. They told
(27 "Do I have to wait for them at school?")

me _____.
(28 "While the kids are in school, you can take English classes at a local college.")

I told them _____,
(29 "I don't have enough money to pay for school.")

but they told me _____. So that's what
(30 "We will pay for your classes.")

I did. I met students from all over the world. I also had a chance to
travel to many American cities with other au pairs. When the year was

over, I was very sad to leave my new family, but we promised _____

_____. They told me

(31 "We will stay in touch.")

_____.

(32 "You will always be welcome in our house.")

Now I am back home and in college, majoring in early childhood

education. My parents told me _____.

(33 "We are happy we let you go to America.")

They can see that I've become much more confident and mature. Becoming an au pair in America was one of the best experiences of my life.

SUMMARY OF LESSON 9

Direct statement or question	Sentence with included statement or question	Use of noun clause or infinitive
She loves kids. She is patient.	I know **that she loves kids.** I'm sure **that she is patient.**	A noun clause is used after verbs and adjectives.
Talk to your children. Don't be so strict.	It is essential **that you talk to your children.** He recommends **that we not be so strict.**	A noun clause is used after expressions of importance. The base form is used in the noun clause.
Is the baby sick? What does the baby need?	If don't know **if the baby is sick or not.** I'm not sure **what the baby needs.**	A noun clause is used as an included question.
What should I do with the crying baby? Where can I get information about the "au pair" program?	I don't know **what to do with the crying baby.** Can you tell me **where to get information about the "au pair" program?**	An infinitive can replace *should* or *can*.
You know more than you think you do. Do you have children?	Dr. Spock said, **"You know more than you think you do."** **"Do you have children?"** asked the doctor.	A noun clause is used in an exact quote to report what someone has said.
I will read a book about child care. Do you have experience with children?	She said **that she would read a book about child care.** She asked me **if I had experience** with children.	A noun clause is used in reported speech to paraphrase what someone has said.
Trust yourself. Don't give the child candy.	He told us **to trust ourselves.** He told me **not to give the child candy.**	An infinitive is used to report an imperative.

1. Use *that* or nothing to introduce an included statement. Don't use *what*.

   > *that*
   > I know ~~what~~ she likes to swim.

2. Use statement word order in an indirect question.

   >   *it is*
   > I don't know what time ~~is it~~.
   >
   > I don't know where (lives) your brother.

3. We *say* something. We *tell* someone something.

   > *told*
   > He ~~said~~ me that he wanted to go home.
   >
   > *said*
   > He ~~told~~, "I want to go home."

4. Use *tell* or *ask*, not *say*, to report an imperative. Follow *tell* and *ask* with an object.

   > *told*
   > I ~~said~~ you to wash your hands.
   >
   >   *me*
   > She asked ^ to show her my ID card.

5. Don't use *to* after *tell*.

   > He told ~~to~~ me that he wanted to go home.

6. Use *if* or *whether* to introduce an included *yes/no* question.

   >   *if*
   > I can't decide ^ I should buy a car or not.
   >
   >   *whether*
   > I don't know ^ it's going to rain or not.

7. Use *would*, not *will*, to report something that is past.

   >   *would*
   > My father said that he ~~will~~ come to the U.S. in 1995.

8. Follow the rule of sequence of tenses when the main verb is in the past.

   >   *wanted*
   > When I was a child, my grandmother told me that she ~~wants~~ to travel.

9. Don't use *so* before a noun clause.

   > He thinks ~~so~~ the U.S. is a beautiful country.

10. Use the base form after expressions showing importance or urgency.

> *be*
> It is urgent that you ~~are~~ on time for the meeting.

> *review*
> I suggested that the teacher ~~reviewed~~ the last lesson.

11. Use *not* + base form to form the negative after expressions showing importance or urgency.

> *not*
> Doctors recommend that small children ~~don't~~ watch TV.

12. Use a period, not a question mark, if a question is included in a statement.

> I don't know what time it is~~?~~

13. Use correct punctuation in an exact quote.

> He said, "I love you."

14. Don't use a comma before a noun clause (EXCEPTION: an exact quote).

> He knows~~,~~ that you like him.

15. *Don't* isn't used in reporting a negative imperative.

> *not to*
> He told me ~~don't~~ open the door.

LESSON 9 TEST/REVIEW

PART 1 Find the mistakes with the underlined words, and correct them. Not every sentence has a mistake. If the sentence is correct, write *C*.

EXAMPLES   I don't know where ~~does~~ your brother live.
> *s*

"What do you want?" asked the man.   **C**

1. I'd like to know <u>what I need to study</u> for the final exam.

2. She is happy <u>what</u> her daughter got married.

3. I don't know <u>what you want.</u>

4. He <u>said</u> me that he wanted my help.

5. I don't know <u>what time is it.</u>

6. The president said, "There <u>will be</u> no new taxes."

7. I don't know <u>what to do.</u>

8. I don't know where should I go for registration.

9. I told you not to leave the room.

10. The weatherman said that it will rain on Sunday, but it didn't.

11. Do you think so New Yorkers are friendly people?

12. Do you think I'm intelligent?

13. I don't know she understands English or not.

14. He asked me how do I feel.

15. He told that he wanted to speak with me.

16. He said to his father, "I'm an adult now."

17. I didn't know that learning English would be so hard.

18. Before I started looking for a job, I thought that I will find a job right away, but I didn't.

19. He told to me that he wanted to buy a car.

20. He said me to open the window.

21. She told me don't use her computer.

22. I didn't understand what did I need to do.

23. It is important that you be here before 9 o'clock.

24. I recommend that you not give the answers to anyone.

25. I suggest that my friend visits me during vacation.

26. My counselor advised that I didn't take so many credit hours.

PART 2 Find the mistakes with **punctuation** in the following sentences. Not every sentence has a mistake. If the sentence is correct, write *C*.

EXAMPLES He said, "I can't help you."

He said, "I have to leave now." **C**

1. I don't know what time it is?

2. Do you know what time it is?

3. I'm sure, that you'll find a job soon.

4. The teacher said I will return your tests on Monday.

5. I didn't realize, that you had seen the movie already.

6. He asked me, "What are you doing here?"

7. "What do you want," he asked.

8. "I want to help you," I said.

9. I told him that I didn't need his help.

10. Can you tell me where I can find the bookstore.

PART 3 Fill in the blanks with an included question.

EXAMPLE   How old is the president?

Do you know _____ *how old the president is?* _____

1. Where does Jack live?

I don't know _____

2. Did she go home?

I don't know _____

3. Why were they late?

Nobody knows _____

4. Who ate the cake?

I don't know _____

5. What does "liberty" mean?

I don't know _____

6. Are they working now?

Can you tell me _____

7. Should I buy the car?

I don't know _____

8. Has she ever gone to Paris?

I'm not sure _____

9. Can we use our books during the test?

Do you know _____

10. What should I do?

I don't know _____

PART 4 Change the following sentences to reported speech. Follow the rule of sequence of tenses or use the infinitive where necessary.

EXAMPLE   He said, "She is late."

He said that she was late. _____

1. She said, "I can help you."

_____

_____

2. He said, "Don't go away."

_____

3. He said, "My mother left yesterday."

_____

4. She said, "I'm learning a lot."

_____

5. He said, "I've never heard of Dr. Spock."

_____

6. He said, "Give me the money."

_____

7. They said to me, "We finished the job."

_____

8. He said to us, "You may need some help."

_____

9. He said to her, "We were studying."

_____

10. He said to her, "I have your book."

_____

11. He said to us, "You should have called me."

_____

12. He said to his wife, "I will call you."

_____

13. He asked me, "Do you have any children?"

_____

14. He asked me, "Where are you from?"

_____

15. He asked me, "What time is it?"

_____

16. He asked me, "Did your father come home?"

_____

17. He asked me, "Where have you been?"

_____

18. He asked me, "Will you leave tomorrow?"

_____

19. He asked me, "What do you need?"

_____

20. He asked me, "Are you a student?"

_____

21. He asked us, "Can you help me today?"

_____

22. He asked us, "Who needs my help?"

_____

EXPANSION ACTIVITIES

Classroom Activities

1. Write questions you have about the topics in the readings of this lesson. Express your questions with _"I wonder . . . "_ Compare your questions in a small group.

EXAMPLES I wonder why parents spend so much less time with their children than they used to.

I wonder why it is so hard to raise a child.

2. What advice did your parents, teachers, or other adults give you when you were younger? Write three sentences. Share them in a small group.

EXAMPLES My mother told me to be honest.

My grandfather told me that I should always respect older people.

_____

_____

_____

Talk About it

1. How is your philosophy of raising children different from your parents' philosophy or methods?

2. Do you think parents should or shouldn't hit children when they misbehave?

3. Did your parents read to you when you were a child?

4. Did you have a lot of toys when you were a child?

5. Do you think children today behave differently from when you were a child?

6. Is it hard to raise children? Why?

7. Read the following poem. Discuss the meaning.

> Your children are not your children.
> They are the sons and daughters of Life's longing for itself.
> They come through you but not from you,
> And though they are with you, yet they belong not to you.
> You may give them your love but not your thoughts.
> For they have their own thoughts.
> You may house their bodies but not their souls,
> For their souls dwell in the house of tomorrow, which you cannot
>   visit, not even in your dreams.
> You may strive to be like them, but seek not to make them like you.
> For life goes not backward nor tarries with yesterday.
> You are the bows from which your children as living arrows are
>   sent forth.
> . . .
> Let your bending in the archer's hand be for gladness;
> For even as he loves the arrow that flies, so he loves also the bow
>   that is stable.
>
> Kahlil Gibran (From *The Prophet*)

Write About it

1. Write a paragraph about an interesting conversation or argument that you had or that you heard recently.

   EXAMPLE   Last week I had a conversation with my best friend about having children. I told her that I didn't want to have children. She asked me why I was against having kids. . . .

2. Write about an unpopular belief that you have. Explain why you have this belief and why it is unpopular.

   EXAMPLES   I believe that there is life on other planets.

   I believe that schools shouldn't have tests.

3. Write about a belief you used to have that you no longer have. Explain what this belief was and why you no longer believe it to be true.

   EXAMPLES   I used to believe that communism was the best form of government.

   I used to believe that marriage made people happy.

4. Write about a general belief that people in your native culture have. Explain what this belief means. Do you agree with it?

   EXAMPLES   In my native country, it is said that it takes a village to raise a child.

   In my native culture, it is believed that wisdom comes with age.

5. Write a short fable or fairy tale that you remember. Include the characters' words in quotation marks. See the folk tale on page 393 for an example.

6. Write about an incident from your childhood, like the one in Exercise 32.

Outside Activities

1. Interview a classmate, coworker, or neighbor about his or her childhood. Find out about this person's family, school, house, activities, and toys. Tell the class what this person said, using reported speech.

2. Interview a friend, coworker, or neighbor who has a child or children. Ask him or her these questions:

   What's the hardest thing about raising a child?
   What's the best thing about raising a child?

   Report this person's answers to the class.

Internet Activities

1. At a search engine, type in *parents*, *parenting*, or *family*. What kind of information can parents get about raising children from a Web site? Bring this information to class.

2. At a search engine, type in *au pair*. Find out how to apply for an au pair program. Bring an application to class.

3. For information about parenting and children, find these Web sites by typing in their names at a search engine:

   Zero to Three
   I am your child

   Find some information about children that surprises you. Bring this information to class.

4. At a search engine, type in *day care center* and the name of the city where you live. Find out five facts about a specific day care center. Bring this information to class.

 Additional Activities at **http://elt.thomson.com/gic**

GRAMMAR

Unreal Conditions—Present
Real Conditions vs. Unreal Conditions
Unreal Conditions—Past
Wishes

CONTEXT: Science or Science Fiction?

Time Travel
Traveling to Mars
Life 100 Years Ago
Science or Wishful Thinking?

Before You Read

1. Do you think time travel is a possibility for the future?

2. Can you name some changes in technology or medicine that happened since you were a child?

 Read the following article. Pay special attention to unreal conditions.

If you **could travel** to the past or the future, which time period **would** you **visit?** What would you like to see? **Would** you **want** to come back to the present? If you **could travel** to the past and prevent your grandfather from meeting your grandmother, then you **wouldn't be** here, right? These ideas may seem the subject of science fiction movies and novels now, but believe it or not, physicists are studying the possibility of time travel seriously.

About 100 years ago, Albert Einstein proved that the universe has not three dimensions but four—three of space and one of time. He proved that time changes with motion. A moving clock ticks more slowly than one that does not move. Einstein believed that, theoretically, time travel is possible. If

Albert Einstein 1879–1955

you **wanted** to visit the Earth in the year 3000, you **would have to** get on a rocket ship going at almost of the speed of light,[1] go to a star 500 light years away, turn around and come back at that speed. When you got back, the Earth **would be** 1,000 years older, but you **would** only **be** ten years older. You **would** be in the future.

However, using today's technologies, if you **wanted** to travel to the nearest star, it **would take** 85,000 years to arrive. (This assumes the speed of today's rockets, which is 35,000 miles per hour.) According to Einstein, you can't travel faster than the speed of light. While most physicists believe that travel to the future is possible, many believe that travel to the past will never happen.

Science and technology are evolving at a rapid pace. **Would** you **want** to travel to the future to see all the changes that will occur? **Would** you **be** able to come back to the present and warn people of future earthquakes or accidents? These ideas, first presented in a novel called *The Time Machine*, written by H.G. Wells over 100 years ago, are the subject not only of fantasy but of serious scientific exploration. In fact, many of today's scientific discoveries and explorations, such as traveling to the moon, had their roots in science fiction novels and movies.

Did You Know?

In 1955, Albert Einstein died at the age of 76. He had requested that his body be cremated but that his brain be saved and studied for research.

Read what people have said in the past about the future.

"Heavier-than-air flying machines are impossible."
  (Lord Kelvin, president, Royal Society, 1895)

"There is no reason for any individual to have a computer in their home."
  (Ken Olsen, president, chairman, and founder of Digital Equipment Corp., 1977)

"The telephone has too many shortcomings to be seriously considered as a means of communication. The device is inherently of no value to us."
  (Western Union internal memo, 1876)

"Airplanes are interesting toys but of no military value."
  (Marshal Ferdinand Foch, French commander of Allied forces during the closing months of World War I, 1918)

"Who . . . wants to hear actors talk?"
  (Harry M. Warner, Warner Brothers, 1927)

"Everything that can be invented has been invented."
  (Charles H. Duell, commissioner, U.S. Office of Patents, 1899)

[1] The *speed of light* is 299,792,458 meters per second (or 186,000 miles per second).

10.1 | Unreal Conditions—Present

An unreal condition is used to talk about a hypothetical or imagined situation.

Examples	Explanation

If we **had** a time machine, we **could travel** to the future or past.
    (Reality: We **don't have** a time machine.)
 	
If I **could travel** to the past, I **would visit** my ancestors.
    (Reality: I **can't travel** to the past.)
 	
If we **didn't have** computers, our lives **would be** different.
    (Reality: We **have** computers.)
	An unreal condition in the **present** describes a situation that is not real now.
	
	Use a past form in the *if* clause and *would* or *could* + base form in the main clause.

If we **could travel** at the speed of light, we**'d be able** to visit the future. If I **visited** my great-great-great-grandparents, they**'d be** very surprised to meet me.	All pronouns except *it* can contract with *would*: *I'd, you'd, he'd, she'd, we'd, they'd.*
If time travel **were** possible, many people **would do** it. If we **were** time travelers, we**'d see** the future.	*Were* is the correct form in the condition clause for all subjects, singular and plural. However, you will often hear native speakers use *was* with *I, he, she*, and *it*.
If I **were** you, I**'d study** more science.	We often give advice with the expression *"If I were you . . ."*
What if you could travel to the future? **What if** you had the brain of Einstein?	We use *what if* to propose a hypothetical situation.
If you **had** Einstein's brain, what **would** you **do?** If you **could** fly to another planet, **would** you **go?**	When we make a question with conditionals, the *if* clause uses statement word order. The main clause uses question word order.

Punctuation Note:
When the *if* clause precedes the main clause, a comma is used to separate the two clauses. When the main clause precedes the *if* clause, a comma is not used.

    If I had Einstein's brain, I would be smarter. (Comma)
    I would be smarter if I had Einstein's brain. (No comma)

EXERCISE **1** ABOUT YOU Answer the following questions with *I would*. Give an explanation for your answers.

EXAMPLE If you could meet any famous person, who would you meet?

I would meet Einstein. I would ask him how he discovered his theory

of relativity.

1. If you could travel to the past or the future, which direction would you go?

   _____

2. If you could make a clone of yourself, would you do it? Why or why not?

   _____

3. If you could travel to another planet, would you want to go?

   _____

4. If you could change one thing about today's world, what would it be?

   _____

5. If you could find a cure for only one disease, what would it be?

   _____

6. If you could know the day of your death, would you want to know it?

   _____

7. If you could have the brain of another person, whose brain would you want?

   _____

8. If you could be a child again, what age would you be?

   _____

9. If you could change one thing about yourself, what would it be?

   _____

10. If you could meet any famous person, who would it be?

    _____

11. If you could be any animal, what animal would you be?

    _____

EXERCISE 2 Fill in the blanks with the correct form of the verb in parentheses ( ) to complete these conversations. Use *would* + base form in the main clause. Use the past tense in the *if* clause.

EXAMPLE A: What _____would you do_____ if you _____were_____
(you/do)   (be)

the mayor of this city?

B: If I _____were_____ the mayor, I
(be)

_____would create_____ enough parking spaces for everyone.
(create)

1. A: If you _____ make a copy of yourself,
(can)

_____ it?
(you/do)

B: My wife says that one of me is enough. If she _____
(have)

two of me, it _____ her crazy.
(drive)

2. A: If you _____ come back to Earth in any form
(can)

after you die, how _____ back?
(you/come)

B: I _____ back as a dog. Dogs have such an easy life.
(come)

A: Not in my native country. There are many homeless dogs.

B: I _____ as an American dog.
(only/come back)

3. A: If you _____ choose to have a boy or girl baby,
(can)

what _____?
(you/choose)

B: I _____. I _____ to
(not/choose)   (not/want)

interfere with nature.

4. A: What _____ if you _____
(you/do)   (have)

a lot of money?

B. I _____ my family first. Then I
(help)

_____ a nice house and car.
(buy)

5. A: If you _____ look like any movie star,
(can)

who _____?
(you/look like)

B: I _____ a young Harrison Ford.
(look like)

6. A: If I _____ find a way to teach a person a
(can)

foreign language in a week, I _____ a million
(make)

dollars.

B: And I _____ your first customer.
(be)

7. A: If you _____ be invisible for a day,
(can)

what _____?
(you/do)

B: I _____ to my teacher's house the day she
(go)

writes the final exam.

8. A: What _____ if you _____
(you/do)   (not/have)

a TV?

B: I think I _____ crazy if
(go)

I _____ a TV.
(not/have)

9. A: Why are you writing your composition by hand?

B: I don't know how to type. I _____ my
(type)

compositions on the computer if I _____ type fast.
(can)

A: If I _____ you, I _____ a
(be)   (take)

keyboarding class to learn to type.

10. A: What _____ if you _____
(you/do)   (can/travel)

to the past or future?

B: I _____ to the past.
(go)

A: How far back _____?
(you/go)

B: I _____ to the nineteenth century and stay there.
_(go)_

A: Why?

B: If I _____ in the nineteenth century, I
(live)

_____ work. My life _____ easy.
(not/have to) _(be)_

A: Yes, but if you _____ in the nineteenth
(live)

century, you _____ vote.
(not/be able to)

11. A: It _____ nice if people _____
_(be)_ _(can)_

live forever.

B: If people _____, the world
(not/die)

_____ overpopulated. There
_(be)_

_____ enough resources for everybody.
(not/be)

A: I didn't think of that. If the world _____
_(be)_

overpopulated, I _____ a parking space!
(never/find)

EXERCISE 3 Fill in the blanks with the correct form of the verb in parentheses ( ) to complete this conversation.

A: If you ___could___ change one thing about yourself,
(example: can)

what _____?
_(1 it/be)_

B: I _____ thinner. If I _____
_(2 be)_ _(3 lose)_

about 30 pounds, I _____ much happier—
_(4 be)_

and healthier. If I _____ so much, I
(5 not/eat)

_____ weight.
(6 lose)

A: Diet is not enough. You need to get exercise too. You can start right now with exercise. Let's go jogging every day after work.

B: If I _____ so tired after work,
(7 be/not)

I _____ jogging with you. But I work
_(8 go)_

nine hours a day and it takes me two hours to commute[2]. So I'm too tired at the end of the day.

A: Can't you get any exercise at your job?

B: If I _____ a different kind of job,
(9 have)

I _____ more exercise. But I sit at a desk all day.
(10 get)

A: How about going swimming with me on Saturdays? I go every Saturday. Swimming is great exercise.

B: If I _____ how to swim, I _____
(11 know) _(12 go)_

with you. The problem is I don't know how to swim.

A: You can take lessons. My gym has a pool and they give lessons on the weekends. Why don't you sign up for lessons?

B: I'm too busy with the kids on the weekends. If I

_____ kids, I _____ much
(13 not/have) _(14 have)_

more free time.

A: If I _____ you, I _____ to
_(15 be)_ _(16 try)_

simplify my life.

EXERCISE 4 ABOUT YOU Make a list of things you would do if you had more time. You may share your sentences in a small group or with the entire class.

EXAMPLES _If I had more free time, I'd read more novels._

I'd visit my grandmother more often if I had more free time.

1. _____

2. _____

3. _____

4. _____

[2] To _commute_ means to travel from home to work and back.

EXERCISE 5 ABOUT YOU Make a list of things you would do differently if you spoke or understood English better. You may share your sentences in a small group or with the entire class.

EXAMPLES   *If I spoke English fluently, I wouldn't come to this class.*

I wouldn't be so nervous when I talk on the telephone if I

understood English better.

1. _____

2. _____

3. _____

EXERCISE 6 Fill in the blanks to tell what the following people are thinking.

EXAMPLE   One-year-old: If I ___*could*___ walk, I ___*would walk*___ into the kitchen
                         (can)   (walk)
and take a cookie out of the cookie jar.

1. Two-year-old: If I _____ talk,
                              (can)

   I _____ my mother that I hate peas.
              (tell)

2. 14-year-old: I _____ happier if
                           (be)

   I _____ drive.
           (can)

3. 16-year-old: If I _____ a car, my friends and
                            (have)

   I _____ out every night.
            (go)

4. 19-year-old: I _____ a private university if
                          (attend)

   I _____ a lot of money.
           (have)

5. 25-year-old: If I _____ married, my parents
                            (be)

   _____ about me so much.
        (not/worry)

6. 35-year-old mother: I _____ more time for
                                    (have)

   myself if my kids _____ older.
                               (be)

7. 60-year-old grandmother: If I _____

   (not/have)

grandchildren, my life _____ so interesting.

   (not/be)

8. 90-year-old: If I _____ young today,

   (be)

I _____ learn all about computers and other

   (have to)

high-tech stuff.

9. 100-year-old: If I _____ you the story of

   (tell)

my life, you _____ it.

   (not/believe)

10. The dog: If I _____ talk, I

   (can)

_____ "Feed me a steak."

   (say)

EXERCISE 7 ABOUT YOU Complete each statement.

EXAMPLES If I studied harder, *I would get better grades.*

If I were the president, *I would lower taxes.*

1. If I were the English teacher, _____

2. If I could live to be 200 years old, _____

3. If I could predict the future, _____

4. If I were rich, _____

5. If I could be a child again, _____

6. If I could change places with any other person in the world, _____

_____

7. My life would be better if _____

8. I'd be learning English much faster if _____

9. I'd study more if _____

10. I'd travel a lot if _____

11. I'd be very unhappy if _____

12. I wouldn't borrow money from a friend unless _____

_____

EXERCISE 8 ABOUT YOU Answer each question with *yes* or *no*. Then make a statement with an unreal condition.

EXAMPLES Do you have the textbook?

Yes. If I didn't have the textbook, I wouldn't be able to do this exercise.

Is this lesson easy?

No. If it were easy, we wouldn't have to spend so much time on it.

1. Are you an American?

2. Do you know how to use the Internet?

3. Do you work on Sundays?

4. Do all the students in this class speak the same language?

5. Does the teacher speak your native language?

6. Are you taking other courses this semester?

7. Do you have a high school diploma?

8. Do you have a car?

9. Do you live far from school?

10. Do you have a job?

11. Do you speak English perfectly?

12. Do you have a computer?

10.2 | Implied Conditions

Examples	Explanation
I **would** never lie to a friend. **Would** you jump in a river to save a drowning person? She **would** never leave her children with a babysitter.	Sometimes the condition (the *if* clause) is implied, not stated. In the examples on the left, the implication is "if you had the opportunity" or "if the possibility presented itself."
Would you **want** to live without today's technologies? **Would** you **want** to travel to another planet? **Would** you **want** to have Einstein's brain? I **wouldn't want** to live for 500 years, **would** you?	*Would want* is used to present hypothetical situations. The *if* clause is implied.

EXERCISE 9 ABOUT YOU Answer these questions and discuss your answers.

1. Would you give money to a beggar?

2. Would you marry someone from another country?

3. Would you buy a used computer?

4. Would you lend a large amount of money to a friend?

5. Would you open someone else's mail?

6. Would you lie to protect a friend?

7. Would you tell a dying relative that he or she is dying?

8. Would you want to travel to the past or the future?

9. Would you want to live more than 100 years?

10. Would you want to visit another planet?

11. Would you want to live on the top floor of a hundred-story building?

12. Would you want to go on an African safari?

EXERCISE 10 ABOUT YOU Answer these questions.

EXAMPLE What would you do if a stranger on the street asked you for money?
I would say, "I'm sorry. I can't give you any."

1. What would you do if you found a wallet in the street with a name and phone number in it?

2. What would you do if you lost your money and didn't have enough money to get home by public transportation?

3. What would you do if you saw a person in a public park picking flowers?

_____

4. What would you do if a cashier in a supermarket gave you a ten-dollar bill in change instead of a one-dollar bill?

_____

5. What would you do if you hit a car in a parking lot and no one saw you?

_____

6. What would you do if you saw another student cheating on a test?

_____

7. What would you do if your doctor told you that you had six months left to live?

_____

8. What would you do if you lost your job and couldn't pay your rent?

_____

9. What would you do if your best friend borrowed money from you and didn't pay you back?

_____

10. What would you do if your best friend told your secret to another person?

_____

TRAVELING TO MARS

Before You Read

1. Are you interested in exploration of different planets?

2. Do you think there is life on other planets?

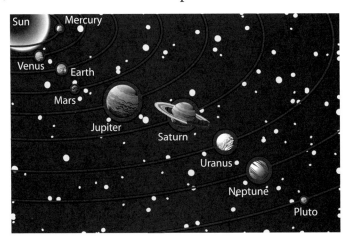

Read the following article. Pay special attention to conditions beginning with *if*.

Exploration on Mars, our closest planetary neighbor, has already begun. In 2004, Spirit Rover landed on Mars to gather information about possible life-forms there, to study the climate and geology of the planet, and to prepare for human exploration in the not-so-distant future of our neighbor. Before anyone goes to Mars, however, more needs to be learned.

Going to Mars is more difficult than going to the moon. **If** astronauts go to Mars, they **will be have** to return within a given time period. **If** they **don't come** back within this period of time, they **will miss** their chance. **If** astronauts have a problem with their equipment, they **will not be able** to rely on a message from Earth to help them. Because of the distance from Earth, it can take about 40 minutes from the time a message goes out from Earth until it is received on Mars. Also, a visitor to Mars will have to be gone for at least three years because of the distance and time necessary to travel.

If you **had** the chance to go to Mars, **would** you go?

Spirit Rover

10.3 | Real Conditions vs. Unreal Conditions

Examples	Explanation
If astronauts **go** to Mars, they **will have** to return within a given time period. **If** they **have** problems, they **will have** to solve them by themselves. **If** a person goes to Mars, he **will be** gone for three years.	The sentences on the left describe a real possibility for the **future**. Notice that for real possibilities, we use the present tense in the *if* clause and the future tense in the main clause.

If you **were** on Mars, you **would weigh** about one-third of what you weigh on Earth.
If you **could** go to Mars, **would** you **go**?
If you **met** a Martian, what **would** you **do** or **say**?
	The statements to the left are about hypothetical or imaginary situations in the **present**. They are not plans for the future.
	    Reality: You are not on Mars now.
	    Reality: You can't go to Mars now.
	Notice that we use the past tense in the *if* clause and *would* or *could* in the main clause.

EXERCISE 11   Fill in the blanks with the correct form of the verb in parentheses ( ). Both real conditions and unreal conditions are used.

EXAMPLES   The government is planning to send astronauts to Mars in the near

future. If an astronaut _____*decides*_____ to go to Mars, he or she
  (decide)

_____*will be*_____ away from family for at least three years.
  (be)

If I _____*saw*_____ a Martian, I _____*would shake*_____ his hand.
  (see)   (shake)

1. I'm thinking of going to California next month. If I

   _____, I _____ back
     (go)   (bring)

   a souvenir for you.

2. If I _____ go to Mars, I _____
       (can)   (bring)

   back a rock as a souvenir.

3. If the weather _____ nice today,
                    (be)

   I _____ out. But it's raining now.
     (go)

4. If the weather _____ nice this weekend,
                    (be)

   we _____ for a walk in the forest.
      (go)

5. The temperature on Mars is very cold. If it _____
(not/be)

so cold, maybe it _____ sustain life.
(can)

6. My sister is thinking about getting married soon. If she

_____ married in the summer, she
(get)

_____ an outdoor wedding.
(have)

7. My brother hates the woman next door. He _____
(not/marry)

her if she _____ the last woman on Earth.
(be)

8. My mother may visit me next week. If she _____
(come)

here, I _____ her to an art museum.
(take)

9. Sue's father died when she was a child. If her father

_____ here, he _____
(be)   (be)

so proud of her.

10. Our cat just had six kittens. If you _____ a kitten,
(want)

we _____ you one.
(give)

11. We love our dog. She's like a member of the family. We

_____ our dog if you _____
(not/sell)   (pay)

us a million dollars.

12. She may get some money from her parents. If her parents

_____ her some money, she
(send)

_____ some new clothes.
(buy)

13. She's always dreaming about winning the lottery. If she

_____ the lottery, she _____
(win)   (quit)

her job.

14. If I _____ a child, I _____
(be)   (play)

video games all day.

15. My son is thinking about a career in medicine. If my son

_____ a doctor when he grows up, we
        (become)

_____ so happy.
        (be)

16. I study a lot. If I _____ , I _____
             (not/study)   *(not/pass)*

this course.

17. My brother is a great student and will probably get a scholarship.

If he _____ a scholarship, he _____
        (get)   *(go)*

to the University of Wisconsin.

EXERCISE 12   *Combination Exercise.* Fill in the blanks with the correct form of the verb in parentheses ( ).

A: If you ___*could*___ change one thing in your life,
        (example: can)

what _____ ?
        (1 you/change)

B: I _____ younger.
        (2 be)

A: You're not very old now. You're just in your 30s.

B: But if I _____ younger,
        (3 be)

I _____ so many responsibilities.
        (4 not/have)

Now I have two small children who need all my attention.

A: What _____ if you _____ kids?
        (5 you/do)   *(6 not/have)*

B: I _____ golf all day on Saturday. And I
        (7 play)

_____ late on Sunday mornings.
        (8 sleep)

A: Are you sorry you had kids?

B: Of course not. I love them very much. If I _____
                                                       (9 not/have)

them, I _____ very unhappy. But I'm just
        (10 be)

dreaming about a simpler, easier time.

A: It _____ nice if we _____
        (11 be)   *(12 can)*

go back in time and make some changes.

Before You Read

1. Can you imagine what life was like 100 years ago? 1,000 years ago?

2. Would you want to live at a different time in history? Would you want to visit a different time in history? What period in history would you want to visit?

 Read the following article. Pay special attention to unreal conditions in the past.

Did You Know?

The average life expectancy for someone born in the U.S. in the year 1900 was 47 years. For someone born in the year 2000 it was 75. Today the leading cause of death is heart disease.

Most of us are amazed by the rapid pace of technology at the beginning of the twenty-first century. We often wonder what life will be like 20 or 50 or 100 years from now. But do you ever wonder what your life **would have been** like if you **had been** alive 100 years ago?

If you **had lived** around 1900 in the U.S., you **would have earned** about $200–$400 a year. You probably **wouldn't have graduated** from high school. Only 6 percent of Americans had a high school diploma at that time. If you **had been** a dentist or an accountant, you **would have made** $2,500 a year. If you **had been** a child living in a city, you **might have had** to work in a factory for 12–16 hours a day.

If you **had gone** to a doctor, he probably **would not have had** a college education. Only 10 percent of doctors at that time had a college degree. And if you **had had** a baby at that time, it **would have been** born at home. If you **had gotten** an infection at that time, you probably **would have died** because antibiotics had not yet been discovered. The leading causes of death at that time were pneumonia, influenza, and tuberculosis.

What about your home? If you **had been living** 100 years ago, you probably **wouldn't have had** a bathtub or a telephone. You **would have washed** your hair about once a month.

Do you think you **would have been** happy with life 100 years ago?

10.4 | Unreal Conditions—Past

Examples	Explanation
If you **had been** alive 100 years ago, you **would have made** about $200 a year. If you **had lived** 100 years ago, you probably **wouldn't have graduated** from high school.	An unreal condition can describe a situation that is not real in the **past.** Use the past perfect in the *if* clause and *would have* + past participle in the main clause.
If you **had gotten** an infection, you **could have died.** If you **had had** a baby, it **might have died** young.	*Could* or *might* can be used in the main clause instead of *would.*
If I **had known** that learning English ***was going*** to be so hard, I **would have studied** it in my country. If **I had realized** how hard I ***would have to*** work as a waitperson, I **would have gone** to college.	A noun clause can be used within an *if* clause (after *know, realize,* etc.). Follow the rule of sequence of tenses in the noun clause. (See Section 9.9.)
If my great-grandparents **had been able to** come to the U.S. 100 years ago, our lives **would have been** easier.	In the *if* clause, use *had been able to* for the past perfect of *could.*
a. If you **were** born 100 years ago, your life **would have been** different. OR b. If you **had been** born 100 years ago, your life **would have been** different.	Sometimes we don't change to the past perfect, especially with the verb *be,* if it is clear that the action is past. It is clear that you *were* born in the past. Sentences (a) and (b) have the same meaning.

Language Notes:

1. In informal speech, *have* after *could, would,* or *might* is pronounced like *of* or /ə/. Listen to your teacher pronounce the sentences above with fast, informal pronunciation.

2. In very informal conversational English, you often hear *would have* in both clauses.

   If I *would have known* about the problem, I *would have told* you. (Informal)

   If I *had known* about the problem, I *would have told* you. (Formal)

EXERCISE 13 Fill in the blanks with the correct form of the verb about life in the U.S. 100 years ago.

EXAMPLE If you _____*had been*_____ a doctor 100 years ago, you
(be)

_____*wouldn't have been*_____ rich.
(not/be)

1. If you _____ a baby 100 years ago, it probably
(have)

_____ at home.
(be/born)

2. If you _____ an infection, you
   (get)

   probably _____.
            (die)

3. If you _____ around 1900,
   (live)

   you probably _____ high school.
                (not/finish)

4. You _____ a car if you
       (not/have)

   _____ in the U.S. 100 years ago.
   (live)

5. Your president _____ Theodore Roosevelt if you
                  (be)

   _____ in the U.S. 100 years ago.
   (live)

6. If you _____ to travel to another city,
   (need)

   you _____ by train.
       (travel)

7. You probably _____ if you
               (work)

   _____ child 100 years ago.
   (be)

EXERCISE 14 A middle-aged woman is telling her daughter how the young lady's life would have been different if she had grown up in the late fifties. Fill in the blanks with the correct form of the verb in parentheses ( ) to complete the story.

It's great that you're thinking about becoming a doctor or astronaut. When I was your age, I didn't have the opportunity you have today.

You can be anything you want, but if you ___*had been*___ a woman
                                          (example: be)

growing up in the fifties, your opportunities _____ limited.
                                              (1 be)

If you _____ to college, you probably
       (2 go)

_____ in nursing or education, or you
(3 major)

_____ a secretarial course.
(4 take)

You probably _____ married in your
             (5 get)

early twenties.

If you _____ pregnant, you probably
                (6 get)

_____ your job. You probably
        (7 quit)

_____ two or more children. Your husband
        (8 have)

_____ to support you and the children. But today,
        (9 work)

you have the opportunity to continue working after you have children.

Technology _____ different too. Your house
                    (10 be)

_____ one TV and one phone. Because we had only
        (11 have)

one TV, the family spent more time together. You _____
                                                        (12 not/have)

a computer or a cell phone.

If you _____ up in the fifties, your life
            (13 grow)

_____ completely different.
        (14 be)

10.5 | Mixed Tenses in Condition Statements

We can mix a present condition with a past result, or a past condition with a present result.

Present Condition (Use simple past)	Past Result (Use *would have* + past participle)
If I **were** you,	I **wouldn't have bought** that old computer.
If I **had** a car,	I **would have taken** you to the airport last week.
If I **were** rich,	I **would have bought** a big house when I came to the U.S.

Past Condition (Use past perfect)	Present Result (Use *would* + base form)
If you **had lived** during the fifties,	you **would have** a different way of looking at the world now.
If I **hadn't come** to the U.S.,	I **would be living** with my parents now.
If she **hadn't lost** her job last month,	she **would be able** to take a vacation now.

EXERCISE 15 Fill in the blanks with the correct form of an appropriate verb. These sentences have mixed tenses.

EXAMPLE She just came to the U.S., so she doesn't speak English perfectly. If she
_____*had come*_____ here a long time ago, she _____*would speak*_____
English much better.

1. He invested a lot of money in a good stock, and now he's rich.

   If he _____ in that stock, he _____

   rich today.

2. Luckily she didn't marry her high school boyfriend. If she

   _____ him, she _____

   happy now.

3. I passed the last course, and now I'm in this course.

   I _____ in this course if I _____

   the last course.

4. The car you bought is terrible. If I _____ you,

   I _____ that car.

5. She didn't see the accident, so she can't tell you what happened.

   She _____ you what happened if she

   _____ the accident.

6. You didn't come to class yesterday, so you don't understand the

   teacher's explanation today. You _____ the

   teacher's explanation today if you _____ to class
   yesterday.

7. She has a lot of work to do, so she got up early. If she

   _____ so much work, she

   _____ in bed all morning.

8. She doesn't have a car, so she didn't drive you to the hospital. If she

   _____ a car, she _____

   you to the hospital yesterday.

9. I didn't learn English as a child. If I _____

   English as a child, I _____ so many problems
   with it now.

EXERCISE 16 ABOUT YOU Complete each statement with a past or present
result.

EXAMPLES If I had taken the TOEFL test last year, _I wouldn't have passed it._

If I hadn't brought my book to class today, _I wouldn't be able to do_
this exercise.

1. If I hadn't taken this course, _____

2. If I hadn't taken beginning English, _____

3. If I hadn't come to class today, _____

4. If I hadn't studied for the last test, _____

5. If I hadn't paid last month's rent, _____

6. If I had been born 200 years ago, _____

EXERCISE 17 ABOUT YOU Complete each statement with a past or present condition.

EXAMPLES I would have saved money if _I had bought a used book._____

I would have studied last night if _we were having a test today._____

1. I would have stayed after class yesterday if _____

_____

2. I would have stayed home today if _____

_____

3. I would have done better on the last test if _____

_____

4. The teacher would have explained the last lesson again if _____

_____

5. I would have taken an easier course if _____

_____

6. I would have studied English when I was a child if _____

_____

7. My parents would have been disappointed in me if _____

_____

EXERCISE 18 Fill in the blanks with the correct form of an appropriate verb. Some sentences have mixed tenses.

EXAMPLES I took a wrong turn on the highway. I arrived at the meeting one hour late.

If I _____hadn't taken_____ a wrong turn on the highway, I

_____would have arrived_____ at the meeting on time.

1. I forgot to set my alarm clock, so I didn't wake up on time.

I _____ on time if I

_____ my alarm clock.

2. She didn't pass the final exam, so she didn't pass the course. If she

_____ the final exam, she

_____ the course.

3. I didn't see the movie, so I can't give you any information about it.

If I _____ the movie, I

_____ you some information about it.

4. He loves her, so he married her. If he _____

her, he _____ her.

5. She didn't hear the phone ring, so she didn't answer it. She

_____ the phone

if she _____ it ring.

6. He left his keys at the office, so he couldn't get into the house. If he

_____ his keys at the office,

he _____ into the house.

7. I don't have much money, so I didn't buy a new coat. I

_____ a new coat if I

_____ more money.

8. He didn't take the medicine, so his condition didn't improve. If he

_____ the medicine, his

condition _____ .

9. I didn't have my credit card with me, so I didn't buy the computer I

saw last week. I _____ the computer

if I _____ my credit card with me.

EXERCISE 19 Complete each statement.

EXAMPLES If I had a million dollars, *I would travel around the world.*

If I had a computer, *I would have typed my last composition.*

1. People would live longer if _____

_____

2. I wouldn't have to work if _____

_____

3. If we had had a test on this lesson last week, _____

_____

4. If I could visit any country in the world, _____

_____

5. If everyone lived to be 150 years old, _____

_____

6. If I had lived in the nineteenth century, _____

_____

SCIENCE OR WISHFUL THINKING?

Before You Read

1. Do you wish for things you don't have in your life?

2. Would you want to live for 150 years?

 Read the science news articles and the conversation that follows. Pay special attention to *wish* and the verbs that follow it.

In laboratory experiments, scientists at the University of Connecticut have been able to double the life span of fruit flies from 70 days to 140 days. They have been able to produce mice that live 30 percent longer than the average mouse. If these experiments worked in humans, it would mean that we would be able to live up to 150 years.

A 63-year-old California woman gave birth to a baby. The woman is believed to be the oldest woman ever to give birth. She went through a program of in-vitro fertilization[3] at the University of Southern California.

If you wish your loving cat had nine lives, you can make your dream come true. A U.S. company announced the start of its cat-cloning service. For $50,000 you can have your darling cat cloned.

[3] *In-vitro fertilization* is a surgical procedure to help a woman conceive a baby.

A: I **wish** I **were** younger. I **wish** I **didn't have to** get old and sick. Science can do so much these days. I **wish** they **could find** a way to keep us young.

B: I read an article about how scientists are working to extend our lives. It's possible that soon people will be able to live 150 years.

A: I wouldn't want to be 150 years old and sick. I **wish** I **could be** 21 forever.

B: I don't think scientists will ever find a way to make us any younger than we are now. The best they can do is extend our lives and keep us healthier longer. What would you do differently if you were 21?

A: I would be going to parties on weekends. I wouldn't have so many responsibilities. I **wouldn't have to** take care of children. I started to have my children when I was in my early twenties. I **wish** I **had waited** until I was older.

B: My aunt is 55 and just got married for the first time a few years ago. She **wishes** she **had gotten** married when she was young and she **wishes** she **had had** children. But now she's too old.

A: I'm not so sure about that. I read an article about a 63-year-old woman who gave birth to a baby with the help of science.

B: That's amazing! What will science do for us next?

A: Scientists have started to clone animals.

B: I used to have a wonderful dog. I miss her. I **wish** I **could have** cloned her. But it's too late. She died 10 years ago.

A: Technology in the twenty-first century is moving so fast, isn't it? Don't you **wish** you **could come** back in 1,000 years and see all the changes in the world after that period of time?

B: I read an article that says that if we could travel at almost the speed of light, we could leave the Earth and come back a thousand years from now.

A: I wouldn't want to live in the future. I just **wish** I **could visit** the future. All our friends and relatives would be long dead if we left the present.

10.6 | Wishes

We often wish for things that are not real or true.

Examples	Explanation
Present	Use a **past** tense verb to wish for something in the **present**.
Reality: I **don't have** a dog.	
Wish: I wish (that) I **had** a dog.	After *wish*, you can use *that* to introduce the clause, but it is usually omitted.
Reality: We **have** to get old.	
Wish: I wish (that) we **didn't have** to get old.	
Reality: I **can't live** 150 years.	
Wish: I wish I **could live** 150 years.	
Past	Use a **past perfect** verb to wish for something in the **past**.
Reality: I **didn't know** my grandparents.	
Wish: I wish I **had known** them.	If the real situation uses *could*, use *could have* + past participle after *wish*.
Reality: My aunt **didn't have** kids when she was young.	
Wish: She wishes she **had had** kids when she was young.	
Reality: My favorite dog died years ago. I **couldn't clone** my dog.	
Wish: I wish I **could have cloned** her.	
Formal: I wish I **were** younger.	With *be*, *were* is the correct form for all subjects. In conversation, however, you will often hear native speakers use *was* with *I, he, she,* and *it*.
Informal: I wish I **was** younger.[4]	
Formal: I wish it **were** Sunday.	
Informal: I wish it was Sunday.	
I'm not young, but I wish I were.	We can use an auxiliary verb (were, did, had, etc.) to shorten the *wish* clause.
I don't have a car, but I wish I **did.**	
I didn't bring my photo album to the U.S., but I wish I **had.**	
I couldn't go to the party last week, but I wish I **could have.**	
	When people on vacation send postcards to friends and relatives, they sometimes write these words.

Wish you were here!
John Smith
123 Bay Road
Cutchogue NY 11935

Usage Note:

In conversation, you often hear Americans use *would have* + past participle for past wishes.

Formal: I wish you *had told* me the truth.

Informal: I wish you *would have told* me the truth.

---

[4]Many native speakers consider *was*, in this case, to be incorrect.

EXERCISE 20   Fill in the blanks to make a wish about the present.

EXAMPLE   Today isn't Friday. I wish it _____ *were* _____ Friday.

1. You're not here with me. I wish you _____ here.

2. I have to work 60 hours a week. I wish I _____ work so much.

3. I can't speak English perfectly. I wish I _____ English perfectly.

4. I don't have a car. I wish I _____ a car.

5. You're going on vacation to Hawaii, but I can't go with you. I wish

   I _____ with you.

6. I'm not rich. I wish I _____ rich.

7. I have a lot of responsibilities. I wish I _____ so many responsibilities.

8. I don't have time to read much. I wish I _____ more time to read.

9. I'm not 18 years old. I wish I _____.

10. Do you wish you _____ to be 150 years old?

11. I can't speak French. I wish _____ French.

EXERCISE 21   ABOUT YOU Fill in the blanks to complete each statement.

EXAMPLE   I wish I had *more time to spend with my family.* _____

1. I wish I were _____

2. I wish I knew how to _____

3. I wish I didn't have to _____

4. I wish I had _____

5. I wish I could _____

EXERCISE 22   Fill in the blanks to make a wish about the past.

EXAMPLE   You didn't see the movie. I wish you *had seen it.* _____

1. I didn't know it was your birthday. I wish I _____. I would have baked you a cake.

2. I didn't go to the concert. Everyone said it was wonderful. I wish

   I _____.

3. I didn't see the parade. I wish I _____ it.

4. I studied German in high school. I wish I _____ _____ English instead.

5. I didn't see his face when he opened the present. I wish I _____ _____ his face.

6. I lost my favorite ring. I was wearing it at the party. I wish I _____ _____ it at home.

7. I told Larry my secret, and he told all his friends. I wish I _____ _____ him my secret.

8. I forgot to bring my photo album when I moved to this city. I wish I _____ it.

EXERCISE 23 *Combination Exercise.* Fill in the blanks with the correct form of the verb in parentheses ( ) in each of the conversations below. Some wishes are about the present, some are about the past.

EXAMPLE **A:** I wish I _____*had*_____ good vision.
                        (have)

B: You *can* have perfect or near perfect vision. Why don't you try laser surgery?

A: What can that do for me?

B: A lot. I had it two years ago, and I don't need glasses anymore. I wore glasses since I was a child. I wish they ____*had had*____ this surgery
                                                              (have)
years ago. Now I can see first thing in the morning, read, drive, and play sports without wondering where my glasses are.

1. **A:** I wish I _____ thin.
                                  (be)

   B: Why don't you try a diet?

   A: I've tried every diet. Nothing works.

   B: You need to exercise every day.

   A: I'm too tired when I get home from work. I wish scientists _____ find a pill that would make me thin
                          (can)
   with no effort on my part.

2. **A:** I've been bald since I was 25 years old. I wish I _____ bald.
                          (be/not)

   B: They say bald men are very manly.

A. I don't care what they say. I wish I _____ hair.
(have)

I wish someone _____ find a cure for
(can)

baldness.

3. **A:** It's so expensive to call my country. I wish I

   _____ talk to my family every day.
   (can)

   B: You can. Just get a microphone for your computer and you can
   chat with them online for free.

   A: I wish I _____ how to do that.
   (know)

   B: Don't worry. I'll show you.

4. **A:** I wish I _____ older.
   (be)

   B: Why? No one wants to get old.

   A: I didn't say old. I just said "older." Older people have more
   experience and wisdom.

   B: I wish we _____ have the wisdom of old
   (can)

   people and the bodies of young people.

   A: If everyone stayed young and no one died, where would we find
   space on the Earth for all the new babies born every day?

   B: We could colonize Mars.

5. **A:** Wish I _____ travel to the future.
   (can)

   B: Why?

   A: I would be able to see future problems and then come back and
   warn people about them.

   B: I wish I _____ go to the past.
   (can)

   A: Why?

   B: I would like to meet my grandparents. I never knew them. I wish

   I _____ them, but they died before I was born.
   (knew)

6. **A:** We saw a great movie last night about time travel.

   B: I wish I _____ with you, but I had to study
   (can/go)

   for my biology test.

7. **A:** I studied Italian when I was a child. I wish I

    _____ English.
    (study)

    B: I wish I _____ born in the U.S. Then English
    (be)

    would be easy.

8. **A:** I wish I _____ college before getting married.
    (finish)

    B: But you have a great husband.

    A: I know. But I wish I _____ a few years. Now
    (wait)

    I have no education and a lot of responsibilities.

    B: You can finish college now.

    A: I wish I _____, but with my two kids, there's no
    (can)

    time.

9. **A:** I'm an only child. I wish I _____ a sister or brother.
    (have)

    B: Maybe you will someday.

    A: I don't think so. My mom is in her fifties already.

    B: With today's biological technologies, older women can still have
    kids.

    A: Maybe so. But she doesn't have the energy to raise a small child.

10.7 | Wishing for a Desired Change

Examples	Explanation
I wish you **wouldn't watch** so many science fiction movies. I wish you **would take** a science course. Your hair is too long. I wish you **would cut** it.	*Would* + base form is used after *wish* to show that a person wants something different to happen in the future. It shows a desire for change.
Compare: a. I wish I **could** travel to the past. (I can't travel to the past.) a. I wish I **were** young. (I'm not young.) b. I wish my parents **would come** to the U.S. (I want them to come to the U.S.) b. I wish you **wouldn't talk** so much about the past. (I want you to stop talking about the past.)	a. *Wish* without *would* is not a desire for change but an expression of discontent with the present situation. b. *Wish* with *would* shows a desire for change.

EXERCISE 24   Fill in the blanks to show a desire that someone do something differently. Answers may vary.

EXAMPLE   My parents are going back to my country. I wish they _would stay here._

1. Are you leaving so soon? I wish you _____ for a few more hours.

2. My son doesn't want to clean his room. I wish he _____ _____ his room.

3. My daughter wants to use the Internet all day. I wish she _____ _____ with her friends instead of sitting in front of the computer all day.

4. Some students are talking so loudly in the library that I can't think. I wish they _____.

5. My son's hair is so long. I don't like long hair on a boy. I wish he _____ his hair.

6. The teacher gives a lot of homework. I wish she _____ _____ so much homework.

7. My friend doesn't want to go to the party with me. I wish he _____ _____ to the party with me.

EXERCISE 25   A man is complaining about his apartment situation. Fill in the blanks with the correct form of the verb in parentheses ( ). Include *would* if you think he is hoping for a change. Don't include *would* if you think there is no possibility of change.

EXAMPLES   I wish my neighbors _would be_ more quiet.
                                      (be)

   I wish the walls _were_ thicker.
                        (be)

1. I wish my landlord _____ more heat.
                        (give)

2. I wish the people upstairs from me _____ around so much at night.
                                        (no/walk)

3. I wish the landlord _____ the hallways more often.
                          (clean)

4. I wish the building _____ an elevator.
                        (have)

5. I wish there _____ more trees and flowers around the building.
                     (be)

6. I wish the landlord _____ my rent every year.
$\qquad$*(not/raise)*

7. I wish my kitchen _____ larger.
$\qquad$*(be)*

8. I wish I _____ a gas stove, not an electric stove.
$\qquad$*(have)*

9. I wish the apartment _____ sunnier.
$\qquad$*(be)*

10. I wish I _____ rich enough to buy a house.
$\qquad$*(be)*

11. I wish I _____ air-conditioning.
$\qquad$*(have)*

12. I wish I _____ move, but I can't.
$\qquad$*(can)*

EXERCISE 26 ABOUT YOU Fill in the blanks to complete these statements. Your wish can include a desire for a change (by using *would*) or it can simply state that you're unhappy with the way things are right now.

EXAMPLES I wish the class *didn't have so many students.* _____

I wish my parents *would let me go out with my friends.* _____

1. I wish my family _____

2. I wish the teacher _____

3. I wish my neighbors _____

4. I wish the government _____

5. I wish more people _____

6. I wish my apartment _____

EXERCISE 27 A student is complaining about her class. Fill in the blanks with the correct form of the verb. Include *would* if you think she hopes for a change. Don't include *would* if you think there is no possibility of change. Both present and past wishes are included.

EXAMPLES I wish the teacher ___*didn't give*___ so much homework.
$\qquad$*(not/give)*

I wish the teacher ___*would spend*___ more time on conditionals.
$\qquad$*(spend)*

1. I wish I _____ skip ESL and go into regular
$\qquad$*(can)*

English.

2. I wish the book _____ the answers in the back.
  (have)

3. I wish I _____ more attention to learning
  (pay)
  English when I was in my native country.

4. I wish I _____ a dictionary in my native country.
  (buy)
  Dictionaries are much cheaper there.

5. I wish I _____ my counselor's advice and
  (take)
  registered early. I couldn't get into the biology class I wanted.

6. I wish I _____ my dictionary to class today.
  (bring)
  We're going to write a composition, and I need to check my
  spelling.

7. I wish the teacher _____ us use our books
  (let)
  during a test.

8. I wish we _____ write so many compositions.
  (not/have to)

9. I wish the students in the back _____ quiet.
  (be)
  They're always making so much noise.

10. I wish I _____ the teacher's brain. Then I would
  (have)
  know English perfectly.

EXERCISE 28 *Combination Exercise.* A mother (M) is complaining to her son (S).
Fill in the blanks with the correct form of the words in parentheses
( ) to express their wishes.

M: You never visit. I wish you _____*would visit*_____ me more
  (example: visit)
  often. I'm not going to live forever, you know.

S: I *do* visit you often. Isn't once a week often enough?

M: Some day I won't be here, and you'll say to yourself, "I wish I

  _____ my mom more often."
  (1 visit)

S: Mom, you're only 48 years old.

M: Who knows how long I'll be here? There are no guarantees in life.
  My own mother died when I was a teenager. I wish she

  _____ to see you and your sister.
  (2 live)

S: I do too. But what can we do?

M: I wish you _____ married already.
(3 be)

S: Mom, I'm only 25 years old. There's plenty of time to get married.

M: Well, your sister's only 23, and she's already married.

S: I wish you _____ comparing me to my sister.
(4 stop)

　　 She has different goals in life. Besides you don't like Shari's husband.

M: You're right. I wish she _____ a better man.
(5 marry)

S: There's nothing wrong with Paul. He's a good husband to her.

M: We'll see. You know, I wish you _____ your hair.
(6 cut)

　　 It's too long.

S: Mom. I'm old enough to decide how long to wear my hair.

M: You're too thin. I wish you _____ more.
(7 eat)

S: I eat enough. When I was a teenager, you said I was too fat.

M: I'm still your mother. I wish you _____ to me.
(8 listen)

S: I *do* listen to you. But I've got to live my own life.

M: Sometimes you act like a child and tell me you're old enough to make your own decisions. Then you tell me you're too young to get married.

S: I'm not too young to get married. I just don't want to now. I want to be a rock musician.

M: I wish you _____ a real job.
(9 find)

S: It *is* a real job.

M: You didn't finish college. I wish you _____ your
(10 get)

　　 degree. How are you ever going to find a real job?

S: You don't need a college degree to be a rock musician.

M: Well, I hope I live long enough to see you married, with a good job.

S: With today's technologies, you'll probably live to be 150 years old and not only see me married, but also see your great-great-great-grandchildren married.

M: I wouldn't want to live so long.

S: You wouldn't? Just think, you'll be 150 years old and I'll be 127. You'll still be telling me how to live my life. That would make you happy, wouldn't it?

SUMMARY OF LESSON 10

1.

Unreal Conditions—Present	
Verb → Past	**Verb → *Would / Might / Could* + Base Form**
If I **were** an astronaut,	I **would go** to Mars.
If I **could** live to be 150 years old,	I **would know** my great-great-grandchildren.
If I **spoke** English perfectly,	I **might have** more opportunities.
If I **could** travel to the past,	I **could meet** my ancestors.
If she **didn't have** children,	she **would have** more free time.
If I **were** in Hawaii,	I **would be** on a beach right now.
If we **didn't have** advanced technology,	we **wouldn't be** able to explore space.

2.

Unreal Conditions—Past	
Verb → Past Perfect	**Verb → *Would / Might / Could* + Have + Past Participle**
If you **had lived** 100 years ago,	you **wouldn't have had** a computer.
If a doctor **had lived** 100 years ago,	he **could have practiced** medicine without a college degree.
If you **had gotten** an infection,	you **might have died.**
If my father **had** not **met** my mother,	I **wouldn't have been** born.

3.

Mixed Tenses	
Present Condition	**Past Result**
If she **were** rich,	she **would have sent** her kids to private school.
If I **had** your phone number,	I **would have called** you yesterday.
If I **were** you,	I **would have quit** my job a long time ago.
Past Condition	**Present Result**
If she **had married** him,	she **would be** very unhappy now.
If I **had stayed** home today,	I **wouldn't be reviewing** this lesson.

4.

Real Possibilities for the Future	
Condition	**Future Result**
If we **explore** Mars,	we **will learn** a lot.
If I **go** to New York,	I **will send** you a postcard.
If she **is** late,	she **will miss** the meeting.

5.

Wishes	
Present	**Past**
I wish I **were** younger.	I wish I **had studied** English when I was younger.
I wish I **could** be a child again.	I wish I **had been** a better student when I was a child.
I wish you **would** cut your hair.	I wish my parents **would have let** me go to the party last week.

EDITING ADVICE

1. Don't use *will* with an unreal condition.

   were
   If I ~~will be~~ rich, I would buy a house.

2. Don't include *be* if you have another verb.

   If I knew more English, I would ~~be~~ find a better job.

3. Always use the base form after a modal.

   have
   She would ~~has~~ called you if she had your phone number.

4. Use the past perfect, not the present perfect, for unreal conditions and wishes.

   had
   If she ~~has~~ studied harder, she wouldn't have failed the test.

   had
   I wish I ~~have~~ seen that movie.

5. For a real condition, use the simple present tense in the *if* clause.

   If I ~~will~~ have time tomorrow, I will write my composition.

PART 1 Find the mistakes with the underlined words, and correct them. Not every sentence has a mistake. If the sentence is correct, write *C*.

EXAMPLES   What ~~will~~ *would* you do if you had a million dollars?

              I wouldn't be able to visit my friends if I <u>didn't have</u> a car. **C**

1. I don't have much money. If I <u>have</u> a lot of money, I'd travel around the world.

2. I <u>will be</u> happier if my family were here.

3. I don't have any time. If I had time, <u>I'd help</u> my friend today.

4. If I <u>could meet</u> the president, I would tell him that he's doing a great job.

5. I'm unhappy because my daughter can't come here. I <u>will be</u> happy if my daughter could live with me.

6. I wish I <u>could speak</u> English perfectly.

7. If I <u>will be</u> you, I would buy a new car.

8. If I didn't have to study English, I <u>would be have</u> more free time.

9. I have a car. I wouldn't be able to find a job here if I <u>don't have</u> a car.

10. If she hadn't repaired the brakes on her car, she <u>might have had</u> an accident.

11. The teacher <u>would has explained</u> the grammar more slowly if she had had more time.

12. I came here when I was 40 years old. I wish I <u>had come</u> here when I was younger.

13. Can you help me?—Sorry. If I could, I <u>would</u>.

14. If I <u>would be</u> young, I would have more energy.

15. I'm sorry I didn't call you yesterday. I <u>would call</u> you if I hadn't been so busy.

16. I didn't know about the party so I didn't go. I wish I <u>have known</u> about it.

17. Mary hates Paul. She wouldn't marry him even if he <u>were</u> the last man on Earth.

18. I wish you <u>would call</u> me more often.

19. If you <u>are</u> late for tomorrow's test, you will not have enough time to finish it.

20. What would you do if you <u>find</u> a wallet with a lot of money in it?

21. I got an invitation to my sister's graduation. I <u>wouldn't have been able to</u> go without the invitation.

22. I heard you saw a great movie last night. I wish I <u>have gone</u> with you.

23. If he <u>has been</u> more careful, the accident wouldn't have happened.

24. If he <u>will have</u> time next weekend, he will help his brother.

PART 2 Fill in the blanks to complete the conversation.

A: Are you happy you came to the U.S.?

B: Yes, I'm glad I'm here. But I wish I _____*had come*_____ here when
                                      (example)

my brother came here 15 years ago.

A: Why?

B: Well, now I'm 40 years old, and it's harder to learn English and find a
good job. I didn't study English when I was a child. I wish I

_____ it when I was younger.
            (1)

A: But your brother learned English quickly.

B: He was only 18 when he came here. Now he speaks English well, has

a small business, and owns a big house. If I _____
                                                   (2)

here when he came here, I _____ _____ successful
                                  (3)

now. But now I have to start everything from the beginning. I wish

I _____ to start so many new things at my age.
            (4)

A: Did your parents come here too?

B: No. My parents are alone in my country. I've asked them to come

here. I wish they _____ here, but they're too old
                           (5)

to make such a big change. If they _____ here,
                                 (6)

they _____ have to go to school to learn English.
       (7)

They're in their late seventies. If they _____ here,
                               (8)

their life _____ much more difficult than it is now.
         (9)

A: There are a lot of things I wish _____ different
                                        (10)

in my life too.

B: What, for example?

A: I got married when I was only 18. I wish I _____
(11)
married so young. And I had my first son when I was only 20. I'm attending college now, and it's hard with so many family responsibilities. I wish I _____ to college when I
(12)
was 18.

B: It's too bad we can't go back and start our lives again. I wish I

_____ back and use the knowledge I have now
(13)
to make better choices.

A: Who knows . . . we may live to be 150 years old and have time to do

all the things we wish we _____ do.
(14)

B: If everyone _____ to be 150 years old, the world
(15)

_____ very crowded and there _____
(16)   (17)
enough food or other resources for everybody.

A: Maybe you're right. We should just do the best we can with the time we have.

PART 3 Some of the following sentences contain real conditions; some contain unreal conditions. Write the letter of the correct words to fill in the blanks.

1. I _____ drive to Canada if I had a car.
   a. were **b.** will **c.** would **d.** would be

2. I might go shopping next Saturday. If I _____
   shopping next Saturday, I'll buy you a scarf.
   a. will go **b.** went **c.** would go **d.** go

3. If I _____ you, I'd move to a different apartment.
   a. were **b.** am **c.** will be **d.** would be

4. I can't help you. I would help you if I _____.
   a. can **b.** could **c.** will be able to **d.** would

5. I might have to work next Monday. If I have to work,
   I _____ be able to come to class.
   a. wouldn't **b.** won't **c.** weren't **d.** wasn't

6. My life would be easier if I _____ more English.
   a. knew **b.** know **c.** will know **d.** would know

7. She has three children. She has no time to study. If she

    _____ children, she would have more time to study.
    a. doesn't have   **b.** weren't have
    c. wouldn't have   **d.** didn't have

8. It's raining now. If it _____ now, I'd go for a walk.
    a. isn't raining   **b.** doesn't raining
    c. weren't raining   **d.** wouldn't raining

9. She wouldn't tell you the secret even if you _____
    her a million dollars.
    a. would be pay   **b.** paid   **c.** will pay   **d.** pay

10. If I could live in any city in the world, I _____
    in Paris.
    a. will live   **b.** would have lived   **c.** would live   **d.** live

11. I don't have a house. I wish I _____ a house.
    a. had   **b.** will have   **c.** have had   **d.** have

12. I can't drive a car. I wish I _____ a car.
    a. could drive   **b.** can drive   **c.** would drive   **d.** will drive

13. If I had known how difficult it was to learn English,
    I _____ it when I was young.
    a. would study   **b.** would studied
    c. would had studied   **d.** would have studied

14. He never exercised and was overweight. He had a heart attack and
    died when he was 50 years old. If he _____
    better care of himself, he might have lived much longer.
    a. would take   **b.** took   **c.** had taken   **d.** will take

15. He needs more driving lessons before he can take the driver's
    license test. If he _____ the test last week, he
    would have failed it.
    a. were taken   **b.** would take   **c.** has taken   **d.** had taken

16. I didn't have time to call you yesterday. I _____
    you if I had had more free time.
    a. would call   **b.** will call   **c.** would have called   **d.** would called

17. He was driving without a seat belt and had a car accident. He
    was seriously injured. If he had been wearing his seat belt, he
    _____ such a serious injury.
    a. might not have had   **b.** wouldn't had
    c. didn't have   **d.** hadn't had

18. Nobody told me we were going to have a test today. I wish
    someone _____ me.
    a. would tell   **b.** had told   **c.** would told   **d.** were told

19. Why didn't you tell me about your move last week? If you had told me, I _____ you.
- **a.** could have helped
- **b.** could help
- **c.** could helped
- **d.** could had helped

20. My roommate talks on the phone all the time. I wish he _____ on the phone so much.
- **a.** won't talk
- **b.** wouldn't talk
- **c.** doesn't talk
- **d.** wouldn't have talked

EXPANSION ACTIVITIES

Classroom Activities

1. Do you think the world would be better or worse if . . . ? Form a small group and discuss your reasons.

- **a.** If there were no computers?
- **b.** If everyone were the same religion or race?
- **c.** If everyone spoke the same language?
- **d.** If we could live to be about 150 years old?
- **e.** If people didn't have to work?
- **f.** If families were allowed to have only one child?
- **g.** If every job paid the same salary?

2. Fill in the blanks. Share your sentences in a small group.

- **a.** If I could change one thing about myself (or my life), I'd change
  _____

- **b.** If I lost my _____, I'd be very upset.

- **c.** Most people would be happier if _____

- **d.** If I could travel to the past, _____

- **e.** If I could travel to the future, _____

- **f.** The world would be a better place if _____

- **g.** I wish I were _____ years old.

3. Fill in the blanks and explain your answers.

If I had known _____,

I would (not) have _____

EXAMPLE If I had known that I needed computer skills in the U.S., I would have studied computers in my native country.

4. Fill in the blanks and explain your answer.

- **a.** I didn't _____, but I wish I had.
- **b.** I _____, but I wish I hadn't.

5. Write some sentences about your job, your school, your apartment, or your family. What do you wish were different? Share your answers in a small group.

   EXAMPLES I have to work on Saturdays. I wish I didn't have to work on Saturdays.

   My son watches TV all day. I wish he would play with his friends more.

6. On a piece of paper or index card, finish this sentence:

   I would be happier if _____.

   The teacher will collect the cards or papers and read each statement. The rest of the class has to guess who wrote it. (Many people will write "*if I were rich,*" or "*if I knew more English,*" so try to think of something else.)

7. Name something. Form a small group and discuss your responses.

   EXAMPLE Name something you wish had never happened.
   I wish the war had never happened.

   a. Name something you wish you had done when you were younger.

   b. Name something you wish you had studied when you were younger.

   c. Name something your family wishes you had done differently.

   d. Name something you wish you had known before you came to this city.

   e. Name something you wish your parents had done or told you.

   f. Name something you wish you had never done.

   g. Name something you wish had never happened.

Talk About it

1. If you could meet anyone in the world, who would you want to meet?

2. If you had the brain of another person, who would you be?

3. Since Albert Einstein's death in 1955, his brain has been kept in a jar for study. If it were possible to create a new Einstein from a brain cell, would it be a good idea to do so? Why or why not?

4. If you had the possibility of making a clone of yourself or a member of your family, would you do it? Why or why not?

5. If you could live 200 years, would you want to?

6. If we could eliminate all diseases, would the Earth be overpopulated?

7. In Lesson Six, we read about Tim Berners-Lee, the creator of the World Wide Web. He has never made any money from the Web. Do you think he would have tried to make money on his idea if he had known how popular the Web was going to become?

8. What entirely new things do you think might be possible in the future?

9. Read the following poem and discuss its meaning.

> There was a young lady named Bright,
> Who traveled far faster than light.
> She left one day
> In a relative way
> And returned the previous night.

Write About it

1. Write about personality traits or bad habits you have. Write how your life would be different if you didn't have these traits or habits. (Or you can write about the habits or traits of another person you know well.)

   EXAMPLES If I exercised, my health would be better.
   If my son weren't so lazy, he'd be able to accomplish much more in his life.

2. Write about an important event in history. Tell what the result would or might have been if this event hadn't happened.

3. Write about how your life would have been different if you had stayed in the same place your whole life.

4. Write about some things in your life that you are not happy about. How would you want to change your life?

Outside Activities

1. Ask a native speaker of English to answer the questions in the first classroom activity. Report this person's answers to the class.

2. Rent one of these movies: *Cocoon, Sleeper, Back to the Future, AI (Artificial Intelligence), Contact,* or *Kate and Leopold.* Write a summary.

Internet Activities

1. At a search engine, type in *time travel.* Find an interesting article to bring to class.

2. At a search engine, type in *H.G. Wells The Time Machine.* Find a summary of this 1895 novel.

3. At a search engine, type in *aging.* Find an interesting article to bring to class. Summarize it.

Additional Activities at **http://elt.thomson.com/gic**

Appendices

Noncount Nouns

The following groups of words are classified as noncount nouns.				
Group A. Nouns that have no distinct, separate parts. We look at the whole				
air	cheese	lightning	paper	tea
blood	cholesterol	meat	pork	thunder
bread	coffee	milk	poultry	water
butter	electricity	oil	soup	yogurt

Group B. Nouns that have parts that are too small or insignificant to count				
corn	hair	rice	sand	sugar
grass	popcorn	salt	snow	

Note: Count and noncount nouns are grammatical terms, but they are not always logical. *Rice* is very small and is a noncount noun. *Beans* and *peas* are also very small but are count nouns.

Group C. Nouns that are classes or categories of things	
food (vegetables, meat, spaghetti)	makeup (lipstick, rouge, eye shadow)
furniture (chairs, tables, beds)	homework (compositions, exercises, reading)
clothing (sweaters, pants, dresses)	jewelry (necklaces, bracelets, rings)
mail (letters, packages, postcards, fliers)	housework (washing dishes, dusting, cooking)
fruit (cherries, apples, grapes)	money or cash (nickels, dimes, dollars)

Group D. Nouns that are abstractions				
advice	experience	intelligence	nature	trouble
art	fun	knowledge	noise	truth
beauty	happiness	life	nutrition	unemployment
crime	health	love	patience	work
education	help	luck	pollution	
energy	information	music	time	

Group E. Subjects of study		
biology	geometry	history
chemistry	grammar	math (mathematics)*

***Note:** Even though *mathematics* ends with *s*, it is not plural.

Notice the quantity words used with count and noncount nouns

Singular Count	Plural Count	Noncount
a tomato	tomatoes	coffee
one tomato	**two** tomatoes	**two cups of** coffee
	some tomatoes	**some** coffee
no tomato	**no** tomatoes	**no** coffee
	(with questions and negatives) **any** tomatoes	**any** coffee
	a lot of tomatoes	**a lot of** coffee
	(with questions and negatives) **many** tomatoes	**much** coffee
	a few tomatoes	**a little** coffee
	several tomatoes	**several** cups of coffee
	How many tomatoes?	**How much** coffee?

The following words can be used as either count nouns or noncount nouns. However, the meaning changes according to the way the nouns are used.

Count	Noncount
Oranges and grapefruit are **fruits** that contain a lot of vitamin C.	I bought some **fruit** at the fruit store.
Ice cream and butter are **foods** that contain cholesterol.	We don't need to go shopping today. We have a lot of **food** at home.
He wrote a **paper** about hypnosis.	I need some **paper** to write my composition.
He committed three **crimes** last year.	There is a lot of **crime** in a big city.
I have 200 **chickens** on my farm.	We ate some **chicken** for dinner.
I don't want to bore you with all my **troubles.**	I have some **trouble** with my car.
She went to Puerto Rico three **times.**	She spent a lot of **time** on her project.
She drank three **glasses** of water.	The window is made of bulletproof **glass.**
I had a bad **experience** during my trip to Paris.	She has some **experience** with computer programming.
I don't know much about the **lives** of my grandparents.	**Life** is sometimes happy, sometimes sad.
I heard a **noise** outside my window.	Those children are making a lot of **noise.**

Uses of Articles

Overview of Articles

Articles tell us if a noun is definite or indefinite.			
	Count		**Noncount**
	Singular	**Plural**	
Definite	**the** book	**the** books	**the** coffee
Indefinite	**a** book	**(some / any)** books	**(some / any)** coffee

Part 1. Uses of the Indefinite Article

A. To classify a subject	
Examples	**Explanation**
Chicago is **a** city. Illinois is **a** state. Abraham Lincoln was **an** American president. What's that? It's **a** tall building.	• Use *a* before a consonant sound. • Use *an* before a vowel sound. • You can put an adjective before the noun.
Chicago and Los Angeles are cities. Lincoln and Washington were American presidents. What are those? They're tall buildings.	Do not use an article before a plural noun.

B. To make a generalization about a noun	
Examples	**Explanation**
A dog has sharp teeth. **Dogs** have sharp teeth. **An elephant** has big ears. **Elephants** have big ears.	Use the indefinite article (*a / an*) + a singular count noun or no article with a plural noun. Both the singular and plural forms have the same meaning.
Coffee contains caffeine. **Milk** is white. **Love** makes people happy. **Money** can't buy **happiness.**	Do not use an article to make a generalization about a noncount noun.

C. To introduce a new noun into the conversation

Examples	Explanation
I have **a cell phone.** I have **an umbrella.**	Use the definite article *a / an* with singular count nouns.
Count: I have **(some) dishes.** Do you have **(any) cups?** I don't have **(any) forks.** **Noncount:** I have **(some) money** with me. Do you have **(any) cash** with you? I don't have **(any) time.**	Use *some* or *any* with plural nouns and noncount nouns. Use *any* in questions and negatives. *Some* and *any* can be omitted.
There's **an elevator** in the building. Are there **any restrooms** on this floor? There isn't **any money** in my checking account.	*There* + a form of *be* can introduce an indefinite noun into a conversation.

Part 2. Uses of the Definite Article

A. To refer to a previously mentioned noun

Examples	Explanation
There's **a dog** in the next apartment. **The dog** barks all the time.	We start by saying *a dog*. We continue by saying *the dog*.
We bought **some grapes.** We ate **the grapes** this morning.	We start by saying *some grapes*. We continue by saying *the grapes*.
I need **some sugar.** I'm going to use **the sugar** to bake a cake.	We start by saying *some sugar*. We continue by saying *the sugar*.
Did you buy **any coffee?** Yes. **The coffee** is in the cabinet.	We start by saying *any coffee*. We continue by saying *the coffee*.

B. When the speaker and the listener have the same reference

Examples	Explanation
The dog has big ears. **The cats** are sleeping. **The milk** is sour. Don't drink it.	The object is present, so the speaker and listener have the same object in mind.
a. **The teacher** is writing on **the blackboard** in **the classroom.** b. **The president** is talking about taxes. c. Please turn off **the lights** and shut **the door** and **the windows** before you leave **the house.**	a. Students in the same class have things in common. b. People who live in the same country have things in common. c. People who live in the same house have things in common.
The house on the corner is beautiful. I spent **the money you gave me.**	The listener knows exactly which one because the speaker defines or specifies which one.

C. When there is only one in our experience

Examples	Explanation
The sun is bigger than **the moon.** There are many problems in **the world.**	The *sun*, the *moon*, and the *world* are unique objects. There is only one in our immediate experience.
Write your name on **the top** of the page. Sign your name on **the back** of the check.	The page has only one top. The check has only one back.
The Amazon is **the longest** river in the world. Alaska is **the biggest** state in the U.S.	A superlative indicates that there is only one.

D. With familiar places

Examples	Explanation
I'm going to **the store** after work. Do you need anything? **The bank** is closed now. I'll go tomorrow.	We use *the* with certain familiar places and people—*the bank, the zoo, the park, the store, the movies, the beach, the post office, the bus / train, the doctor, the dentist*—when we refer to the one that we habitually visit or use.

Language Notes:

1. Omit *the* after a preposition with the words *church, school, work,* and *bed.*

>   He's **in church.**
>   I'm going **to school.**
>   They're **at work.**
>   I'm going **to bed.**

2. Omit *to* and *the* with *home* and *downtown.*

>   I'm going **home.**
>   Are you going **downtown** after class?

E. To make a formal generalization

Examples	Explanation
The shark is the oldest and most primitive fish. **The bat** is a nocturnal animal.	To say that something is true of all members of a group, use *the* with singular count nouns.
The computer has changed the way people deal with information. **The cell phone** uses radio waves.	To talk about a class of inventions, use *the*.
The heart is a muscle that pumps blood to the rest of the body. **The ear** has three parts: outer, middle, and inner.	To talk about an organ of the body in a general sense, use *the*.

Language Note:

For informal generalizations, use *a* + a singular noun or no article with a plural noun.

Compare:

>   **The computer** has changed the way we deal with information.
>   **A computer** is expensive.
>   **Computers** are expensive.

Part 3: Special Uses of Articles

No Article	Article

Personal names:
    John Kennedy
    George Bush
	The whole family:
	    the Kennedys
	    the Bushes

Title and name:
    Queen Elizabeth
    Pope John Paul
	Title without name:
	    the Queen
	    the Pope

Cities, states, countries, continents:
    Cleveland
    Ohio
    Mexico
    South America
	Places that are considered a union:
	    the United States
	    the former Soviet Union
	Place names: the _____ of _____
	    the Republic of China
	    the District of Columbia

Mountains:
    Mount Everest
    Mount McKinley
	Mountain ranges:
	    the Himalayas
	    the Rocky Mountains

Islands:
    Coney Island
    Staten Island
	Collectives of islands:
	    the Hawaiian Islands
	    the Philippines

Lakes:
    Lake Superior
    Lake Michigan
	Collectives of lakes:
	    the Great Lakes
	    the Finger Lakes

Beaches:
    Palm Beach
    Pebble Beach
	Rivers, oceans, seas, canals:
	    the Mississippi River
	    the Atlantic Ocean
	    the Dead Sea
	    the Panama Canal

Streets and avenues:
    Madison Avenue
    Wall Street
	Well-known buildings:
	    the Sears Tower
	    the Empire State Building

Parks:
    Central Park
    Hyde Park
	Zoos:
	    the San Diego Zoo
	    the Milwaukee Zoo

Seasons:
    summer   fall   spring   winter
    Summer is my favorite season.
Note: After a preposition, *the* may be used.
    In (the) winter, my car runs badly.
	Deserts:
	    the Mojave Desert
	    the Sahara Desert

Continued

Directions:
   north   south
   east   west
	Sections of a piece of land:
	   the Southwest (of the U.S.)
	   the West Side (of New York)

School subjects:
   history   math
	Unique geographical points:
	   the North Pole the Vatican

Name + *college* or *university*:
   Northwestern University
   Bradford College
	The University (College) of _____
	   the University of Michigan
	   the College of DuPage County

Magazines:
   Time   *Sports Illustrated*
	Newspapers:
	   the *Tribune* the *Wall Street Journal*

Months and days:
   September
   Monday
	Ships:
	   the *Titanic*
	   the *Queen Elizabeth II*

Holidays and dates:
(month + day):
   Thanksgiving   July 4   Mother's Day
	The day of (month):
	   the Fourth of July
	   the fifth of May

Diseases:
   cancer   AIDS
   polio   malaria
	Ailments:
	   a cold a toothache
	   a headache the flu

Games and sports:
   poker   soccer
	Musical instruments, after *play*:
	   the drums the piano
	Note: Sometimes *the* is omitted.
	   She plays (the) drums.

Languages:
   French
   English
	The _____ language:
	   the French language
	   the English language

Last month, year, week, etc. = the one before this one:
   I forgot to pay my rent last month.
   The teacher gave us a test last week.
	The last month, the last year, the last week, etc. = the last in a series:
	   December is the last month of the year.
	   Summer vacation begins the last week in May.

In office = in an elected position:
   The president is in office for four years.
	In the office = in a specific room:
	   The teacher is in the office.

In back / in front:
   She's in back
   of the car.
	In the back / in the front:
	   He's in the back of the bus.

The Verb *Get*

***Get* has many meanings. Here is a list of the most common ones:**

• get something = receive
    I got a letter from my father.
• get + (to) place = arrive
    I got home at six.
    What time do you get to school?

• get + object + infinitive = persuade   She got him to wash the dishes.

• get + past participle = become
    get accustomed to   get dressed   get scared
    get acquainted   get engaged   get tired
    get bored   get hurt   get used to
    get confused   get lost   get worried
    get divorced   get married
    They got married in 1989.

• get + adjective = become
    get angry   get nervous   get upset
    get dark   get old   get well
    get fat   get rich
    get hungry   get sleepy
    It gets dark at 6:30.

• get an illness = catch   While she was traveling, she got malaria.

• get a joke or an idea = understand
    Everybody except Tom laughed at the joke. He didn't get it.
    The boss explained the project to us, but I didn't get it.

• get ahead = advance   He works very hard because he wants to get ahead in his job.

• get along (well) (with someone) = have a good relationship
    She doesn't get along with her mother-in-law.
    Do you and your roommate get along well?

• get around to something = find the time to do something   I wanted to write my brother a letter yesterday, but I didn't get around to it.

Continued

- get away = escape

  The police chased the thief, but he got away.

- get away with something = escape punishment

  He cheated on his taxes and got away with it.

- get back = return

  He got back from his vacation last Saturday.

- get back at someone = get revenge

  My brother wants to get back at me for stealing his girlfriend.

- get back to someone = communicate with someone at a later time

  The boss can't talk to you today. Can she get back to you tomorrow?

- get by = have just enough but nothing more

  On her salary, she's just getting by. She can't afford a car or a vacation.

- get in trouble = be caught and punished for doing something wrong

  They got in trouble for cheating on the test.

- get in(to) = enter a car

  She got in the car and drove away quickly.

- get out (of) = leave a car

  When the taxi arrived at the theater, everyone got out.

- get on = seat yourself on a bicycle, motorcycle, horse; enter a train, bus, airplane

  She got on the motorcycle and left.

  She got on the bus and took a seat in the back.

- get off = leave a bicycle, motorcycle, horse, train, bus, airplane

  They will get off the train at the next stop.

- get out of something = escape responsibility

  My boss wants me to help him on Saturday, but I'm going to try to get out of it.

- get over something = recover from an illness or disappointment

  She has the flu this week. I hope she gets over it soon.

- get rid of someone or something = free oneself of someone or something undesirable

  My apartment has roaches, and I can't get rid of them.

- get through (to someone) = communicate, often by telephone

  She tried to explain the harm of eating fast food to her son, but she couldn't get through to him.

  I tried to call my mother many times, but her line was busy. I couldn't get through.

- get through with something = finish

  I can meet you after I get through with my homework.

Continued

- get together = meet with another person
  I'd like to see you again. When can we get together?

- get up = arise from bed
  He woke up at 6 o'clock, but he didn't get up until 6:30.

APPENDIX D

Gerund and Infinitive Patterns

1. Verb + Infinitive

They need **to leave.**
I learned **to speak English.**

agree	claim	know how	seem
appear	consent	learn	swear
arrange	decide	manage	tend
ask	demand	need	threaten
attempt	deserve	offer	try
be able	expect	plan	volunteer
beg	fail	prepare	want
can afford	forget	pretend	wish
care	hope	promise	would like
choose	intend	refuse	

2. Verb + Noun / Object Pronoun + Infinitive

I want you **to leave.**
He expects me **to call** him.

advise	convince	hire	require
allow	dare	instruct	select
appoint	enable	invite	teach
ask	encourage	need	tell
beg	expect	order	urge
cause	forbid	permit	want
challenge	force	persuade	warn
choose	get	remind	would like
command	help*		

*Note: After *help*, *to* is often omitted: "He helped me (to) move."

3. Adjective + Infinitive

They are happy **to be** here.
We're willing **to help** you.

afraid	disturbed	lucky	sorry
ashamed	eager	pleased	surprised
amazed	foolish	prepared	upset
careful	fortunate	proud	willing
content	free	ready	wrong
delighted	glad	reluctant	
determined	happy	sad	
disappointed	likely	shocked	

4. Verb + Gerund

I enjoy **dancing**.
They don't permit **drinking**.

admit	detest	miss	resent
advise	discuss	permit	resist
anticipate	dislike	postpone	risk
appreciate	enjoy	practice	stop
avoid	finish	put off	suggest
can't help	forbid	quit	tolerate
complete	imagine	recall	understand
consider	keep (on)	recommend	
delay	mention	regret	
deny	mind	remember	

5. Expressions with *go* + Gerund

He **goes fishing** every Saturday.
They **went shopping** yesterday.

go boating	go hiking	go sightseeing
go bowling	go hunting	go skating
go camping	go jogging	go skiing
go dancing	go sailing	go swimming
go fishing	go shopping	

6. Preposition + Gerund

Verb + Preposition + Gerund
We talked about **moving.**
I look forward to **having** my own apartment.

adjust to	concentrate on	forget about	refrain from
argue about	depend on	insist on	succeed in
believe in	(dis)approve of	look forward to	talk about
care about	dream about	object to	think about
complain about	feel like	plan on	worry about

Adjective + Preposition + Gerund
I'm fond of **traveling.**
She's not accustomed to **eating** alone.

accustomed to	famous for	interested in	sure of
afraid of	fond of	lazy about	surprised at
appropriate for	good at	proud of	tired of
ashamed of	grateful to . . . for	responsible for	upset about
concerned about	guilty of	sorry about	used to
excited about	(in)capable of	suitable for	worried about

Verb + Object + Preposition + Gerund
I thanked him for **helping** me.
I apologized to him for **forgetting** his birthday.

accuse . . . of	devote . . . to	prevent . . . from	suspect . . . of
apologize to . . . for	forgive . . . for	prohibit . . . from	thank . . . for
blame . . . for	keep . . . from	stop . . . from	warn . . . about

Gerund After Preposition in Certain Expressions
Who's in charge of **collecting** the papers?
What is your reason for **coming** late?

impression of	in favor of	in the middle of	requirement for
in charge of	instead of	need for	technique for
in danger of	interest in	reason for	the point of

7. Noun + Gerund

He has difficulty **speaking** English.
She had a problem **finding** a job.
She spent three weeks **looking** for an apartment.

Use a gerund after the noun in these expressions:

have a difficult time	have a hard time
have difficulty	have a problem
have experience	have trouble
have fun	spend time / money
have a good time	there's no use

8. Verb + Gerund or Infinitive (with little or no difference in meaning)

They like **to sing.**
They like **singing.**

I started **to read.**
I started **reading.**

attempt	intend
begin	like
can't stand	love
continue	neglect
deserve	prefer
hate	start
hesitate	

APPENDIX E

Verbs and Adjectives Followed by a Preposition

Many verbs and adjectives are followed by a preposition.

accuse someone of	(be) ashamed of	count on
(be) accustomed to	(be) aware of	deal with
adjust to	believe in	decide on
(be) afraid of	blame someone for	depend on / upon
agree with	(be) bored with / by	(be) different from
(be) amazed at / by	(be) capable of	disapprove of
(be) angry about	care about / for	(be) divorced from
(be) angry at / with	compare to / with	dream about / of
apologize for	complain about	(be) engaged to
approve of	concentrate on	(be) excited about
argue about	(be) concerned about	(be) familiar with
argue with	consist of	(be) famous for

Continued

Many verbs and adjectives are followed by a preposition.

feel like	(be) mad about	(be) sorry about
(be) fond of	(be) mad at	(be) sorry for
forget about	(be) made from / of	speak about
forgive someone for	(be) married to	speak to / with
(be) glad about	object to	succeed in
(be) good at	(be) opposed to	(be) sure of / about
(be) grateful to someone for	participate in	(be) surprised at
(be) guilty of	plan on	take care of
(be) happy about	pray to	talk about
hear of	(be) prepared for	talk to / with
hope for	prevent someone from	thank someone for
(be) incapable of	prohibit someone from	(be) thankful to someone for
insist on / upon	protect someone from	think about / of
(be) interested in	(be) proud of	(be) tired of
(be) involved in	recover from	(be) upset about
(be) jealous of	(be) related to	(be) upset with
(be) known for	rely on / upon	(be) used to
(be) lazy about	(be) responsible for	wait for
listen to	(be) sad about	warn someone about
look at	(be) satisfied with	(be) worried about
look for	(be) scared of	worry about
look forward to	(be) sick of	

APPENDIX F

Direct and Indirect Objects

Word Order with Direct and Indirect Objects

The order of direct and indirect objects depends on the verb you use.

        IO   DO
He told his friend the answer.

            DO   IO
He explained the answer to his friend.

The order of the objects sometimes depends on whether you use a noun or a pronoun object.

  S V   IO   DO
He gave the woman the keys.

  S V   DO   IO
He gave them to her.

Each of the following groups of words follows a specific pattern of word order and preposition choice. In some cases, the connecting preposition is *to*; in some cases, *for*. In some cases, there is no connecting preposition.

She'll serve lunch *to* her guests.
She reserved a seat *for* you.
I asked him a question.

Group 1	**Pronouns affect word order. The preposition is *to*.**				
Patterns:	He gave a present to his wife. (DO to IO)				
	He gave his wife a present. (IO / DO)				
	He gave it to his wife. (DO to IO)				
	He gave her a present. (IO / DO)				
	He gave it to her. (DO to IO)				
Verbs:	bring	lend	pass	sell	show	teach
	give	offer	pay	send	sing	tell
	hand	owe	read	serve	take	write

Group 2	**Pronouns affect word order. The preposition is *for*.**				
Patterns:	He bought a car for his daughter. (DO for IO)				
	He bought his daughter a car. (IO / DO)				
	He bought it for his daughter. (DO for IO)				
	He bought her a car. (IO / DO)				
	He bought it for her. (DO for IO)				
Verbs:	bake	buy	draw	get	make	
	build	do	find	knit	reserve	

Group 3	**Pronouns don't affect word order. The preposition is *to*.**			
Patterns:	He explained the problem to his friend. (DO to IO)			
	He explained it to her. (DO to IO)			
Verbs:	admit	introduce	recommend	say
	announce	mention	repeat	speak
	describe	prove	report	suggest
	explain			

Group 4	**Pronouns don't affect word order. The preposition is *for*.**			
Patterns:	He cashed a check for his friend. (DO for IO)			
	He cashed it for her. (DO for IO)			
Verbs:	answer	change	design	open	prescribe
	cash	close	fix	prepare	pronounce

Group 5	**Pronouns don't affect word order. No preposition is used.**			
Patterns:	She asked the teacher a question. (IO / DO)			
	She asked him a question. (IO / DO)			
	It took me five minutes to answer the question. (IO / DO)			
Verbs:	ask	charge	cost	wish	take (with time)

Spelling and Pronunciation of Verbs

Spelling of the -s Form of Verbs

Rule	Base Form	-s Form
Add *s* to most verbs to make the -*s* form.	hope eat	hopes eats
When the base form ends in *s*, *z*, *sh*, *ch*, or *x*, add *es* and pronounce an extra syllable, /əz/.	miss buzz wash catch fix	misses buzzes washes catches fixes
When the base form ends in a consonant + *y*, change the *y* to *i* and add *es*.	carry worry	carries worries
When the base form ends in a vowel + *y*, do not change the *y*.	pay obey	pays obeys
Add *es* to *go* and *do*.	go do	goes does

Pronunciation of the -s Form
The -s form has three pronunciations.

We pronounce /**s**/ if the verb ends in these voiceless sounds: /**p t k f**/.

hope—hopes	pick—picks
eat—eats	laugh—laughs

We pronounce /**z**/ if the verb ends in most voiced sounds.

live—lives	read—reads	sing—sings
grab—grabs	run—runs	borrow—borrows

When the base form ends in *s*, *z*, *sh*, *ch*, *x*, *se*, *ge*, or *ce*, we pronounce an extra syllable, /əz/.

miss—misses	watch—watches	change—changes
buzz—buzzes	fix—fixes	dance—dances
wash—washes	use—uses	

These verbs have a change in the vowel sound.

do /**du**/—does /**dʌz**/
say /**sei**/—says /**sɛz**/

Spelling of the *-ing* Form of Verbs

Rule	Base Form	*-ing* Form
Add *-ing* to most verbs. **Note:** Do not remove the *-y* for the *-ing* form.	eat go study	eating going studying

For a one-syllable verb that ends in a consonant + vowel + consonant (CVC), double the final consonant and add *ing*.	p l a n
	  │ │ │
	  C V C
	
	s t o p
	│ │ │
	C V C
	
	s i t
	│ │ │
	C V C
		planning
		
		stopping
		
		sitting

Do not double a final *w*, *x*, or *y*.	show mix stay	showing mixing staying
For a two-syllable word that ends in CVC, double the final consonant only if the last syllable is stressed.	refér admít begín	referring admitting beginning
When the last syllable of a two-syllable word is not stressed, do not double the final consonant.	lísten ópen óffer	listening opening offering
If the word ends in a consonant + *e*, drop the *e* before adding *ing*.	live take write	living taking writing

Spelling of the Past Tense of Regular Verbs

Rule	Base Form	*-ed* Form
Add *ed* to the base form to make the past tense of most regular verbs.	start kick	started kicked
When the base form ends in *e*, add *d* only.	die live	died lived
When the base form ends in a consonant + *y*, change the *y* to *i* and add *ed*.	carry worry	carried worried
When the base form ends in a vowel + *y*, do not change the *y*.	destroy stay	destroyed stayed

Continued

Rule	Base Form	-ed Form
For a one-syllable word that ends in a consonant + vowel + consonant (CVC), double the final consonant and add -ed.	s t o p | | | C V C p l u g | | | C V C	stopped plugged
Do not double a final *w* or *x*.	sew fix	sewed fixed
For a two-syllable word that ends in CVC, double the final consonant only if the last syllable is stressed.	occúr permít	occurred permitted
When the last syllable of a two-syllable word is not stressed, do not double the final consonant.	ópen háppen	opened happened

Pronunciation of Past Forms That End in -ed
The past tense with -ed has three pronunciations.

We pronounce a /t/ if the base form ends in these voiceless sounds: /p, k, f, s, š, č/.

jump—jumped	cough—coughed	wash—washed
cook—cooked	kiss—kissed	watch—watched

We pronounce a /d/ if the base form ends in most voiced sounds.

rub—rubbed	charge—charged	bang—banged
drag—dragged	glue—glued	call—called
love—loved	massage—massaged	fear—feared
bathe—bathed	name—named	free—freed
use—used	learn—learned	

We pronounce an extra syllable /əd/ if the base form ends in a /t/ or /d/ sound.

wait—waited	want—wanted	need—needed
hate—hated	add—added	decide—decided

APPENDIX H

Capitalization Rules

- The first word in a sentence: **M**y friends are helpful.

- The word "I": My sister and **I** took a trip together.

- Names of people: **M**ichael **J**ordan; **G**eorge **W**ashington

- Titles preceding names of people: **D**octor (**Dr.**) **S**mith; **P**resident **L**incoln; **Q**ueen **E**lizabeth; **Mr. R**ogers; **Mrs.** Carter

- Geographic names: the United States; Lake Superior; California; the Rocky Mountains; the Mississippi River

  Note: The word "the" in a geographic name is not capitalized.

- Street names: Pennsylvania Avenue (Ave.); Wall Street (St.); Abbey Road (Rd.)

- Names of organizations, companies, colleges, buildings, stores, hotels: the Republican Party; Heinle Thomson; Dartmouth College; the University of Wisconsin; the White House; Bloomingdale's; the Hilton Hotel

- Nationalities and ethnic groups: Mexicans; Canadians; Spaniards; Americans; Jews; Kurds; Eskimos

- Languages: English; Spanish; Polish; Vietnamese; Russian

- Months: January; February

- Days: Sunday; Monday

- Holidays: Christmas; Independence Day

- Important words in a title: Grammar in Context; The Old Man and the Sea; Romeo and Juliet; The Sound of Music

  Note: Capitalize "the" as the first word of a title.

APPENDIX I

Plural Forms of Nouns

Regular Noun Plurals

Word Ending	Example Noun	Plural Addition	Plural Form	Pronunciation
Vowel	bee banana	+ s	bees bananas	/z/
s, ss, sh, ch, x, z	church dish box watch class	+ es	churches dishes boxes watches classes	/əz/
Voiceless consonants	cat lip month book	+ s	cats lips months books	/s/

Continued

Word Ending	Example Noun	Plural Addition	Plural Form	Pronunciation
Voiced consonants	card pin stove	+ s	cards pins stoves	/z/
Vowel + *y*	boy day key	+ s	boys days keys	/z/
Consonant + *y*	lady story party	*y* + *ies*	ladies stories parties	/z/
Vowel + *o*	video radio	+ s	videos radios	/z/
Consonant + *o*	potato hero	+ *es*	potatoes heroes	/z/
Exceptions: photos, pianos, solos, altos, sopranos, autos, avocados				
f or fe	leaf knife	*f* + *ves*	leaves knives	/vz/
Exceptions: beliefs, chiefs, roofs, cliffs, chefs, sheriffs				

Irregular Noun Plurals

Singular	Plural	Explanation
man woman mouse tooth foot goose	men women mice teeth feet geese	Vowel change (**Note:** The first vowel in *women* is pronounced /I/.)
sheep fish deer	sheep fish deer	No change
child person	children people (OR persons)	Different word form

Continued

Singular	Plural	Explanation
	(eye)glasses belongings clothes goods groceries jeans pajamas pants / slacks scissors shorts	No singular form
alumnus cactus radius stimulus syllabus	alumni cacti OR cactuses radii stimuli syllabi OR syllabuses	*us* → *i*
analysis crisis hypothesis oasis parenthesis thesis	analyses crises hypotheses oases parentheses theses	*is* → *es*
appendix index	appendices OR appendixes indices OR indexes	*ix* → *ices* OR → *ixes*
bacterium curriculum datum medium memorandum criterion phenomenon	bacteria curricula data media memoranda criteria phenomena	*um* → *a* *ion* → *a* *on* → *a*
alga formula vertebra	algae formulae OR formulas vertebrae	*a* → *ae*

Metric Conversion Chart

Length

When You Know	Symbol	Multiply by	To Find	Symbol
inches	in	2.54	centimeters	cm
feet	ft	30.5	centimeters	cm
feet	ft	0.3	meters	m
yards	yd	0.91	meters	m
miles	mi	1.6	kilometers	km

Metric

When You Know	Symbol	Multiply by	To Find	Symbol
centimeters	cm	0.39	inches	in
centimeters	cm	0.03	feet	ft
meters	m	3.28	feet	ft
meters	m	1.09	yards	yd
kilometers	km	0.62	miles	mi

Note:
1 foot = 12 inches
1 yard = 3 feet or 36 inches

Area

When You Know	Symbol	Multiply by	To Find	Symbol
square inches	in^2	6.5	square centimeters	cm^2
square feet	ft^2	0.09	square meters	m^2
square yards	yd^2	0.8	square meters	m^2
square miles	mi^2	2.6	square kilometers	km^2

Metric

When You Know	Symbol	Multiply by	To Find	Symbol
square centimeters	cm^2	0.16	square inches	in^2
square meters	m^2	10.76	square feet	ft^2
square meters	m^2	1.2	square yards	yd^2
square kilometers	km^2	0.39	square miles	mi^2

Weight (Mass)

When You Know	Symbol	Multiply by	To Find	Symbol
ounces	oz	28.35	grams	g
pounds	lb	0.45	kilograms	kg
Metric				
grams	g	0.04	ounces	oz
kilograms	kg	2.2	pounds	lb

Note: 16 ounces = 1 pound

Volume

When You Know	Symbol	Multiply by	To Find	Symbol
fluid ounces	fl oz	30.0	milliliters	mL
pints	pt	0.47	liters	L
quarts	qt	0.95	liters	L
gallons	gal	3.8	liters	L
Metric				
milliliters	mL	0.03	fluid ounces	fl oz
liters	L	2.11	pints	pt
liters	L	1.05	quarts	qt
liters	L	0.26	gallons	gal

Temperature

When You Know	Symbol	Do This	To Find	Symbol
degrees Fahrenheit	°F	Subtract 32, then multiply by $\frac{5}{9}$	degrees Celsius	°C
Metric				
degrees Celsius	°C	Multiply by $\frac{9}{5}$, then add 32	degrees Fahrenheit	°F

Sample temperatures

Fahrenheit	Celsius	Fahrenheit	Celsius
0	− 18	60	16
10	− 12	70	21
20	− 7	80	27
30	− 1	90	32
40	4	100	38
50	10		

Comparative and Superlative Forms

Comparative and Superlative Forms			
	Simple	Comparative	Superlative
One-syllable adjectives and adverbs	tall	taller	the tallest
	fast	faster	the fastest
Exceptions:	bored	more bored	the most bored
	tired	more tired	the most tired
Two-syllable adjectives that end in -y	easy	easier	the easiest
	happy	happier	the happiest
	pretty	prettier	the prettiest
Other two-syllable adjectives	frequent	more frequent	the most frequent
	active	more active	the most active
Some two-syllable adjectives have two forms.	simple	simpler	the simplest
		more simple	the most simple
	common	commoner	the commonest
		more common	the most common
Note: These two-syllable adjectives have two forms: *handsome, quiet, gentle, narrow, clever, friendly,* and *angry.*			
Adjectives with three or more syllables	important	more important	the most important
	difficult	more difficult	the most difficult
-*ly* adverbs	quickly	more quickly	the most quickly
	brightly	more brightly	the most brightly
Irregular adjectives and adverbs	good / well	better	the best
	bad / badly	worse	the worst
	far	farther / further*	the farthest / furthest
	little	less	the least
	a lot	more	the most
* Note: *Farther* is for distances. *Further* is for ideas. 　　I live *farther* from school than you do. 　　She doesn't want to discuss the matter *further.*			

The Superlative Form

Subject	Verb	Superlative Form + Noun	Prepositional Phrase
Alaska	is	the biggest state	in the U.S.
California	is	the most populated state	in the U.S.

The Comparative Form

Subject	Linking Verb[1]	Comparative Adjective	*Than*	Noun / Pronoun
She	is	taller	than	her sister (is).
She	seems	more intelligent	than	her sister.

Subject	Verb Phrase	Comparative Adverb	*Than*	Noun / Pronoun
I	speak English	more fluently	than	my sister (does).
I	sleep	less	than	you (do).

Comparisons with Nouns

Subject	Verb	Comparative Word + Noun	*Than*	Noun / Pronoun
I	work	fewer hours	than	you (do).
I	have	more time	than	you (do).

Equatives with Adjectives and Adverbs

Subject	Linking Verb	*As*	Adjective	*As*	Noun / Pronoun
She	isn't	as	old	as	her husband (is).
She	looks	as	pretty	as	a picture.

Subject	Verb Phrase	*As*	Adverb	*As*	Noun / Pronoun
She	speaks English	as	fluently	as	her husband (does).
He	doesn't work	as	hard	as	his wife (does).

Equatives with Quantities

Subject	Verb	*As Many / Much*	Noun	*As*	Noun / Pronoun
She	works	as many	hours	as	her husband (does).
Milk	doesn't have	as much	fat	as	cream (does).

Subject	Verb	*As Much As*	Noun / Pronoun
Chicken	doesn't cost	as much as	meat (does).
I	don't drive	as much as	you (do).

---

[1] The linking verbs are *be, look, seem, feel, taste, sound,* and *seem.*

Equatives with Nouns

Pattern A

Subject	Verb	*The Same*	Noun	*As*	Noun / Pronoun
She	wears	the same	size	as	her mother (does).
She	isn't	the same	height	as	her brother (is).

Pattern B

Subject & Subject	Verb	*The Same*	Noun
She and her mother	wear	the same	size.
She and her brother	aren't	the same	height.

Similarities using *Like / Alike*

Pattern A

Subject	Linking Verb	*Like*	Noun / Pronoun
Sugar	looks	like	salt.
Regular coffee	tastes	like	decaf.

Pattern B

Subject & Subject	Linking Verb	*Alike*
Sugar and salt	look	alike.
Regular coffee and decaf	taste	alike.

Glossary of Grammatical Terms

- **Adjective** An adjective gives a description of a noun.

  It's a *tall* tree.   He's an *old* man.   My neighbors are *nice*.

- **Adverb** An adverb describes the action of a sentence or an adjective or another adverb.

  She speaks English *fluently*.   I drive *carefully*.

  She speaks English *extremely* well.   She is *very* intelligent.

- **Adverb of Frequency** An adverb of frequency tells how often the action happens.

  I *never* drink coffee.   They *usually* take the bus.

- **Affirmative** means *yes*.

- **Apostrophe** ' We use the apostrophe for possession and contractions.

  My *sister's* friend is beautiful.   Today *isn't* Sunday.

- **Article** The definite article is *the*. The indefinite articles are *a* and *an*.

  I have *a* cat.   I ate *an* apple.   *The* president was late.

- **Auxiliary Verb** Some verbs have two parts: an auxiliary verb and a main verb.

  He *can't* study.   We *will* return.

- **Base Form** The base form, sometimes called the "simple" form, of the verb has no tense. It has no ending (-*s* or -*ed*): *be, go, eat, take, write*.

  He doesn't *know* the answer.   I didn't *go* out.

  You shouldn't *talk* loudly.

- **Capital Letter** A B C D E F G . . .

- **Clause** A clause is a group of words that has a subject and a verb. Some sentences have only one clause.

  She found a good job.

  Some sentences have **a main clause** and a **dependent clause.**

MAIN CLAUSE	DEPENDENT CLAUSE (**reason clause**)
She found a good job	because she has computer skills.
MAIN CLAUSE	DEPENDENT CLAUSE (**time clause**)
She'll turn off the light	before she goes to bed.
MAIN CLAUSE	DEPENDENT CLAUSE (***if* clause**)
I'll take you to the doctor	if you don't have your car on Saturday.

- **Colon** :

- **Comma** ,

- **Comparative Form** A comparative form of an adjective or adverb is used to compare two things.

  My house is *bigger* than your house.

  Her husband drives *faster* than she does.

- **Complement** The complement of the sentence is the information after the verb. It completes the verb phrase.

  He works *hard.*   I slept *for five hours.*   They are *late.*

- **Consonant** The following letters are consonants: *b, c, d, f, g, h, j, k, l, m, n, p, q, r, s, t, v, w, x, y, z.*

  NOTE: *y* is sometimes considered a vowel, as in the world *syllable.*

- **Contraction** A contraction is made up of two words put together with an apostrophe.

  He's my brother.   *You're* late.   They *won't* talk to me.

  (*He's = he is*)   (*You're = you are*)   (*won't = will not*)

- **Count Noun** Count nouns are nouns that we can count. They have a singular and a plural form.

  1 pen — 3 pens   1 table — 4 tables

- **Dependent Clause** See **Clause.**

- **Direct Object** A direct object is a noun (phrase) or pronoun that receives the action of the verb.

  We saw *the movie.*   You have *a nice car.*   I love *you.*

- **Exclamation Mark !**

- **Frequency Words** Frequency words are *always, usually, often, sometimes, rarely, seldom,* and *never.*

  I *never* drink coffee.   We *always* do our homework.

- **Hyphen –**

- **Imperative** An imperative sentence gives a command or instructions. An imperative sentence omits the word *you.*

  Come here.   *Don't be* late.   Please *sit* down.

- **Indefinite Pronoun** An indefinite pronoun (*one, some, any*) takes the place of an indefinite noun.

  I have a cell phone. Do you have *one?*

  I didn't drink any coffee, but you drank *some.* Did he drink *any?*

- **Infinitive** An infinitive is *to* + base form.

  I want *to leave.*   You need *to be* here on time.

- **Linking Verb** A linking verb is a verb that links the subject to the noun or adjective after it. Linking verbs include *be, seem, feel, smell, sound, look, appear,* and *taste.*

  She *is* a doctor.   She *seems* very intelligent.   She *looks* tired.

- **Modal** The modal verbs are *can, could, shall, should, will, would, may, might,* and *must.*

    They *should* leave.   I *must* go.

- **Negative** means *no.*

- **Nonaction Verb** A nonaction verb has no action. We do not use a continuous tense (*be* + verb *-ing*) with a nonaction verb. The nonaction verbs are: *believe, cost, care, have, hear, know, like, love, matter, mean, need, own, prefer, remember, see, seem, think, understand,* and *want.*

    She *has* a laptop.   We *love* our mother.

- **Noncount Noun** A noncount noun is a noun that we don't count. It has no plural form.

    She drank some *water.*   He prepared some *rice.*

    Do you need any *money?*

- **Noun** A noun is a person (*brother*), a place (*kitchen*), or a thing (*table*). Nouns can be either count (*1 table, 2 tables*) or noncount (*money, water*).

    My *brother* lives in California.   My *sisters* live in New York.

    I get *mail* from them.

- **Noun Modifier** A noun modifier makes a noun more specific.

    fire department   *Independence* Day   *can* opener

- **Noun Phrase** A noun phrase is a group of words that forms the subject or object of the sentence.

    A very nice woman helped me at registration.

    I bought *a big box of candy.*

- **Object** The object of the sentence follows the verb. It receives the action of the verb.

    He bought *a car.*   I saw *a movie.*   I met *your brother.*

- **Object Pronoun** Use object pronouns (*me, you, him, her, it, us, them*) after the verb or preposition.

    He likes *her.*   I saw the movie. Let's talk about *it.*

- **Paragraph** A paragraph is a group of sentences about one topic.

- **Parentheses ( )**

- **Participle, Present** The present participle is verb + *-ing.*

    She is *sleeping.*   They were *laughing.*

- **Period .**

- **Phrase** A group of words that go together.

    Last month my sister came to visit.

    There is a strange car *in front of my house.*

- **Plural** Plural means more than one. A plural noun usually ends with *-s*.
  She has beautiful *eyes.*

- **Possessive Form** Possessive forms show ownership or relationship.
  Mary's coat is in the closet.   *My* brother lives in Miami.

- **Preposition** A preposition is a short connecting word: *about, above, across, after, around, as, at, away, back, before, behind, below, by, down, for, from, in, into, like, of, off, on, out, over, to, under, up, with.*
  The book is *on* the table.

- **Pronoun** A pronoun takes the place of a noun.
  I have a new car. I bought *it* last week.
  John likes Mary, but *she* doesn't like *him.*

- **Punctuation** Period . Comma , Colon : Semicolon ; Question Mark ? Exclamation Mark !

- **Question Mark ?**

- **Quotation Marks " "**

- **Regular Verb** A regular verb forms its past tense with *-ed.*
  He *worked* yesterday.   I *laughed* at the joke.

- ***s* Form** A present tense verb that ends in *-s* or *-es.*
  He *lives* in New York.   She *watches* TV a lot.

- **Sense-Perception Verb** A sense-perception verb has no action. It describes a sense.
  She *feels* fine.   The coffee *smells* fresh.   The milk *tastes* sour.

- **Sentence** A sentence is a group of words that contains a subject[2] and a verb (at least) and gives a complete thought.
  SENTENCE: She came home.
  NOT A SENTENCE: When she came home

- **Simple Form of Verb** The simple form of the verb, also called the base form, has no tense; it never has an *-s, -ed,* or *-ing* ending.
  Did you *see* the movie?   I couldn't *find* your phone number.

- **Singular** Singular means one.
  She ate a *sandwich.*   I have one *television.*

- **Subject** The subject of the sentence tells who or what the sentence is about.
  My sister got married last April. *The wedding* was beautiful.

- **Subject Pronouns** Use subject pronouns (*I, you, he, she, it, we, you, they*) before a verb.
  They speak Japanese.   *We* speak Spanish.

---

[2] In an imperative sentence, the subject *you* is omitted: *Sit down. Come here.*

- **Superlative Form** A superlative form of an adjective or adverb shows the number one item in a group of three or more.

    January is the *coldest* month of the year.

    My brother speaks English the *best* in my family.

- **Syllable** A syllable is a part of a word that has only one vowel sound. (Some words have only one syllable.)

    change (one syllable)   after (af·ter = two syllables)

    look (one syllable)   responsible (re·spon·si·ble = four syllables)

- **Tag Question** A tag question is a short question at the end of a sentence. It is used in conversation.

    You speak Spanish, *don't you?*   He's not happy, *is he?*

- **Tense** A verb has tense. Tense shows when the action of the sentence happened.

    SIMPLE PRESENT: She usually *works* hard.

    FUTURE: She *will work* tomorrow.

    PRESENT CONTINUOUS: She *is working* now.

    SIMPLE PAST: She *worked* yesterday.

- **Verb** A verb is the action of the sentence.

    He *runs* fast.   I *speak* English.

    Some verbs have no action. They are linking verbs. They connect the subject to the rest of the sentence.

    He *is* tall.   She *looks* beautiful.   You *seem* tired.

- **Vowel** The following letters are vowels: *a, e, i, o, u. Y* is sometimes considered a vowel (for example, in the word *syllable*).

APPENDIX M

Alphabetical List of Irregular Verb Forms

Base Form	Past Form	Past Participle	Base Form	Past Form	Past Participle
be	was / were	been	bid	bid	bid
bear	bore	born / borne	bind	bound	bound
beat	beat	beaten	bite	bit	bitten
become	became	become	bleed	bled	bled
begin	began	begun	blow	blew	blown
bend	bent	bent	break	broke	broken
bet	bet	bet	breed	bred	bred

Continued

Base Form	Past Form	Past Participle	Base Form	Past Form	Past Participle
bring	brought	brought	grow	grew	grown
broadcast	broadcast	broadcast	hang	hung	hung[3]
build	built	built	have	had	had
burst	burst	burst	hear	heard	heard
buy	bought	bought	hide	hid	hidden
cast	cast	cast	hit	hit	hit
catch	caught	caught	hold	held	held
choose	chose	chosen	hurt	hurt	hurt
cling	clung	clung	keep	kept	kept
come	came	come	know	knew	known
cost	cost	cost	lay	laid	laid
creep	crept	crept	lead	led	led
cut	cut	cut	leap	leapt / leaped	leapt / leaped
deal	dealt	dealt	leave	left	left
dig	dug	dug	lend	loaned / lent	loaned / lent
dive	dove / dived	dove / dived	let	let	let
do	did	done	lie	lay	lain
draw	drew	drawn	light	lit / lighted	lit / lighted
drink	drank	drunk	lose	lost	lost
drive	drove	driven	make	made	made
eat	ate	eaten	mean	meant	meant
fall	fell	fallen	meet	met	met
feed	fed	fed	mistake	mistook	mistaken
feel	felt	felt	overcome	overcame	overcome
fight	fought	fought	overdo	overdid	overdone
find	found	found	overtake	overtook	overtaken
fit	fit	fit	overthrow	overthrew	overthrown
flee	fled	fled	pay	paid	paid
fly	flew	flown	plead	pleaded / pled	pleaded / pled
forbid	forbade	forbidden	prove	proved	proven / proved
forget	forgot	forgotten	put	put	put
forgive	forgave	forgiven	quit	quit	quit
freeze	froze	frozen	read	read	read
get	got	gotten	ride	rode	ridden
give	gave	given	ring	rang	rung
go	went	gone	rise	rose	risen
grind	ground	ground	run	ran	run

Continued

[3] *Hanged* is used as the past form to refer to punishment by death. *Hung* is used in other situations: She *hung* the picture on the wall.

Base Form	Past Form	Past Participle	Base Form	Past Form	Past Participle
say	said	said	swear	swore	sworn
see	saw	seen	sweep	swept	swept
seek	sought	sought	swell	swelled	swelled / swollen
sell	sold	sold	swim	swam	swum
send	sent	sent	swing	swung	swung
set	set	set	take	took	taken
sew	sewed	sown / sewed	teach	taught	taught
shake	shook	shaken	tear	tore	torn
shed	shed	shed	tell	told	told
shine	shone / shined	shone / shined	think	thought	thought
shoot	shot	shot	throw	threw	thrown
show	showed	shown / showed	understand	understood	understood
shrink	shrank / shrunk	shrunk / shrunken	uphold	upheld	upheld
shut	shut	shut	upset	upset	upset
sing	sang	sung	wake	woke	woken
sink	sank	sunk	wear	wore	worn
sit	sat	sat	weave	wove	woven
sleep	slept	slept	wed	wedded / wed	wedded / wed
slide	slid	slid	weep	wept	wept
slit	slit	slit	win	won	won
speak	spoke	spoken	wind	wound	wound
speed	sped	sped	withhold	withheld	withheld
spend	spent	spent	withdraw	withdrew	withdrawn
spin	spun	spun	withstand	withstood	withstood
spit	spit	spit	wring	wrung	wrung
split	split	split	write	wrote	written
spread	spread	spread			
spring	sprang	sprung			
stand	stood	stood			
steal	stole	stolen			
stick	stuck	stuck			
sting	stung	stung			
stink	stank	stunk			
strike	struck	stuck / stricken			
strive	strove	striven			

Note:

The past and past participle of some verbs can end in -ed or -t.

burn	burned or burnt
dream	dreamed or dreamt
kneel	kneeled or knelt
learn	learned or learnt
spill	spilled or spilt
spoil	spoiled or spoilt

The United States of America: Major Cities

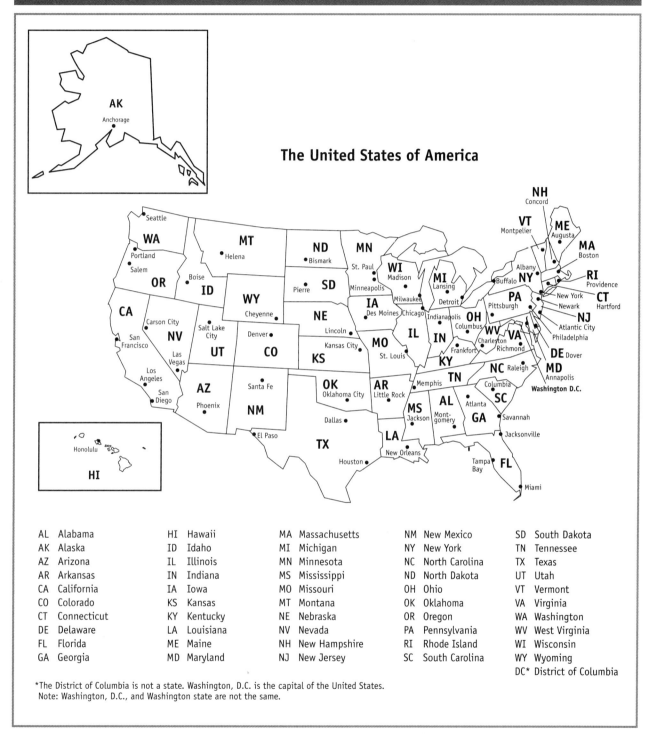

AL Alabama	HI Hawaii	MA Massachusetts	NM New Mexico	SD South Dakota
AK Alaska	ID Idaho	MI Michigan	NY New York	TN Tennessee
AZ Arizona	IL Illinois	MN Minnesota	NC North Carolina	TX Texas
AR Arkansas	IN Indiana	MS Mississippi	ND North Dakota	UT Utah
CA California	IA Iowa	MO Missouri	OH Ohio	VT Vermont
CO Colorado	KS Kansas	MT Montana	OK Oklahoma	VA Virginia
CT Connecticut	KY Kentucky	NE Nebraska	OR Oregon	WA Washington
DE Delaware	LA Louisiana	NV Nevada	PA Pennsylvania	WV West Virginia
FL Florida	ME Maine	NH New Hampshire	RI Rhode Island	WI Wisconsin
GA Georgia	MD Maryland	NJ New Jersey	SC South Carolina	WY Wyoming
				DC* District of Columbia

*The District of Columbia is not a state. Washington, D.C. is the capital of the United States.
Note: Washington, D.C., and Washington state are not the same.

North America

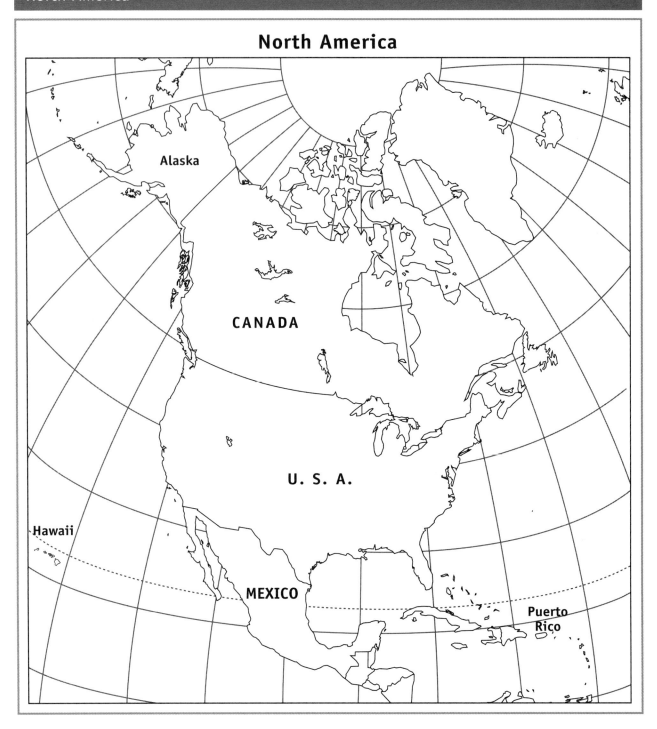

Alaska

CANADA

U. S. A.

Hawaii

MEXICO

Puerto
Rico

Index

Photo Credits